THE
ETHICS OF
MARTIN LUTHER

THE
ETHICS
OF
MARTIN
LUTHER

PAUL
ALTHAUS

*Translated and
with a Foreword by
Robert C. Schultz*

FORTRESS PRESS PHILADELPHIA

This book is a translation of *Die Ethik Martin Luthers* © 1965 by Gütersloher Verlagshaus Gerd Mohn in Gütersloh, Germany.

Biblical quotations from the Revised Standard Version of the Bible, copyrighted 1946 and 1952 by the Division of Christian Education of the National Council of the Churches of Christ in the United States of America, are used by permission.

Quotations from the American Edition of *Luther's Works* published by Concordia Publishing House in St. Louis and Fortress Press in Philadelphia are used by permission. Grateful acknowledgment is hereby made to Concordia Publishing House for textual material quoted from volumes appearing under their copyright.

Library of Congress Catalog Card Number 72–164552

ISBN 0-8006-0047-9

Second printing 1978

7390H78   Printed in the United States of America   1-47

"Having been justified by grace,

we then do good works,

yes, Christ himself does all in us."

(*WA* 39^I, 46; *LW* 34, 111)

FOREWORD

The Ethics of Martin Luther appears at a particularly significant
point in the church's encounter with Luther. After some fifteen
years, the American Edition of Luther's Works is close to completion. For the first time, nearly the full scope of Luther's thought
will be available to the English-speaking world. No one can know
what this will mean for the future development of Christianity
outside the homeland of the Reformation, or even what the
gradual appearance of these volumes over the years has already
meant. For it lies in the very nature of this edition that its effects
will be felt primarily not in publications but in sermons, in church
school classes, in pastoral care, and in the conversation of the
brethren.

When plans for the American Edition were first announced,
there was a question whether the church could muster the editorial
patience and translating skill to complete so great a task. There
was also reasonable doubt as to whether Americans would buy
enough copies of such an extensive edition to make the project
economically feasible. All such questions have been resolved by
the appearance of the Edition itself. Indeed its quality and wide-
spread acceptance raise a far more serious kind of question about
the relationship between Luther and his American readers.

During the past few years, we have seen the handsome series
of volumes in a multitude of pastors' studies and church libraries.
And whereas we were once pleased by its unexpected presence,
we are now more likely to speculate about the reasons for its
absence. But another more subtle impression remains: bright and
colorful rows of books, always in sequence, dust jackets sometimes
faded but rarely frayed, the earliest volumes showing no more
sign of use than the most recent, in short, orderly and respected
nonuse. If these impressions are valid, then we need now—now
that the task of making Luther available has been resolved—to
lead people into a fruitful encounter with the Reformer himself.
There is a sense, of course, in which that is really beyond our do-

ing for there can be no genuine encounter with Luther that is not existential encounter with the gospel. But some things can be done to facilitate access to Luther's thought. This volume, together with its companion,[1] is presented as a contribution to that end.

It is not necessary to explore the reasons for the practical aliena-tion of pastors and people from Luther's own writings. It is enough to know that the separation is broader than the mere language gap. Nor need we do more than note the fact that many theologians today find Luther's opponents in the left wing of the Reformation more attractive than Luther himself, while others are focusing on the theologians of and conditions in the church before the Reformation which combined to make the Reformation such a tragic necessity. It is enough to know that such scholarly research is—for the present at least—so specialized and technical that it is more likely to conceal Luther from rather than reveal him to the interested but nonscholarly reader. In any case, it seems that we cannot expect the current generation of theological scholar-ship to lead us into our own personal encounter with Luther in the way that theologians of the previous generation so frequently did.

We do not apologize then for offering the reader this mature fruit of Paul Althaus's intensive lifelong encounter with Luther. Althaus, who was born in 1888 and died in 1966, clearly belongs to the previous generation of theologians. The problems which he encountered were burning issues in another place and time. Yet as a guide into Luther, his continuing relevance is matched by few other theologians of this century. Althaus began the study of theology in the age of liberal theology which remembered Luther more for his historical significance than for his mature theological position. But for Althaus, as for many of his generation, the suf-fering and chaos produced by World War I raised questions to which liberal theology could not adequately respond. In this situa-tion Althaus's own experience of the power of the Reformer's theology convinced him that Luther remains a very fruitful partner in any theological conversation. This conclusion was repeatedly tested as Althaus confronted the kaleidoscopic variety of situations that arose in his more than fifty years as an active theologian. His

---

[1] Paul Althaus, *The Theology of Martin Luther* (Philadelphia: Fortress Press, 1966).

companion volumes on Luther, *The Theology* and *The Ethics,* are a summary statement of what he learned from and about Luther in the process of letting Luther speak to those situations and problems. However, the books are far more than a collection of occasional essays on specific topics. They actually provide us with a systematic, comprehensive, and well-balanced introduction that can lead us to our own encounter with Luther himself.

The close relationship between the author's own theological work and his conversation with Luther will become clearer if we sketch some of the major foci of Althaus's theological thought in chronological order without attempting to detail fully his theological position. The reader of his two volumes on Luther will immediately note the intimate connection between the author's own personal development and the focal points of his conversations with Luther. Throughout these conversations, Althaus consistently raises two questions: (1) Did Luther really understand the Bible? (2) Is Luther's understanding of the two governments still relevant?[2]

At least three of Althaus's teachers focused their attention on Luther's theology before such interest was common. Althaus was thus prepared very early in his career to make independent contributions to the Luther-Renaissance of the 1920s. His own father, Paul Althaus, Sr., a representative of the Erlangen School, would probably have been the first to draw his son's attention to Theodosius Harnack's two volume study of *Luther's Theology,* a then

---

2 In preparing the following, I have freely used other summaries of Althaus's work without attempting to identify specific points of indebtedness. The following essays have been most helpful and contain further references.

Hans Grass, "Die Theologie von Paul Althaus," *Neue Zeitschrift für Systematische Theologie und Religionsphilosophie* 8 (1966), no. 3: 213–41.

Wilfried Joest, "Paul Althaus als Lutherforscher," *Luther* 29 (1958): 1–11.

Walther von Loewenich, "Paul Althaus als Lutherforscher," *Luther-Jahrbuch* (1968): 9–47.

Wenzel Lohff, "Paul Althaus," in *Theologians of Our Time,* ed. Leonhard Reinisch (Notre Dame, Indiana: University of Notre Dame Press, 1964), pp. 48–64.

Bibliographies of Althaus's work have been prepared by Gottfried Petzold, "Veröffentlichungen von Paul Althaus über Luther, eine Auswahl," *Luther* 29 (1958), no. 1: 12–13, and by Wenzel Lohff, "Bibliographie der Veröffentlichungen von Professor D. Paul Althaus," in *Dank an Paul Althaus,* ed. Walter Künneth and Wilfried Joest (Gütersloh: Bertelsmann, 1958), pp. 246–72. A supplement to the Lohff bibliography was prepared by Joachim Kahl and published as note 62 in Hans Grass, "Die Theologie von Paul Althaus," pp. 236–41.

almost forgotten work.[3] Carl Stange, pioneer in the study of Luther's early Latin writings long before the publication of Luther's Commentary on Romans, acquainted Althaus with this little-known side of Luther's work. The most influential of Althaus's teachers, Adolf Schlatter, drew Althaus's attention to Luther with his frequent criticism of Luther's doctrine of justification.

In 1920 Althaus joined the theological faculty of the University of Rostock. His lectures on Luther—we might call them the first draft of his two Luther books—were from the first well attended. By 1926 his reputation as a Luther scholar was so well established that the members of the *Luthergesellschaft* chose him to succeed Karl Holl as president of their scholarly society.

Like most of his contemporaries, Althaus came out of the disaster and suffering of World War I with the certainty that theology had to speak of both the grace and the wrath of God with radically new seriousness. The mood of the times was eschatological bordering on apocalytic. Althaus responded to this in his book *The Last Things*.[4] The Luther studies growing out of this theme were published later.

Germany, however, faced the need for total political, social, and economic reorganization. The situation demanded an immediate response. Many felt that Lutherans were so limited by conservative presuppositions that they could not play a significant role in social reorganization. Althaus responded to these problems with *Religious Socialism* in 1921.[5] This study of basic questions of Christian social ethics closes with an analysis of Luther's doctrine of the two kingdoms. The four hundredth anniversary of the Peasants' War provided the occasion for a more thorough consideration of Luther's social ethics, "Luther's Response to the Peasants' War."[6] In these and in later studies on Luther's doctrine of the two kingdoms, Althaus shows that Luther's decisions in the Peasants' War were entirely in harmony with his theology. But he also shows that

---

[3] Theodosius Harnack, *Luthers Theologie* (Erlangen: Blaesing, 1862–1886), 2nd. ed. (Munich: Kaiser, 1927).

[4] Paul Althaus, *Die Letzten Dinge. Entwurf einer christlichen Eschatologie* (Gütersloh: Bertelsmann, 1922). The third and fourth editions (1926 and 1933) are substantial reworkings of the theme. A tenth edition appeared in 1970.

[5] Paul Althaus, *Religiöser Sozialismus. Grundfragen der christlichen Sozialethik* (Gütersloh: Bertelsmann, 1921).

[6] Paul Althaus, "Luthers Haltung im Bauernkriege," *Jahrbuch der Luthergesellschaft* 7 (1925): 1–34.

these same theological principles under other political conditions provide the basis for a flexible and even radical response to the issues of the time.

A series of quadricentennials of significant Reformation events provided the stimulus for a number of studies that pioneered in the analysis of Luther's theology. In 1926, Althaus published a brief essay on "The Significance of the Cross for Luther's Thought" that focused attention on Luther's theology of the cross.[7] The titles of other publications describe their own themes: "Obedience and Freedom in Luther's Use of the Bible," *Communio Sanctorum: The Congregation in the Lutheran Understanding of the Church,* and "Luther's Doctrine of the Lord's Supper."[8] None of these is a merely historical study of the sixteenth century Reformation. Rather they are "applied Luther studies"[9] which engage Luther in the discussion of these problems as they appear in the twentieth century.

Althaus was now ready to come to terms with Adolf Schlatter's massive criticism that Luther's doctrine of justification was not faithful to the biblical witness. To Schlatter's assertion that it was man-centered rather than God-centered Althaus responded in 1931 with an essay, "Let God be God: The Meaning of Luther's Doctrine of Justification."[10] Schlatter had also criticized Luther's teaching that the Christian is at one and the same time totally a righteous man and totally a sinner; Schlatter felt that Luther's pessimism on this point was unfaithful to Paul. Althaus responded to this criticism in *Paul and Luther: A Comparison of their Teachings about Man.*[11] In this study of Romans 7, Althaus concludes that Luther's own deep experience of the Christian life has led

(1)

(2)

---

[7] Paul Althaus, "Die Bedeutung des Kreuzes im Denken Luthers," *Luther* 7 (1926): 97–107. The theme is developed in great detail by Walther von Loewenich, *Luthers Theologia Crucis* (Munich: Kaiser, 1929).

[8] Paul Althaus, "Gehorsam und Freiheit in Luthers Stellung zur Bibel," *Luther* 9 (1927): 74–86, *Communio Sanctorum. Die Gemeinde im lutherischen Kirchengedanken. I. Luther* (Munich: Kaiser, 1929), and "Luthers Abendmahlslehre," *Jahrbuch der Luthergesellschaft* 11 (1929): 2–42.

[9] Joest, "Paul Althaus als Lutherforscher," p. 2.

[10] Paul Althaus, "Gottes Gottheit als Sinn der Rechtfertigungslehre Luthers," *Jahrbuch der Luthergesellschaft* 13 (1931): 1–28.

[11] Paul Althaus, *Paulus und Luther über den Menschen. Ein Vergleich* (Gütersloh: Bertelsmann, 1938). A second expanded edition appeared in 1951; a fourth edition in 1963. Althaus's own commentary on Paul's Letter to the Romans (*Der Brief an die Römer*) was published as volume 6 of *Das Neue Testament Deutsch* (Göttingen: Vandenhoeck & Ruprecht, 1932; 10th ed., 1966).

him to extend Paul's statements in a way that did not contradict
Paul but went well beyond Paul's own intention. This study
provides an excellent example of Althaus's style of creative inter-
action with Luther.

But the 1930s left little time for quiet theological reflection.
Life demanded personal response and political decisions. During
these years, no Christian failed to gather rich experience of what
it means to be simultaneously a righteous man and a sinner. Like
many of his contemporaries, Althaus had a deep appreciation of
the tragic situation of Germany after World War I. His thinking
even into the 1930s must be understood in the context of the
sense of tragic despair that prevailed. The experience of death and
suffering during the war was reinforced by the ensuing chaos and
corruption of civilian life.[12] The impending collapse of the Weimar Republic further heightened the continuing awareness of a
need for basic political rebirth.

Like many of his colleagues in university life, Althaus was a
member of the German National Party, which in 1931 responded
to the threat of the Socialist and Communist parties by entering
into a coalition with the National Socialists. These two parties
were held together by their common concern for a regeneration of
the German nation and by the certainty on the part of each that it
could control the other and thus decisively influence the outcome
of that rebirth. Thus the German National Party, which contrib-
uted some eighteen percent of Hitler's bare majority in 1933, did
so with realistic hopes of determining the policies of the resulting
coalition government. In this historical context and as a contribution to the welfare of the nation, Althaus wrote *The Church's*

---

12 Heinrich Böhmer's *Road to Reformation,* trans. John W. Doberstein and
Theodore G. Tappert (Philadelphia: Muhlenberg Press, 1946) originally appeared as the first (and apparently only) volume in a series on "German
Leaders" (Die deutschen Führer). In its original edition the very first sentence
of Erich Brandenburg's "Series Foreword" reflects the mood of the times:
"Toppled from the heights of its position as a great-power to the depths of
defeat—as has so often happened in its history—and groaning under the heavy
burden of its wartime losses and its present economic problems, the German
people once again begins to look toward the future and to devote all its strength
and resources to the task of rebuilding what has been destroyed." Heinrich
Böhmer, *Der junge Luther* (Gotha: Flamberg, 1925). Professor Heinrich
Schmidt of the University of Heidelberg first drew my attention to this statement in a very helpful conversation about Althaus's relationship to the political
events of the 1930s.

German Hour,[13] a pamphlet in which he summoned the Christians of Germany to play an active and decisive role in the rebirth of the nation. It was a call to involvement, to political and social action. And it is as such a call, within the context and possibilities of its own time, that it deserves to be evaluated.[14] Althaus's theology had allowed broad freedom of action to the Religious Socialists in the twenties. He could not now, without reason, deny similar freedom to the coalition government and even to the National Socialists.

In addition, Althaus was characteristically most charitable in putting the best construction on everything, and willing to cooperate as long as possible—even when he himself would have done it differently. He made every effort to identify and support what was good in all his opponents, both in theology and in politics. And there was in fact much that initially seemed positive and healthy about what was happening under the new regime. And when—at least as early as 1936—Althaus began to express doubts about the darker side of National Socialism, he no longer had full freedom of expression and publication.[15] While we differ with his political decisions during those years and question whether he saw the full implications of the situation early enough and clearly enough, there should be no doubt of his courage in openly opposing the National Socialists when his personal judgment required that. He expressed his opposition not only privately but in publications opposing emerging policies on race, sterilization, the elimination of "worthless lives," etc. He also spoke out openly against the messianic pretensions of the National Socialists and the attempt of the "German Christians" to gain control of the territorial churches. And even while expressing deepest loyalty to the German nation and people, he affirmed the fallibility of all

---

13 Paul Althaus, *Die deutsche Stunde der Kirche* (Göttingen: Vandenhoeck & Ruprecht, 1933). The first edition appeared as no. 4 in a series called "Dienst des Pfarrers."

14 "Lutheran Christianity knows itself to be responsible for the nation and the country and not merely for the salvation of individual souls. It is responsible for the preservation of God's creation and for the orders of creation. In this sense, our faith results in political involvement and our Christianity is political." Paul Althaus, *Politisches Christentum; Ein Wort über die Thüringer "Deutschen Christen,"* Theologia Militans, no. 5 (Leipzig: Deichert, 1935), p. 2.

15 Althaus speaks of this in the Foreword to the second edition of his *Grundriss der Ethik* (Gütersloh: Bertelsmann, 1953), p. 5.

leaders and the right of revolt. His work made no small contribution to the preservation of the integrity of the Lutheran Church of Bavaria.

Many things could be seen more clearly from the perspective of 1945. But that perspective was not available in 1936—either to Christians in Germany or to Christians in the West, so many of whom were willing to seek peace at any price. But Althaus's experiences during these years permitted him to test Luther's doctrine of the two governments in the crucible of the concrete situation. He learned that while the doctrine allows for making wrong and right decisions, without guaranteeing that we will avoid either guilt or punishment, it always maintains the integrity of Christian liberty and the certainty of God's forgiving love.

The restoration of social and economic stability after World War II gave Althaus the opportunity to revise and summarize his own theological position. These years saw new editions of his outlines of *Ethics* and of *Dogmatics*.[16] He also completed the detailed statement of his own theological position in *The Christian Truth*.[17] The many editions of this major work bear eloquent testimony to Althaus's popularity and influence as a teacher. After 1945, he also devoted much time to the defense of Luther's doctrine of the two governments (see below, pp. 43–82) and to preparing his two volumes on Luther's theology and ethics. Althaus himself has drawn attention to the close relationship in organization and structure between his own dogmatics and ethics and his studies of Luther's theology.[18]

In the 1950s Althaus participated in the heated discussion about the third use of the law in Luther's theology. He developed his own position in *The Divine Command: A New Perspective on Law and Gospel*,[19] a position which is reflected also in the

---

16 Paul Althaus, *Grundriss der Ethik*, 2nd ed. (Gütersloh: Bertelsmann, 1953) [*Leitsätze zur Ethik* (Erlangen: Merkel, 1928) had earlier been published in a revised edition (Erlangen: Merkel, 1931) with the new title *Grundriss der Ethik*].
   Paul Althaus, *Grundriss der Dogmatik*, 2 vols., 5th ed. (Gütersloh: Bertelsmann, 1960).
17 Paul Althaus, *Die Christliche Wahrheit. Lehrbuch der Dogmatik* (Gütersloh: Bertelsmann, 1947; 8th ed., 1969).
18 Althaus, *Theology*, p. viii.
19 Paul Althaus, *The Divine Command: A New Perspective on Law and Gospel*, trans. Franklin Sherman (Philadelphia: Fortress Press, 1966).

present volume. In this little book Althaus uses the distinction between the Christian "ethos" as describing the Christian's personal existence in relationship to God and Christian "ethics" as describing the Christian's activity, a distinction which is preserved here in the *Ethics.* During this period Althaus also focused on the question of the historical Jesus and particularly on the historicity of the resurrection of Jesus.[20]

We have been able to do little more than sketch the breadth of Althaus's conversation with Luther and its significance for his theological work. Even this little, however, illustrates the seriousness with which he engaged Luther as a partner in the contemporary theological conversation. The present volume on Luther's ethics and its companion volume on Luther's theology, taken together, both summarize these conversations and document their results.

We are of course not engaged in the same conversations as Althaus. His encounters with Luther therefore cannot spare us our own, but his summary of the conversations can more frequently than not give us a running start. In any case, the example of his own fruitful encounters with Luther and their stimulating effect on his thinking may give us the confidence to engage Luther as a primary partner in our own theological conversations. This is the stimulation that still needs to be supplied before the so faithfully purchased and shelved volumes of the American Edition of *Luther's Works* will be read and studied with equal faithfulness.

There are many signs that the spirit of rationalism and idealism will dominate the closing decades of the twentieth century as thoroughly as it did the closing decades of previous centuries. Americans who have been struggling with the complexities of Schleiermacher's vocabulary are moving on to the obscurities of Ritschl's grammar. And if history repeats itself, we may expect a growing disaffection with the theology of the mature Luther similar to that produced by Ritschlian theology. Althaus's studies of Luther's theology and ethics, together with similar works, may then be of as little interest to theologians at the end of the twen-

---

[20] Paul Althaus, *Fact and Faith in the Kerygma of Today,* trans. David Cairns (Philadelphia: Muhlenberg Press, 1960).

tieth century as was Theodosius Harnack to their counterparts in
the nineteenth century. If that should happen, a later generation
will have to rediscover Luther out of their own experience. However that may come about, Althaus's studies of Luther's theology
and ethics will have served their purpose well if, during this time,
they continue to work as a quiet ferment among the pastors and
teachers who are the most significant theologians in the life of the
church.

*   *   *

Whenever possible I have tried to quote from the texts of
existing modern translations of Luther's writings. References to
these English translations are given in the notes immediately following Althaus's own references to the Weimar edition, which
usually invite the reader to explore the larger context in which
a particular statement occurs. Occasionally the references for a
series of brief quotations are collated in the next following footnote. "Cf." before a reference to a translated work indicates that
the translation is based on a version of the text different from
that indicated by Althaus in his reference to the Weimar edition.

I wish to express my thanks to both Concordia Publishing
House and Fortress Press for permission freely to use material
from the American Edition of *Luther's Works.* I am even more
grateful to the many individual translators whose work I have
used earlier in *The Theology of Martin Luther* as well as here in
this volume. To have acknowledged their individual contributions
would have impossibly complicated the notes; yet I am deeply
appreciative of their labors. As translators themselves, they will
best know how valuable their help has been to me. Mrs. James
Craig was responsible for the faithful typing and retyping of the
manuscript. Much of my work on the volume was done while I
was a member of the faculty of St. John's University, Jamaica,
New York. My thanks to my chairman, Dr. James Megivern, and
my dean, The Reverend Richard Devine, C.M., for their encour-
agement to complete the work.

My personal gratitude to the author has already been expressed
in the Translator's Note to the *Theology.* I shall not repeat it
here. Wolfgang Trillhaas has spoken for many in pointing out

that the true significance of Paul Althaus's work can best be measured by the standard of Daniel 12:3: "Those who are wise shall shine like the brightness of the firmament; and those who turn many to righteousness like the stars forever and ever."

Valparaiso, Indiana
October, 1971

PREFACE

THIS IS THE BOOK on Luther's ethics which I promised as a supplement to *The Theology of Martin Luther*.[1] *The Theology* and *The Ethics* are closely related to each other because they share the common theme of justification. *The Ethics* reiterates what Luther has to say, particularly in his *Treatise on Good Works*,[2] about the ground of the Christian life: justification through faith alone is of fundamental significance for the proper understanding and realization of the ethical life. Here the Christian's activity is described in terms of justification, the foundation of the Christian ethos. It is here in *The Ethics* that Luther's statement about faith is brought to completion: faith is realized only as it finds concrete expression in the midst of this worldly life. Thus Luther's doctrine of justification and of faith is the clasp that holds these two books together.

In my preface to *The Theology* I spoke about the intention and nature of my arrangement and presentation of the material.[3] What was said there applies here as well.

Critics of *The Theology* expressed the wish that it had contained more references to secondary literature. I have therefore provided more extensive references in this volume. A number of people expressed the hope that the footnote references to the Weimar Edition of *Luther's Works* (*WA*) might have included some brief designation of the particular writing involved. Because of the very large number of such references in the present volume, I could not accede to this request. Instead, I have listed in a footnote at the beginning of each chapter or section the major sources of the references appearing therein, together with their location in *WA*.

Certain themes that might have been included in *The Ethics* have already been treated in *The Theology*—for example, Luther's understanding of the first commandment[4] and of the command-

---

1 Philadelphia: Fortress Press, 1966.
2 *WA* 6, 202–76; *LW* 44, 21–114.
3 *Theology*, v–viii.
4 *Theology*, 130–40.

ment to love our neighbor.⁵ *The Theology* also contains a section
on church and ministry,⁶ to which I have nothing further to add
at this point.

Erlangen
January, 1965

---

⁵ *Theology,* 304–13.
⁶ *Theology,* 287–344. For additional information on this theme see Karl Holl,
"Luther und das landesherrliche Kirchenregiment," *GA* 1, pp. 326–80; Ernst
Kinder, *Der evangelische Glaube und die Kirche. Grundzüge des evang.-luth.
Kirchenverständnisses* (Berlin: Lutherisches Verlagshaus, 1958), pp. 78–144;
Hans Liermann, "Luther ordnet seine Kirche," *Luther-Jahrbuch* 31 (1964):
29–46; and Martin Doerne, "Luthers Kirchenverständnis" in *Fragen zur Kirchen-
reform I* (Göttingen: Vandenhoeck & Ruprecht, 1964), pp. 10–41.

CONTENTS

ABBREVIATIONS

BC   — *The Book of Concord,* translated and edited by Theodore G. Tappert, et al. (Philadelphia, 1959).

GA   — Karl Holl, *Gesammelte Aufsätze zur Kirchengeschichte* (3 vols.; Tübingen: Mohr, 1932), vol. 1, 6th ed., vol. 3, 2nd ed., vol. 3, ed. Hans Lietzmann.

LCC   — *Library of Christian Classics,* John T. McNeill and Henry P. van Dusen, general editors (Philadelphia: Westminster, 1953–).

LCC 18 — *Luther: Letters of Spiritual Counsel,* translated and edited by Theodore G. Tappert. *LCC,* vol. 18 (1955).

LW   — American Edition of *Luther's Works* (Philadelphia and St. Louis, 1955–).

RW   — *Reformation Writings,* translated by Bertram Lee Woolf (New York: Philosophical Library, 1953–).

S-J   — *Luther's Correspondence,* 2 vols., edited by Preserved Smith and Charles M. Jacobs (Philadelphia: United Lutheran Publication House, 1913–1918).

Theology — Paul Althaus, *The Theology of Martin Luther,* translated by Robert C. Schultz (Philadelphia: Fortress Press, 1966).

WA   — *D. Martin Luthers Werke.* Kritische Gesamtausgabe (Weimar, 1883–).

WA Br — *D. Martin Luthers Werke.* Briefwechsel (Weimar, 1930–1948).

WA DB— *D. Martin Luthers Werke. Deutsche Bibel* (Weimar, 1906–).

WA TR — *D. Martin Luthers Werke.* Tischreden (Weimar, 1912–1921).

THE
ETHICS OF
MARTIN LUTHER

1

THE FOUNDATION OF THE CHRISTIAN ETHOS[1]

LUTHER'S ETHICS is determined in its entirety, in its starting point and all its main features, by the heart and center of his theology, namely, by the justification of the sinner through the grace that is shown in Jesus Christ and received through faith alone. Justification by faith determines Christian ethics because, for the Christian, justification is both the presupposition and the source of the ethical life.

JUSTIFICATION AS THE PRESUPPOSITION OF ALL CHRISTIAN ACTIVITY

Everything the Christian does presupposes that he is justified. Justification determines the Christian ethos because it governs the Christian's understanding of what the Christian life is. It does this in two ways: negatively, by what it rules out, and positively, by what it affirms. (1) (2)

In the first place, justification has a negative significance for the Christian ethos. Since fellowship with God—and this is all that salvation really is—is grounded entirely in God's gracious acceptance of the sinner, neither the Christian ethos nor human activity can ever be construed as a way of attaining God's approval and winning salvation.[2] According to Luther's teaching on justification,

---

[1] *Treatise on Good Works, WA* 6, 202–76; *LW* 44, 21–114. Karl Thieme, *Die sittliche Triebkraft des Glaubens bei Luther* (Leipzig: Dörffling & Franke, 1895). Wilhelm Walther, "Die christliche Sittlichkeit nach Luther," *Das Erbe der Reformation im Kampfe der Gegenwart*, Heft 3, 2d ed. (Leipzig: Deichert, 1917). Karl Holl, "Der Neubau der Sittlichkeit" (1919), *GA* 1, 217–87, esp. 217–29. Ragnar Bring, *Das Verhältnis von Glauben und Werken in der lutherischen Theologie*, trans. Karl-Heinz Becker (Munich: Chr. Kaiser, 1955). Albrecht Peters, *Glaube und Werk. Luthers Rechtfertigungslehre im Lichte der Heiligen Schrift* (Berlin: Lutherisches Verlagshaus, 1962).

[2] ". . . so that nobody thinks he is pleasing to God an account of what he does." *WA* 6, 263; *LW* 44, 97.

there are two reasons why such an understanding is impossible.

First, no man ever surrenders his heart to the will of God as completely as the command of God, understood in its most profound sense, requires. A man may do many good things but still not be a good man, because his heart is never pure but always divided and enslaved to sin. A man could be truly good, and he and his works well pleasing to God, only if his heart were free to serve God with undivided loyalty.[3]

Second, even if with the help of grace a man should ever bring himself to the point of such complete devotion, his perfect ethical righteousness still would not motivate God to save him. God wants to bestow salvation as a free act of his own sovereign mercy in Christ. No other way of salvation would allow God to be God! If we regard our own ethos as something we have achieved, a performance we can offer to God as a reason for saving us, we refuse to let God be God—and that is the greatest sin of all. Thus, what I do can never be understood teleologically, that is, as though it had the purpose of winning salvation.[4] Salvation or fellowship with God is granted only to faith. It always precedes all human action. We can relate to God only through faith, never through our own accomplishments. The activity of the Christian whose ethos is based on justification can never be understood in terms of achieving salvation; it can only be understood in terms of gratitude to God for the salvation freely given before we do anything.[5] No one can ever attain a good conscience before God through his works. On the contrary, good works can be done only by the man who already has a good conscience because God has freely forgiven

---

3 *WA* 39[1], 46; *LW* 34, 111. For a more detailed discussion of this point, see *Theology*, 118–29.

4 "Grace cannot stand it when we want to give something to God or establish merit or pay him with our works. This is the greatest of blasphemies and idolatries and is nothing less than the denial and even ridicule of God. These offerings of works spell the elimination of thank-offerings, which cannot exist alongside them. Whoever wants to earn and win by works certainly does not expect to receive anything for nothing or through grace. Instead, he wants to do business and haggle with God. But whoever receives nothing by grace will not give thanks either." *WA* 31[1], 252; *LW* 14, 34.

5 Luther says of men who have done good works in order to gain God's favor: "In all this they have had no faith in the grace of God and no certainty of his approval . . . and they look for good only after the works have been performed. And so they build their confidence not on God's favor, but on the works they have done. That is building on sand and water." *WA* 6, 209; *LW* 44, 29.

his sin. A good conscience is not the product but the source of the
Christian ethos.[6]

Since obedience is required of us, our works are—and are intended to be—nothing more than simple compliance with God's
command. We add nothing beyond what he requires, nothing upon
which salvation could be based.[7] What we do for God can be
described only in terms of obedience, and of thanks and praise to
God. Understood teleologically, however—that is, in terms of their
purpose—our deeds are done not for God but for our neighbor
and for him alone. Whatever we do, we are to concern ourselves
only with our neighbor's needs and not worry about our own
salvation. We are to care for our neighbor and him alone.[8] The
man who does something to gain his own salvation really cares
only for himself. However, God has already provided for my
needs—therefore I do not need to be concerned about myself. Indeed, God gives me what I need in advance when I, through faith,
receive his grace and favor. Beyond that, nothing more is needed.[9]

In the second place, justification as the ground of ethics has a
positive significance. Just as God—paradoxically—accepts me as
righteous and looks upon me with favor even though I am and
remain a sinner, so God also accepts and approves my works. Em-
pirically, what the Christian does is never so good as to be right
and acceptable in the sight of God, for man's sinful nature con-

---

[6] "Sins must be forgiven before good works can be done. For works do not drive out sin, but the driving out of sin leads to good works. For good works must be done with joyful heart and good conscience toward God, that is, out of the forgiveness of guilt." *WA* 2, 715; *LW* 35, 10.

[7] Works should be done "as an exercise of faith, so that nobody thinks he is pleasing to God on account of what he does, but rather by a confident trust in his favor he does such tasks for a gracious and loving God and to his honor and praise alone. And in so doing he serves and benefits his neighbor." *WA* 6, 263; *LW* 44, 97.

[8] "Our own self-imposed good works lead us to and into ourselves, so that we just seek our own benefit and salvation. But God's commandments drive us to our neighbor's need, that by means of these commandments we may be of benefit only to others and to their salvation." *WA* 6, 242; *LW* 44, 71.

[9] "You have frequently heard that we need not do works for God's benefit but only for our neighbor's benefit. We cannot make God stronger or richer through our works—but these works can strengthen and enrich other people. People need them—God doesn't—and people ought to receive them." *WA* 10III, 222. "Therefore I say, 'O God, I do not intend my works to gain merit before you but only to serve my neighbor. I shall depend only on your mercy.'" *WA* 10III, 279. "All our works should be of such a nature that they flow from plea-sure and love, and are all directed toward our neighbor, since for ourselves we need nothing to make us good." *WA* 12, 333; *LW* 30, 79.

tinues to contaminate everything he does. Nevertheless, the deeds
are right in the sight of God because in his grace he approves them
—even as he approves the man who in faith lays hold of his
wondrous grace and favor.[10] It is by virtue of this justifying "yes"
of God that the Christian is given, through faith, a good conscience about his works. In and of itself, in an immanent sense, his
conscience is not good; it only becomes a good conscience in a
paradoxical way—through the word of forgiveness, God's act of
justification.[11]

Christian behavior, therefore, however imperfect and sinful it
may be in and of itself, is good because it is grounded in the
assurance of a prior "yes," in that divine approval which the
Christian does not have to seek because it has already been given.
This is why the Christian can go ahead and act in confidence and
joy, even though his works are still impure and imperfect.[12]

It goes without saying that in all this Luther is thinking of men
who are trying to obey God's commands. He is not speaking of
intentional disobedience but of obedience, however fragmented
and defective that obedience may be in actuality. This brings us to
an important distinction which Luther makes in the meaning of
God's "good pleasure." First, there is the ethical meaning: God is
pleased with all those works which he has himself commanded
and which are therefore right in his sight, whereas he is not
pleased with all those works which men choose for themselves.[13]
Second, Luther makes a metaethical distinction: as a result of
justification God is—paradoxically—pleased with the works he

---

10 "All the works of men are evil and sinful, but God considers the works of
the righteous to be good." *WA* 39[I], 204. Cf. *WA* 39[II], 188; *LW* 34, 304–305.
    11 *WA* 6, 205; *LW* 44, 24.
    12 "Faith is the highest work because it blots out these everyday sins and
still stands fast by never doubting that God is so favorably disposed toward you
that he overlooks such everyday failures and offenses. Yes, even if a deadly sin
arise . . . nonetheless faith always rises again and does not doubt that its sin is
already gone." *WA* 6, 215; *LW* 44, 37. Nobody does the work of this commandment unless he is firm and unshaken in the confidence of divine favor. *WA*
6, 275; *LW* 44, 113.
    13 Those who fulfill the fourth commandment can say: "See, this work is
well pleasing to my God in heaven; this I know for certain. . . . You should
rejoice heartily and thank God that he has chosen and fitted you to perform a
task so precious and pleasing to him. Even though it seems very trivial and
contemptible, make sure that you regard it as great and precious, not on account
of your worthiness but because it has its place within that jewel and holy
treasure, the word and commandment of God." *WA* 30[I], 149; *BC*, 381.

has himself commanded, even though the works actually done are (2)
full of impurity. These two meanings of God's good pleasure
must always be clearly distinguished.[14] All ethical activity that is
right in the sight of God thus presupposes that God is pleased in
two ways.

This twofold meaning of God's good pleasure corresponds to a
twofold meaning of the word *good*. In the ethical sense my action
is good if done in response to God's command. In the metaethical
sense my action is good, despite its constant impurity, because of
God's act of justification. Deeds, therefore, may be ethically good
—because commanded by God—and still have no metaethical
value whatever in the sight of God unless they are done in the
faith that God justifies the sinner.[15]

God's command demands that the substance of our activity be
morally correct. However, our activity is really good in God's
judgment only if we act with the right feeling and attitude toward
God. The word *good* thus designates the right substance of an act
and its right performance, that is, the right attitude toward God.
This right attitude toward God consists in being certain that God
has already given us salvation and that the God who justifies is
already pleased with us before we act.

This means that Christian activity is Christian because it is
carried on in the faith that we are justified. This faith and only
this faith makes it good in the sense of the gospel. Thus Christian
activity is good, despite all the sinfulness that remains within us,

---

[14] Both meanings of God's good pleasure are closely related. They describe the
same reality as faith, insofar as it relies completely on God's activity and is at
the same time concerned with what God has commanded and does not seek to
find good works for itself. If faith were to choose works for itself, it would
thereby break its trust in God's mercy. Since God's mercy gives me my work to
do, such a break could not be reconciled with justifying faith.

[15] "For although such works do not make men righteous before God or save
them, nevertheless it is a joy and comfort to know that these works please God
so very much—and the more so when such a man is a believer and is in the
kingdom of Christ." *WA* 30[II], 560; *LW* 46, 241. Luther also speaks of God's
twofold good pleasure: "Therefore, if according to God's word and command
you live in your station with your husband, wife, child, neighbor, or friend, you
can see God's intention in these things; and you can come to the conclusion that
they please him, since this is not your own dream, but his word and command,
which never deludes or deceives us. It is a wonderful thing, a treasure beyond
every thought or wish, to know that you are standing and living in the right
relationship to God. In this way not only can your heart take comfort and pride
in the assurance of his grace, but you can know that your outward conduct and
behavior is pleasing to him." *WA* 32, 329; *LW* 21, 37–38.

because it is done in faith. Luther describes this very beautifully in his *Treatise on Good Works*. God accepts as good that faith which receives his grace. All Christian activity must proceed "in faith," that is, in the trust that these works, like the man who does them, are right with God because they are justified.[16] Such trust also makes this man's activity right and good in the sight of God. Faith is the "first, highest, and most precious of all good works," the "chief work." Without it all other works are nothing and are dead.[17] Faith alone is true service of God. Works done in this trust share faith's own acceptance by God.[18] "For in this work all good works exist, and from faith these works receive a borrowed goodness."[19] All works done in this faith share the healthy soundness which "makes all works good"; faith is "the man in charge."[20] Thus the ethical substance of works and their moral correctness are not enough in God's judgment. Works must also be done with the right religious attitude. They must be theologically as well as ethically correct, that is, they must be done in the certainty of salvation and with the confidence that God graciously accepts them as valid, just as he accepts the man who does them.[21] This faith is indispensable. A work may be very ethical in terms of its substance even though it is done in unfaith; if so, it is sin in God's judgment (Romans 14:23). Viewed in terms of simple morality, the non-Christian can do everything the Christian does.[22] The true Christian ethos is distinguished from every other ethos because the Christian acts on the basic presupposition of his certainty that he is saved. Modern studies in comparative religion have confirmed this insight of Luther.

Luther says both that works must be done "in faith" and that

---

16 "Good works . . . are not good in themselves, but must be done in faith and in the assurance of God's favor." *WA* 6, 229; *LW* 44, 54; *WA* 6, 204, 263; *LW* 44, 24, 97.

17 *WA* 6, 204–205, 210, 212, 255, 275; *LW* 44, 23–24, 31, 33, 87, 113.

18 *WA* 6, 212; *LW* 44, 33.

19 *WA* 6, 204; *LW* 44, 24.

20 *WA* 6, 263; *LW* 44, 98; *WA* 6, 215–16, 275; *LW* 44, 37–38, 113.

21 "Nobody must think that the training and teaching of his children is sufficient in itself. It must be done in confidence of God's favor. A man must have no doubt that he is well pleasing to God in what he is doing." *WA* 6, 255; *LW* 44, 87.

22 "A heathen, a Jew, a Turk, a sinner may also do all other works; but to trust firmly that he pleases God is possible only for a Christian, who is enlightened and strengthened by grace." *WA* 6, 206; *LW* 44, 25.

"all works remain within the sphere of the first commandment and of faith."[23] These two statements express the same thought. For faith is the fulfilling of the first commandment.[24] Thus the same things that have been said about faith in the preceding paragraphs may be said about the first commandment.[25]

The Christian's justifying faith and his certainty that he is saved give him very great freedom of action.[26] The Christian is free to do joyfully every work required by the situation in which he lives. An ethos that is not based on justification and is not certain that God is well pleased with us, but rather feels we need first to gain God's approval, is compelled to try to find special holy works that are different from common ordinary works. Such an ethos must choose special pious works rather than simply doing what God has commanded.[27] When we are certain that we are justified and that God is graciously pleased with our person and our works, then every distinction between ordinary and special, profane and holy, insignificant and significant, small and great works disappears completely.[28] Such distinctions are made only by the moralist

---

[23] *WA* 6, 249; *LW* 44, 79.

[24] *WA* 6, 209; *LW* 44, 29; *Theology,* 234 ff.

[25] "In all the commandments the first is the captain, and faith the chief work and life of all other works, without which, as has been said, such works cannot be good." *WA* 6, 234; *LW* 44, 60. "The first and chief commandment, from which all the others proceed . . . is to illuminate and impart its splendor to all the others." *WA* 30^I, 180; *BC*, 409.

[26] *WA* 6, 214; *LW* 44, 36.

[27] "There are no good works except those works which God has commanded." *WA* 6, 204; *LW* 44, 23. Luther says that the Christian accepts "any free work which presents itself without his selecting it." *WA* 6, 214; *LW* 44, 36. "He who is not at one with God, or is in a state of doubt, worries and starts looking about for ways and means to do enough and to influence God with his many good works." *WA* 6, 207; *LW* 44, 27.

[28] "In this faith all works become equal, and one work is like another; all distinctions between works fall away, whether they be great, small, short, long, many, or few. For the works are acceptable not for their own sake but because of faith, which is always the same and lives and works in each and every work without distinction, however numerous and varied these works always are. . . . It further follows from this that a Christian man living in this faith has no need of a teacher of good works; he does whatever the occasion calls for, and all is well done. [Luther refers at this point to 1 Samuel 10:6–7; 1:17–18; and Romans 8:2.] For faith does not permit itself to be bound to any work or to refuse any work, but, as the first Psalm says, it 'yields its fruit in its season' [Psalms 1:3], that is, in the normal course of events. We may see this in an everyday example. When a husband and wife really love one another, have pleasure in each other, and thoroughly believe in their love, who teaches them how they are to behave one to another, what they are to do or not to do, say or not to say, what they are to think? Confidence alone teaches them all this, and even more than is necessary. For such a man there is no distinction in works.

who must give meaning and value to his life through what he does. Since the Christian has received the meaning and value of his life through God's gracious act of justification, all tasks and works of life are equally important and holy because they have been assigned to him by God's direction of his life. There are no particularly holy works. Everything that we do is secular. However, it all becomes holy when it is done in obedience to God's command and in the certainty that he will be pleased, that is, when it is done in faith. This gives value and hidden glory to everything we do. As long as a man is trapped in moralism and does not live as a justified man, he seeks out imposing and glorious works. True Christian works, however, do not make a great impression, and their glory is hidden just as God's glory is hidden.[29]

Thus faith sets the Christian free. He is free to do his work with joy, in contrast to the slavish worry, insecurity, and unhappiness of the man who has no faith, doubts how he stands with God, and does not know how he will satisfy God.[30]

JUSTIFICATION AS THE SOURCE OF ALL CHRISTIAN ACTIVITY

Justification does far more ethically than determine the character of the Christian life and regulate its self-understanding. God's relationship to men in justification is nothing less than the basic source of the Christian ethos.

Justification is received in faith. When a man comes to faith, says Luther, Christ enters into him and God's Holy Spirit is given

---

He does the great and the important as gladly as the small and the unimportant, and vice versa. Moreover, he does them all as a free man with a glad, peaceful, and confident heart." *WA* 6, 206–207; *LW* 44, 26–27.

[29] "Lo, all these virtues [such as peacefulness] lie in heaps in this estate; but men do not see them, for they make no show. Because of the goodness and the number of them they cannot make a show. But the empty, worthless, useless works, these make a show!" *WA* 31¹, 202; *LW* 13, 56. "These unnatural and superstitious works, which they decide upon without either the command or the approval of God, they regard as so brilliant and saintly as to surpass and obscure love, which is the sun that outshines all works. . . . Therefore we must battle unremittingly not only against the opinions of our own heart, on which by nature we would rather depend in the matter of salvation than on the word of God, but also against the false front and saintly appearance of self-chosen works." *WA* 40¹¹, 71; *LW* 27, 57.

[30] *WA* 6, 207; *LW* 44, 27.

to him.[31] Man is made new, and this newness is for Luther one and the same whether it be attributed to faith or Christ or the Holy Spirit. How are we to understand this? Justification is a completely new kind of encounter between God and man. God now encounters man in his real nature as God. Before this, of course, man stood under God, before God, and carried God's image in himself. All this, however, was determined by the law, that is, by God's demands and judgment. And as long as a man deals only with the God of the law and with his ethical demands, he does not see and experience the true nature of God. We confront the true God and his real deity only when we hear the gospel of God's spontaneous gift to the sinner: he gives himself to men as a gift in order to enter into a loving relationship with them.[32] God now fully confronts man entirely as the self-giving love he really is. God thus gains a new kind of power over the human heart which previously maintained its inner distance from God through mistrust, slavish fear, and flight. God now enflames this heart with love for God. Through this loving approach to man, God draws him into the process of his own love. God has acted lovingly toward man in the crucified Christ; how could man now do anything other than to cease mistrusting and opposing God and be reconciled to him?[33] All this is the work of Christ or of the Holy Spirit, who enters into a man when he begins to believe.

Now such a man's relationship to the law is also basically changed. As long as man was a sinner the law confronted him only with the unfulfillable demands of God, and man could only respond with hatred and resistance.[34] When the sinner has been

---

[31] *Theology*, 233 ff. "God gives his spirit immediately to him who trusts him." *WA* 6, 206; *LW* 44, 26.

[32] "No one can learn to know such a God through the law but only through the Spirit and word of the gospel." *WA* 15, 726.

[33] "If you see in the crucified Christ that God is so kindly disposed toward you that he even gives his own Son for you, then your heart in turn must grow sweet and disposed toward God." *WA* 6, 216; *LW* 44, 38. "When anyone hears and believes this preaching, he is encouraged and comforted by it; now he no longer flees from God but turns to him. And since he finds and feels such grace and mercy in God, he again begins to be reconciled to God and starts to call upon him from his heart and to respect and honor him as his loving God. The stronger such faith and comfort are, the more he loves God's commands and desires to obey them." *WA* 22, 222.

[34] *Theology*, 175–76.

justified, however, the law takes on new meaning for him: Christ
has fulfilled the law for us. Thereby we are relieved of the terrible
burden that there can be no salvation for us unless we completely
fulfill the law. This one barrier to recognizing the law as the
expression of God's eternal goodwill is now set aside. Now man
is able to love God's law with his whole heart just as he loves God
himself—for the content of the law is the form and expression of
the nature of God. The great and unfulfillable demands of the
law previously made man despair. Now these same demands are
precious and desirable, for they have been fulfilled through Christ;
and Christ, who has fulfilled the whole law, dwells in the hearts
of Christians and motivates and enables them to fulfill the law.[35]
The gospel has made the law "a lovely thing" for man.[36] This is
"the great miracle of transformation" which God's Spirit works
in man's heart.[37] In place of the covetous desires forbidden by
God's law, God's Spirit has now created a new and sweet desire
to love that is greater than any natural desire and simultaneously
hates the flesh.[38] Such a man is now involved in a new process.
The good tree now produces good fruit.[39] This is the impulse and
the motivation of God's Spirit himself. The Holy Spirit is restless
in us and cannot remain idle; and as a result, the Christian is also
not idle but is rather filled with energy and acts in such a way
that he pleases God.[40] As the Holy Spirit himself burns with love,

---

[35] "When our heart hears that Christ has fulfilled the law for us and taken
our sin upon himself, we are no longer concerned that the law demands the
impossible of us and that we must despair and abandon our attempts to keep it.
Rather, the fact that the law is so high and deep, so holy and right and good,
and demands such great things of us is now precious and . . . good; we even
love and praise the law because it demands so many great things of us. The
heart, which through Christ has everything the law demands, would be very
grieved if the law demanded less. See, the law previously was hard and difficult, even impossible; now it becomes light and easy for it lives in our hearts
through the Spirit." *WA* 17[II], 70. Believers "having accepted the Holy Spirit
through the word of faith now joyfully and eagerly do what the law demands."
WA 5, 553.
[36] *WA* 5, 562.
[37] Ibid.
[38] The Holy Spirit "inflames us with a new and sweet concupiscence of love
and makes us hate that concupiscence which the law forbids." *WA* 5, 559,
562–63.
[39] Luther uses this picture very frequently, for example, *WA* 39[I], 46; *LW* 34,
111; *WA* 39[II], 188; *LW* 34, 305.
[40] "There is a spirit of restlessness amid the greatest calm, that is, in God's
grace and peace. A Christian cannot be still or idle. He constantly strives and
struggles with all his might, as one who has no other object in life than to

so he makes the Christian's heart burn with love and desire for
God. He makes the dead heart live.[41]

It is only a change in terminology when Luther describes all
this work of the Holy Spirit as the work of *faith*. For the Holy *(11)*
Spirit is involved in faith. Faith receives the Spirit and is at the
same time his work. Faith and the Spirit are one. Luther's description of faith in his *Preface to the Epistle of St. Paul to the Romans*
clearly describes this relationship:[42]

> Faith is not the human notion and dream that some people call
> faith. When they see that no improvement of life and no good
> works follow—although they can hear and say much about faith—
> they fall into the error of saying, "Faith is not enough; one must
> do works in order to be righteous and be saved." This is due to
> the fact that when they hear the gospel, they get busy and by
> their own powers create an idea in their heart which says, "I
> believe"; they take this then to be a true faith. But as it is a human
> figment and idea that never reaches the depths of the heart,
> nothing comes of it either, and no improvement follows.
>
> Faith, however, is a divine work in us which changes us and
> makes us to be born anew of God, John 1 [:12–13]. It kills the
> old Adam and makes us altogether different men, in heart and
> spirit and mind and powers; and it brings with it the Holy Spirit.
> Oh, it is a living, busy, active mighty thing, this faith. It is im-
> possible for it not to be doing good works incessantly. It does not
> ask whether good works are to be done, but before the question
> is asked, it has already done them, and is constantly doing them.

disseminate God's honor and glory among the people." *WA* 45, 540; *LW* 24,
88. "But after a man is justified by faith, now possesses Christ by faith, and
knows that he is his righteousness and life, he will certainly not be idle but,
like a sound tree, will bear good fruit (Matthew 7:17). For the believer has the
Holy Spirit; and where he is, he does not permit a man to be idle but drives
him to all the exercises of devotion, to thanksgiving, and to the practice of love
toward all men." *WA* 40[I], 265; *LW* 26, 154–55. See below, n. 57.

41 "The Holy Spirit now comes and fills a man's heart and makes him to be a
different kind of man who loves God and enjoys doing what God wills. . . . He
kindles fiery flames in the heart and makes it alive so that it breaks out in
fiery tongues and with an energetic hand. And a new man is created who now
understands, feels, and thinks differently than before. Now his understanding,
insight, emotions, and heart are all alive—all these burn with the desire to do
everything that pleases God." *WA* 21, 440.

42 *WA* DB 7, 10; *LW* 35, 370–71. *Theology*, 234–50. "The kingdom of God
comes . . . only through the gospel and faith in God, through which hearts are
cleansed, comforted, and pacified. For the Holy Spirit fills a man's heart with
love and knowledge of God and unities his spirit with God's Spirit. As a result
his mind is changed so that he wills and desires, seeks and loves, whatever God
wills." *WA* 15, 725.

Whoever does not do such good works, however, is an unbeliever. He gropes and looks around for faith and good works, but knows neither what faith is nor what good works are. Yet he talks and talks, with many words, about faith and good works.

Faith is a living, daring confidence in God's grace, so sure and certain that the believer would stake his life on it a thousand times. This knowledge of and confidence in God's grace makes men glad and bold and happy in dealing with God and with all creatures. And this is the work which the Holy Spirit performs in faith. Because of it, without compulsion, a person is ready and glad to do good to everyone, to serve everyone, to suffer everything, out of love and praise to God who has shown him this grace. Thus it is impossible to separate works from faith, quite as impossible as to separate heat and light from fire. Beware, therefore, of your own false notions and of the idle talkers who imagine themselves wise enough to make decisions about faith and good works, and yet are the greatest fools. Pray God that he may work faith in you. Otherwise you will surely remain forever without faith, regardless of what you may think or do.

We have said that the sinner's experience of God's accepting and justifying love creates love in man. For Luther, our love of God and our love of our neighbor cannot be separated. Luther emphasizes that we must experience God's love for us before we can seriously love our brother;[43] but he also emphasizes that our experience of God's love necessarily results in our loving our brother. Luther uses the picture of a water fountain or a water pipe to describe this relationship between the love which we have experienced from God and our love of the brother: God's love flows into us and then flows out again to our neighbor.[44] Our faith which receives God's love and our love of the brother which passes on God's love are part of a continuous process.

Because the Christian's activity flows out of his experience of God's love and since this activity is itself love, it shares all the characteristics of God's own love. God wants his people to act

---

[43] "Before we can show mercy, we ourselves must previously have received God's mercy from God." *WA* 10[III], 225. "Anyone who does not believe but goes on doubting the grace and love of God will not have the heart to express his love and thanks to God by responding to his neighbor in love. However, this faith which recognizes the great grace and goodness of God which has helped him from death to life, always inflames a man's heart to love and to do good, even to his enemies, just as God has done for him." *WA* 22, 15.

[44] *WA* 7, 37; *RW*[I], 379; cf. *LW* 31, 371; *WA* 10[III], 223; *WA* 17[I], 265.

spontaneously, freely and voluntarily, happily and eagerly.[45] Where the Spirit and faith do their work, the Christian does not respond compulsively or artificially to his neighbor; rather, he acts with an inner necessity comparable to the natural processes by which trees bear fruit.[46] This spontaneity changes the "thou shalt" to an inner "I must." Here the imperative is set aside through the indicative worked by God's Holy Spirit: Christians spontaneously do the good works which they ought to do.

In his Small Catechism, Luther describes faith as the source of life in obedience to God's commands by beginning the explanation of all the commandments with an abbreviated form of the first commandment: "We should fear and love God, and as a result . . ."[47] In his *Treatise on Good Works* and in the Large Catechism he describes how faith does what the commandments say we ought to do and thereby fulfills them. He demonstrates that the actions forbidden by individual commandments flow from mistrust of God and unfaith in Christ; similarly, he shows that it is faith that produces the righteous works which they command.[48] Since faith fulfills the first commandment, Luther can also say that people who keep the first commandment will also keep all the others by virtue of keeping the first commandment.[49]

All this is true for the commandments that deal with our relation to our neighbor as well as those that deal with our relation to God. Luther refers to this in connection with each commandment. For example, in speaking of the fifth commandment he says: "This lofty, noble, satisfying work may be learned very easily, if we do it in faith and bring faith to bear upon it. For if faith does not doubt the favor of God, and a man has no doubt that he has a gracious God, it will be quite easy for him to be gracious and

---

[45] The Christian "does everything gladly and willingly . . . because it is a pleasure for him to please God in doing these things . . . content that his service pleases God." *WA* 6, 207–213; *LW* 4, 27–36; *WA* 213; *LW* 44, 36.

[46] "We confess that good works must follow faith, yes, not only must, but follow voluntarily, just as a good tree not only must produce good fruits, but does so freely (Matthew 7:18)." *WA* 39[I], 46; *LW* 34, 111.

[47] *WA* 30[I], 353–62; *BC*, 342–44.

[48] *WA* 12, 459; *WA* 30[I], 180, *BC*, 409.

[49] "Where the heart is right with God and this commandment is kept, fulfillment of all the others will follow of its own accord." *WA* 30[I], 139; *BC*, 371. "The first commandment is the chief source and fountainhead from which all the others proceed." *WA* 30[I], 181; *BC*, 410.

favorable to his neighbor, however much the neighbor may have
sinned against him.[50] In speaking of the command to be chaste,
Luther says: "In the matter of chastity a good strong faith is a
great help—more noticeably so than in almost any other work.
Faith is a guard of chastity."[51] In speaking of the seventh commandment he says: "Faith teaches this work [of not worrying and
not being greedy] of itself. If the heart expects and puts its trust
in divine favor, how can a man be greedy and anxious? Such a
man is absolutely certain that he is acceptable to God: therefore
he does not cling to money; he uses his money cheerfully and
freely for the benefit of his neighbor. He knows full well that he
will have enough no matter how much he gives away. His God,
whom he trusts, will neither lie to him nor forsake him."[52] In
discussing the eighth commandment, Luther speaks of those who
are ashamed to confess the truth of the gospel when the important
people of this world attack it. "When the pope and the bishops,
as well as princes and kings, attack the truth, then everybody runs
away, keeps quiet, or pretends not to notice so as not to lose his
possessions, his honor, his favor, and his life. Why do they do
this? For the simple reason that they have no faith in God and
expect nothing good from him. For where there is such faith and
confidence, there is also a bold, defiant, fearless heart that risks all
and stands by the truth, no matter what the cost, whether it is
against pope or king, as we see that the dear martyrs did."[53]

LIFE AS THE EXERCISE OF FAITH[54]

The theologians of the Lutheran Reformation liked to describe
works as "following" faith.[55] This phrase establishes the substan-
tive priority of faith but does not suggest a temporal succession,
a separation in time. The relationship of faith to practical life is
much closer; indeed, it is a relationship of immanence. Works

---

[50] *WA* 6, 268; *LW* 44, 103.
[51] *WA* 6, 269; *LW* 44, 105.
[52] *WA* 6, 272; *LW* 44, 108.
[53] *WA* 6, 275; *LW* 44, 112.
[54] Manfred Schloenbach, *Heiligung als Fortschreiten und Wachstum des
Glaubens in Luthers Theologie* (Helsinki: Luther-Agricola Gesellschaft, 1963).
[55] Luther uses this expression, for example, in *WA* 39[I], 46; *LW* 34, 111; and
WA 10[III], 278.

(and suffering) are exercises of our faith: Christians "should exercise faith in all good works."[56]

For Luther, the exercise of faith in practical life is to be understood in a twofold sense. It is both an expression of the Christian's faith before the world and a matter of training whereby that faith is strengthened.

Faith, like human life itself, never stands still but is always energetically active in the present world.[57] Luther does not think of faith as existing in and of itself and thus separate from the activity of life; he thinks of it only in terms of the concrete acts of life in specific existential situations. Luther does not imagine that any moment of life could be lived without faith or in neutrality toward faith. Every situation and every hour of life is lived either in faith or in unfaith. At every moment throughout life, faith is summoned to concrete realization. "Works" are nothing but the concrete realization of faith itself. Faith needs works—that is, concrete, specific acts of life—in order to be itself at any point. Faith always needs secular life—just as secular life in turn always needs faith. Believing is not something I do *alongside* my life in this world but rather in it—in each and every act of living. Faith expresses itself in the form of works. Faith lives *in* works, just as works are done *in* faith.

Only by thus exercising our faith can we begin to recognize what faith is and what it means to believe. This happens when we have to risk or bear something in faith or when we encounter our neighbor or our enemy in faith. Then we really begin to learn what it means to say that we place all our trust in God alone.[58]

As a man through his actions becomes aware of what faith

---

56 *WA* 6, 204; *LW* 44, 23. Luther uses this expression frequently, for example, in the *Treatise on Good Works: WA* 6, 212, 255, 263, 268; *LW* 44, 34, 87, 97–98, 103.

57 "Now, since the being and nature of man cannot exist for an instant unless it is doing or not doing something, putting up with or running away from something (for as we know, life never stands still), well, then, let him who wants to be holy and full of good works begin to exercise himself at all times in this faith in all his life and works. Let him learn to do and to leave undone all things in such continual faith. Then he will find how much work he has to do, and how completely all things are included in faith, and how he may never grow idle because his very idling must be the exercise and work of faith." *WA* 6, 212; *LW* 44, 34.

58 "Nobody knows what a great thing it is to trust God alone except him who begins to trust and tries to do faith's works." *WA* 6, 234; *LW* 44, 61.

(2') means, he also becomes certain *that* he believes.[59] Faith that is
exercised thus becomes certain of itself in a twofold sense. First,
(a) the practice of works is the test of faith.[60] Our works show that
we have faith and thereby make us certain both that we have faith
and that we are saved. Luther repeatedly asserted this on the basis
(b) of 2 Peter 1:10.[61] Second, such exercise also trains faith. As faith
is realized in the concrete situations of life it becomes stronger,
increases, and grows. Since faith is the central element in being a
Christian, everything depends on the strengthening of faith. All
the commands, all the practices of life, and all our works serve
this purpose.[62] The more energetically faith is practiced, the more
it can make us certain of our salvation.

Thus there is a twofold interchange between faith and works:
works flow out of faith, and faith in turn is strengthened by
works.[63]

Luther recognizes that there are steps and stages in the exercise
and strengthening of faith. Alongside works stands suffering—
and both of these together are necessary for the full exercise of
faith.[64] However, it is more significant to confirm our faith through
suffering than through works. For it is more difficult to maintain
our faith in God's eternal love when we are suffering than when
we are actively working. Therefore, faith is greater and stronger

---

[59] *WA* 17^I, 258; *WA* 10^{III}, 95, 278.

[60] "On the basis of this [eighth] commandment, anyone may very easily try
and find out whether he is a Christian and true believer in Christ, and thus
whether he is doing good works or not." *WA* 6, 275; *LW* 44, 113.

[61] For example, *WA* 6, 217; *LW* 44, 40; *WA* 14, 22–24; *LW* 30, 158–59;
WA 32, 423; *LW* 21, 149. For a detailed discussion, see *Theology*, 245–50.

[62] "Such works are to be done and such suffering endured in faith and in the
sure confidence of God's favor, so that all the works remain within the sphere
of the first commandment and of faith, which exercises itself in these sufferings
and grows strong. It is for the sake of this faith that all other commandments
and works have been instituted." *WA* 6, 249; *LW* 44, 79. "One should not let
faith rest and lie still, for it is so constituted that through application and
practice it becomes stronger and stronger, until it is sure of the call and election
and cannot be wanting." *WA* 14, 23; *LW* 30, 158–59.

[63] Luther describes the relationship between the first commandment and the
others as "a pretty golden ring." Praise and worship flow out of faith, and they
in turn strengthen faith. "Thus faith goes out into works and through works
comes back to itself again." *WA* 6, 249; *LW* 44, 79. "Thus you see how the
first commandment is the chief source and fountainhead from which all the
others proceed; again, to it they all return and upon it they depend, so that end
and beginning are all linked and bound together." *WA* 30^I, 181; *BC*, 410.

[64] We should "remain pupils of the first commandment and of faith throughout all works and sufferings, and never cease to learn." *WA* 6, 234; *LW* 44, 61.

when enduring suffering than when simply manifesting itself in works.[65] The greatest and most precious fruit of faith is that I can remain confident that God means well with me and loves me even in the midst of the troubles and suffering of this life. (In discussing suffering, Luther distinguishes between the confirmation *(i)* of faith in temporal and secular suffering and the confirmation of faith in the spiritual suffering of experiencing God's wrath and *(ii)* punishment.)[66] Since God can use our sufferings to produce the highest confirmation and make us aware of the full value of faith, these sufferings themselves are immeasurably precious and valuable.[67]

THE LIFE OF THE CHRISTIAN
AS A STRUGGLE WITH HIMSELF

Through faith the justified man becomes a new man. The Spirit of God moves him. However, faith does not transform the whole person all at once. The old nature with its desires is not yet completely put to death. Thus the Christian is still divided within himself. Luther understands <u>Romans 7</u> as a <u>lamentation over this</u> *(1)* <u>split</u> in the life of the Christian.

This split is not to be confused with the twofold character of the Christian as *simul justus et peccator*, at one and the same time a righteous man and a sinner. Luther uses *simul justus et peccator* *(2)* to describe the *whole* man in the judgment of God at any given time: in and of myself I am and remain throughout my whole life a sinner before God; yet through God's gracious act of justification, I, the sinner, am now righteous. Each of these two statements is a

---

65 "In these works faith is still slight and weak. Let us ask further whether, when everything goes wrong with their life, their goods, their honor, their friends, or whatever they have, they still believe that their works are pleasing to God, and that God in his mercy ordains their sufferings and difficulties for them, whether they be small or great. . . . And just as confidence and faith are better, higher, and stronger at this stage than in the first, so the sufferings which are borne in this kind of faith excel all works of faith. Therefore there is an immeasurable difference between such works and sufferings, and the sufferings are better." *WA* 6, 208; *LW* 44, 28–29.

66 *WA* 6, 208; *LW* 44, 28; *Theology*, 57–58.

67 "They who in such suffering trust God and hold on to a good, firm confidence in him, who believe that he is well pleased with them, see in their sufferings and afflictions nothing but pure and precious merits, the costliest treasures which no man can assess. For faith and confidence make precious before God all that which others think most shameful." *WA* 6, 208; *LW* 44, 28.

characterization of the *whole* person in God's judgment. Thus *simul justus et peccator*, the twofold character of the Christian, is to be distinguished from the coexistence within the Christian of both the old and the new man, that anthropological conflict which Luther, following Paul, describes as a conflict between the Spirit and the flesh.[68]

The Christian lives in faith but he also still lives in the flesh.[69] The flesh is opposed to the life of faith and constantly attacks faith. Therefore the Christian life is a constant struggle of the Spirit with the flesh and of faith with the desires of the old man. If faith does not enter into this battle against the flesh, then the flesh becomes lord over faith and kills it. Only Christians become involved in this battle for the very life of faith.[70] This kind of conflict does not exist in the natural life as long as faith and the Holy Spirit do not yet dwell in a man; such a man follows his evil desires without resisting. But faith and the Spirit resist the desires of the flesh. The Christian life is formed and shaped by this struggle. The mark of Christian existence is that one no longer surrenders to the flesh without resistance but now struggles against it.[71]

How is this struggle carried on? Luther sometimes says that God is at work; at other times he says that man himself is sum-

---

[68] *Theology*, 242 ff.

[69] "Through the law of faith, therefore, Paul lives to God inwardly. At the same time he is dead to the law. In the flesh, however, he does not yet live to God but is made alive to God. He is not yet dead to the law but is being put to death to the law. . . . For it is in the life to come that we live fully to God and are dead to the law." *WA* 2, 498, *LW* 27, 233.

[70] "Even though a man has become righteous, he is not yet completely rid of evil lusts. To be sure, faith has indeed begun to subdue the flesh; but the flesh continues to bestir itself and rages nevertheless in all sorts of lusts that would like to assert themselves again and do what they want. Therefore the Spirit must busy itself daily to tame the flesh and bring it into subjection, must wrestle with it incessantly, and take care that it does not repel faith. . . . Where faith is genuine it must attack the body and hold it in check, lest the body do what it pleases." *WA* 12, 282; *LW* 30, 27. "Faith has not yet completely permeated the old man and still does not have full power over the flesh." *WA* 12, 323; *LW* 30, 68.

[71] Believers "always have trials enough; they must wage war constantly. Those who are without faith and the Spirit do not feel this; or they give in, run away, and follow evil lust. . . . Before he believed, he went his way as he pleased. But now that the Spirit has come and works to make him pure, the battle begins. Then the devil, the world, and the flesh assault the faith." *WA* 12, 325; *LW* 30, 70. For a comparison of Luther's understanding of Romans 7:14 ff. with Paul's intention, see Paul Althaus, *Paulus und Luther über den Menschen*, 4th ed. (Gütersloh: Bertelsmann, 1963).

moned to do battle. For Luther both of these assertions are based
on our baptism. He makes this particularly clear in his *The Holy
and Blessed Sacrament of Baptism.*[72] Baptism means not only that
God has made a promise, but also that man has taken an obligation upon himself. God promises the person who is baptized that   (*i*)
he will put his old man to death throughout his life; and we who
are baptized thereby obligate ourselves for the rest of our lives to   (*ii*)
fulfill the meaning of our baptism in all that we do and in everything that happens to us. This makes us active participators in
God's work of mortifying our old man.

God's (word) puts the old man to death in the hard school of
life, particularly in the context of our vocation and our suffering.[73]
When God sends suffering, he works within the context of the
dialectical relationship of his "alien" and proper work (Isaiah 28:
21).[74] God leads us into precisely those situations that will stimu-
late and tempt our old man to sin. He does this in order to set us
free from sin.[75] Luther emphasizes God's therapeutic action against
the pride and ambition that are so common among pious people.
He sees this as God's most urgent action against man's sin. This
corresponds to Luther's basic understanding of the nature of
human sin.[76] The Bible gives many illustrations of godly people
who have asked God to discipline them in order to preserve them
against this hidden evil of pride. "Against this secret villain we
must pray God daily to suppress our self-esteem."[77]

Thus the Christian needs the cross in order to carry on his

---

72 *WA* 2, 727–37; *LW* 35, 29–43.
73 "God trains and tests you all your life long with many good works and
with all kinds of sufferings. Thereby he accomplishes what you in baptism have
desired." *WA* 2, 730; *LW* 35, 33. Luther also applies this to married life, *WA*
40III, 283; *WA* 2, 736; *LW* 31, 41.
74 *Theology,* 119–20.
75 "Therefore, to destroy such works of ours as well as of the old Adam in
us, God overwhelms us with those things which move us to anger, with many
sufferings which rouse us to impatience, and last of all, even with death and the
abuse of the world. By means of these he seeks nothing else but to drive out of
us anger, impatience, and unrest, and to perfect his own work in us, that is,
his peace." *WA* 6, 248; *LW* 44, 77.
76 *Theology,* 146–47.
77 "Therefore David says 'Prove me.' [Psalms 26:2] It is as though he said:
'Take hold of me, give me something to do, impose shame and persecution,
cross and need upon me.' All the prophets prayed against this villainy." Luther
says that the sin of ambition "has often tripped even those who have grasped
God's word purely. . . . By rushing out and refusing to be content as part of
the common crowd, but wanting to be something special, one wanders from
the path without even noticing it." *WA* 17I, 234–35; *LW* 12, 188–89.

struggle against his old man. God will lay upon us the cross we need. Luther warns us against laying upon ourselves a cross that we have ourselves chosen, thinking it will be good for us—as if we could "take heaven by storm" through an unusual measure of self-discipline. In such efforts autonomous reason is once again at work. God does not want this. We should wait for God's leading and guidance and accept what he lays upon us; we are not to take the initiative and force suffering upon ourselves.[78] Luther's statements on these matters are determined by the basic themes of his preaching of justification: all autonomous human activity in matters relating to salvation is rejected; instead, we are to wait for and completely trust in what God does.

God disciplines the Christian, but he does it in such a way that he also summons the Christian to discipline himself and to struggle actively with his old man throughout his life. As ways of subduing the old man Luther mentions fasting, watching, praying, and working. Clearly Luther is not thinking only of physical lusts— "flesh" refers to more than man's physical nature—although he emphatically includes them. Thus faith struggles against the old man by mortifying the body and by disciplining sensuality.[79] For our physical desires are powerful and, as 1 Peter 2:11 says, they "wage war against your soul." "We should fast, pray, and work, in order to subdue and suppress lust."[80]

Thus Luther seriously encourages physical asceticism. But in contrast to the practices of Roman monasticism, he emphasizes first that asceticism is not meritorious, not a goal in itself, but only a means to the end of controlling and killing the desires of the flesh. All asceticism is to be regulated and limited in terms of this goal.[81]

---

[78] "Reason always wants to extol only its own works." *WA* 12, 272; *LW* 30, 16. "God does not want us to search for misfortune and to choose it ourselves. Walk in faith and love. If the cross comes, accept it. If it does not come, do not search for it." *WA* 12, 364; *LW* 30, 109–110.

[79] "Here the works begin; here a man cannot enjoy leisure; here he must indeed take care to discipline his body by fastings, watchings, labors, and other reasonable discipline and to subject it to the Spirit so that it will obey and conform to the inner man and faith and not revolt against faith and hinder the inner man, as it is the nature of the body to do if it is not held in check." *WA* 7, 30; *LW* 31, 358.

[80] *WA* 12, 325; *LW* 30, 71.

[81] Speaking of the Roman practice, Luther says: "All these people seek nothing beyond the work itself in their fasting. When they have performed that, they think that they have done a good work." *WA* 6, 245; *LW* 44, 74. "In the practice of fasting, vigils, and labors, we are not to look upon the works them-

Asceticism that is practical for its own sake, as a meritorious work, is not controlled but goes far beyond anything that is necessary for the struggle with sensuality. Luther encourages asceticism only insofar as it is helpful in that struggle.[82] Beyond this, all outward discipline and asceticism are limited by the fact that they can control the body but cannot make the soul pure. Here outward abstinence is of no avail; man must be cleansed from the inside out—and only faith can do that.[83]

Luther's second point of emphasis is that ascetic discipline can never be regulated by a universal law of the church. Rather, the individual must freely decide what is necessary and helpful for him. Since every man is different from every other, determining the right form of discipline is an individual task.[84]

The third way in which Luther's understanding of asceticism differs from the Roman understanding is that he wants asceticism —like the Christian life in general—to be completely oriented to the service of our fellowman. We need to keep in shape to help our neighbor. Every egoistic attempt to gain salvation for ourselves is rejected and condemned.[85]

---

selves . . . but only on the wanton and lustful Adam, that by these disciplines a man may be protected from the dominion of Adam." *WA* 6, 246; *LW* 44, 76. See also *WA* 6, 269; *LW* 44, 105.

82 "For no commandment of the church, no rule of any order, can make fastings, vigils, and penances of more worth, or the pursuit of these activities, except inasmuch and insofar as they serve to subdue or destroy the flesh and its lusts." *WA* 6, 246; *LW* 44, 75. "When the lust of the flesh ceases, every reason for fasting, watching, working, eating this or that has already ceased, and there is no longer any commandment whatever that is binding." *WA* 6, 247; *LW* 44, 76. "Everyone is to take upon himself so much of these works as is good and profitable for the suppressing of his sinful nature and for the preparation of it for death. He is to increase or diminish these works according as he sees sin increasing or diminishing." *WA* 2, 735; *LW* 35, 40.

83 In discussing the phrase "having purified your souls" in 1 Peter 1:22, Luther says: "Therefore it is not enough for one to abstain from the deed, to remain chaste outwardly, and to let evil lusts stay in the heart. No, one must strive to purify the soul, so that evil lust and desire depart from our heart and the soul is hostile to them and constantly fights against them until it is rid of them." *WA* 12, 295; *LW* 30, 40. "One can weaken and mortify the body with fasting and works; but one does not expel evil lust in this way. Faith, however, can subdue and restrain it, so that it gives room to the Spirit." *WA* 12, 296; *LW* 30, 41.

84 *WA* 12, 283; *LW* 30, 27. "In Christendom it will not do to issue laws, so that there is a general rule pertaining to self-control. For people are not alike. One is strong, another is weak by nature, and no one is always as fit in every respect as the other person is. Therefore everyone should learn to know himself, what he can do and what he can stand." *WA* 14, 20; *LW* 30, 156.

85 "To what end should we now lead a chaste life? To be saved by doing so? No, but for the purpose of serving our neighbor." *WA* 12, 296; *LW* 30, 41.

The Christian does make progress in the struggle of the Spirit against the flesh but this battle is never finished in this earthly life. The battle ends only with physical death.[86] No one becomes a saint here on earth. "As long as flesh and blood remain, so long sin also remains. Consequently, constant warfare is necessary."[87] In this struggle, original sin can indeed be subdued but it cannot be eliminated. "Thou shalt not covet" remains a goal which we do not reach here on earth.[88] Therefore the Christian longs to be rid of himself through physical death. He desires to die, whereas the world "cannot get enough of this life." "However, he cannot get rid of this life; what it seeks he flees from and what he flees from it seeks."[89] The world has an insatiable desire for this earthly life. The Christian, however, desires the end of this life because it will set his whole person free to serve God with perfect purity of heart.

---

[86] *Theology,* 244–45, 407.

[87] *WA* 12, 326; *LW* 30, 71.

[88] "Above all, he wants our hearts to be pure, even though as long as we live here we cannot reach that ideal. So this [ninth and tenth] commandment remains, like all the rest, one that constantly accuses us and shows just how upright we really are in God's sight." *WA* 30[I], 178; *BC,* 407.

[89] *WA* 17[II], 13.

2

THE KNOWLEDGE OF
GOD'S COMMANDS[1]

THE NATURAL LAW

ON THE BASIS of Paul's statement in Romans 2:15 Luther asserts that man is naturally born with a knowledge of what he is to do and not to do. Luther calls this "natural justice," "natural law," or "law of nature" (he also uses "natural laws" in the plural).[2] In the process of creation God wrote this law in the hearts of all men. Man therefore has the very best law book in his heart and needs no other books in order to know what is right.[3] Natural law is implanted in man, that is, in human reason.[4] Since reason knows it, we may also call it rational law. However, it is given us by God, who has given us our reason and inscribed it with natural law.[5] Luther thus makes no distinction between "natural" and "divine," or between "natural" and "revealed." Although natural law is implanted in our human reason, it still

---

[1] Ernst Troeltsch, *The Social Teaching of the Christian Churches,* trans. Olive Wyon (New York: Harper Torchbook, 1960), 2:529 ff. Karl Holl, "Der Neubau der Sittlichkeit" (1919), in *GA* 1, esp. pp. 243–63. Franz Lau, *"Äusserliche Ordnung" und "weltlich Ding" in Luthers Theologie des Politischen* (Göttingen: Vandenhoeck & Ruprecht, 1933). Georg Wünsch, *Evangelische Ethik des Politischen* (Tübingen: Mohr/Siebeck, 1936), pp. 126 ff. Johannes Heckel, *Lex charitatis. Eine juristische Untersuchung über das Recht in der Theologie Martin Luthers* (Munich: Verlag der Bayerischen Akademie der Wissenschaften, 1953). Ernst Wolf, "Natürliches Gesetz und Gesetz Christi bei Luther," in *Peregrinatio. Studien zur reformatorischen Theologie und zum Kirchenproblem* (Munich: Chr. Kaiser, 1954), pp. 191 ff. Aarne Siirala, *Gottes Gebot bei Martin Luther* (Helsinki: Schriften der Luther-Agricola-Gesellschaft, 1956). Martin Schloemann, *Natürliches und gepredigtes Gesetz bei Luther* (Berlin: Töpelmann, 1961).

[2] *WA* 17^{II}, 102; *WA* 39^{I}, 540; *WA* 18, 80–81; *LW* 40, 97–98. Heinrich Bornkamm tries to establish a distinction between Luther's use of "the law of nature" (*Naturrecht* and *natürliches Recht*) and "natural law" (*natürliches Gesetz*); see *Luther and the Old Testament,* trans. Eric W. Gritsch and Ruth C. Gritsch (Philadelphia: Fortress, 1969), p. 131. I do not find sufficient evidence for such a distinction.

[3] *WA* 40^{II}, 71–72; *LW* 27, 56–57.

[4] Luther says that "all reason is filled" with natural law. *WA* 11, 279; *LW* 45, 128.

[5] *WA* TR 4, no. 3911; *LW* 54, 293.

25

remains God's will and "divine law."[6] God's commands are present and effective in us through the law which has been implanted
in our reason. Thus natural law is a very precious possession.

Sometimes Luther seems to distinguish between the divine and
the natural law. Divine law as the laws given in Scripture, the
word of God, is distinguished from the law written in man's
heart. However, he does not distinguish between these two in
terms of content.[7]

The natural law precedes all written and positive laws and takes
precedence over them.[8] It determines all positive statutes—or at
least it ought to determine them. For all of them have their source
in this natural law and are to be critically evaluated on the basis
of it.[9] This is true not only of the ethical rules formulated by men
but also of positive laws.[10] The natural laws are always and universally valid. Unlike positive regulations and rules whose validity
is limited to a particular time and place, they "prevail and remain
in all lands."[11] These positive laws can and must be changed as
the situation changes. Natural laws, however, are unchangeable.

(Experience itself teaches) that God's will is written in men's
hearts. We feel this norm in our hearts.[12] Our knowledge of the

---

[6] *WA* 41, 639; *WA* TR 2, no. 2243; *WA* 30[III], 207; *LW* 46, 269. Luther
speaks of "the common, divine, and natural law which even the heathen, Turks,
and Jews have to keep if there is to be any peace or order in the world." *WA*
18, 307; *LW* 46, 27.
[7] Thus Luther uses the following series: "Contrary to God's word, contrary
to reason and every sense of justice." *WA* 15, 305; *LW* 45, 261. Elsewhere he
seems to equate "the natural law of all the world" with "the divine law,"
specifically referring to Deuteronomy 32:35. *WA* 18, 303–304; *LW* 46, 25. The
biblical word thus has its own place alongside natural law, but the content of
both is the same. This is also the case in *WA* 18, 307; *LW* 46, 27, where
Luther speaks of struggling "against the divine and natural law." I also understand Luther's comment in *WA* TR 2, no. 2151, to mean that Luther himself
does not see any difference in content between the natural law and the divine
law: "I should like to see someone who was properly able to distinguish between the natural law and the divine law."
[8] *WA* TR 2, no. 2151.
[9] "It was not necessary for Christ to give instruction about this, for it was
implanted in nature and written in their hearts. Furthermore, all books, with
the exception of Holy Writ, are derived from that source and spring. Therefore, Christ's words and doctrine must not be interpreted as though he had
wanted to teach and ordain anything in addition to this or to institute anything
better." *WA* 45, 669; *LW* 24, 228; *WA* TR 4, no. 3911; *LW* 54, 293.
[10] "Therefore, we should keep written laws subject to reason, from which
they originally welled forth as from the spring of justice." *WA* 11, 280; *LW*
45, 129; *WA* 30[II], 562; *LW* 46, 242; *WA* 17[II], 91.
[11] *WA* 18, 81; *LW* 40, 97–98; *WA* 30[III], 225; *LW* 46, 291; *WA* 31[I], 233;
LW 14, 14.
[12] "There is no one who does not feel it. Everyone must acknowledge that

various peoples of the world shows that all people know the natural laws. We do not need the Ten Commandments to know our decisive religious and ethical duties and to know that disobedience is forbidden. As Paul says in Romans 2, these are known to all peoples.[13]

THE NATURAL LAW
WRITTEN AND PREACHED

Mankind's primal fall away from God affected its knowledge of God's law. Since men have denied and corrupted their primal knowledge of God, the law written in their hearts has also been largely obscured and forgotten.[14] Evil lust and desire have darkened the light in men's hearts so that they no longer follow it. Satan has blinded reason to the natural law and has covered this law with a veil.[15] As a result, reason no longer perceives the full and pure form of the natural law implanted in it by God.

God therefore must renew the primal natural law, that is, make people remember it and "reawaken" man's knowledge of the law. He does this through the word, that is, through the law of Moses and the preaching based on this law.[16]

Thus the law written by Moses on the tables of stone takes its place alongside the law written in man's heart. This form of God's law is given only to a particular people, that is, to Israel.[17] However, the content of Moses' law is still basic and universal. The law of Moses is not a new law; it only reminds us of the one

---

what the natural law says is right and true. . . . This light lives and shines in all human reason. If men would only pay attention to it, they would have no need of books or of any other law. For they carry along with them in the depth of their hearts a living book which could give them quite adequate instruction about what they ought to do and not to do, how they ought to judge, and what ought to be accepted and rejected." *WA* 17[II], 102.

13 "Experience itself shows that all nations share this common ordinary knowledge. . . . I feel in my heart that I certainly ought to do these things for God, not because of what traditional written laws say, but because I brought these laws with me when I came into the world. . . . For although the decalogue was given in one way at a single time and place, all nations recognize that there are sins and iniquities." *WA* 39[I], 540.

14 *WA* 16, 447; *WA* 39[I], 539.

15 *WA* 16, 447; *WA* 17[II], 102.

16 "However, the devil so blinds and possesses hearts that they do not always feel this law. Therefore one must preach the law and impress it on the minds of people till God assists and enlightens them, so that they feel in their hearts what the word says." *WA* 18, 80; *LW* 40, 97; *WA* 39[I], 540.

17 *WA* 39[I], 540.

natural law and expresses it in a way that has never been equaled.[18]
The law of Moses also contains specific regulations governing the
people of Israel. These are applicable only to this people and are
not valid for other nations. The Mosaic law is valid only insofar
as it expresses the form of the natural law, that is, only insofar as
it strikes every man in his own conscience and so attests its
validity.[19] As written, Moses' law is of limited validity; but in
terms of its essential content it is universally valid. Insofar as
Moses' law is given only to the Jews—and this is particularly true
of Moses' judicial laws—the rules and laws valid in our own
country take its place for us non-Jews.[20]

If the natural law is to be reawakened in men, it must be
preached on the basis of Scripture.[21] Men no longer carry it in
themselves in such a way that they could get along without the
preaching of the law. At the same time, the preached law strikes
them in their hearts only because the law was originally written
in their hearts.[22]

When governments make laws and use their power to punish
violators of the laws, they take their place alongside the preaching
of the word. Thus the actions of government also remind men of
the natural law in their hearts.

THE CONTENT OF THE NATURAL LAW

The law written in man's heart contains within itself all the
commandments of the First and Second Tables: the commandment
to fear, trust, and obey God as well as all the commandments and
prohibitions of the Second Table governing our relationships to our

---

[18] "The natural laws were never so orderly and well written as by Moses."
WA 18, 80–81; *LW* 40, 97–98; *WA* 39[I], 539–40; *Theology,* 89–92.

[19] *WA* 16, 390; *LW* 35, 172–73. "The written law was given to a specific
nation insofar as it is written—but not insofar as it is spoken, for this knowledge is common to all nations." *WA* 39[I], 540.

[20] "Now that we are under our princes, lords, and emperors, we must outwardly obey their laws instead of the laws of Moses." *WA* 18, 72; *LW* 40, 90.
In a discussion of marriage, Luther says: "This is why Moses' law cannot be
simply and completely valid among us. We have to take into consideration the
character and ways of our land when we want to make or apply laws and
rules." *WA* 30[III], 225; *LW* 46, 291; *WA* Br 3, 484; *S-J* 2, 311.

[21] *WA* 16, 447.

[22] "Otherwise, were it not naturally written in the heart, one would have to
teach and preach the law for a long time before it became the concern of
conscience. The heart must also find and feel the law in itself. Otherwise, it
would not become a matter of conscience for anyone." *WA* 18, 80; *LW* 40, 97.

fellowmen.[23] This means that the natural law contains the basic rules that people need in order to live together with one another. These are summarized in the Golden Rule of Matthew 7:12 and Luke 6:31: I ought to treat my neighbor the way that I would like to have him treat me. This is the same as the commandment to love our neighbor as ourselves.[24] According to Jesus this commandment summarizes all the proclamations of God, those of the law and of the prophets. The natural law is thus nothing else than the commandment or law of love. Precisely this rule of love is the natural law which pervades our reason.[25] Christ and the natural law teach one and the same thing.[26] Luther equates acting according to the Golden Rule with "Christian love."[27] Thus Luther considers that all the rules of the Sermon on the Mount (suffering injustice and not taking revenge, for example) are part of natural law.

Alongside these are other rules of natural law. A husband has the duty of taking care of his wife and children;[28] "he who is able to prevent injury but does not do so is guilty of the injury";[29] we must return property that has been taken unjustly;[30] no one can judge his own case but must submit it to the judgment of the authorities, for only in this way can peace and order be preserved in the world.[31] Thus Luther feels that the elementary moral laws and the basic rules of legal justice stand alongside one another in natural law.

Luther views all these rules as natural law. He makes no conceptual distinctions between various kinds of natural law. He neither speaks of a distinction between absolute and relative natural law,[32] nor does he distinguish "the divine, spiritual, law

---

[23] *WA* 18, 81; *LW* 40, 98; *WA* 39[I], 540; *WA* TR 4, no. 3911; *LW* 54, 293.

[24] *WA* 2, 120; *LW* 42, 68; *WA* 6, 5; *WA* 6, 49; *LW* 45, 292; *WA* 18, 80; *LW* 40, 97; *WA* 19, 638; *LW* 46, 111; *WA* 32, 494–95; *LW* 21, 235–36; *WA* 40[II], 71; *LW* 27, 56.

[25] "For nature teaches—as does love—that I should do as I would be done by (Luke 6:31) . . . that love and natural law may always prevail. . . . Such a free decision is given, however, by love and by natural law with which all reason is filled." *WA* 11, 279; *LW* 45, 128; *WA* 18, 80; *LW* 40, 97.

[26] *WA* 19, 642; *LW* 46, 114.

[27] *WA* 51, 393.

[28] *WA* 40[III], 278.

[29] *WA* 30[II], 544; *LW* 46, 230.

[30] *WA* 11, 278; *LW* 45, 127.

[31] *WA* 18, 306–307; *LW* 46, 26–27; *WA* Br 10, 33.

[32] Troeltsch and Wünsch claimed that Luther made such a distinction. Luther,

of nature" from the "secular natural law."[33] For Luther, natural
law is an undifferentiated unity. There is no special natural law
for Christians. Rather, the same law applies to both Christians and
non-Christians. Secular and spiritual government and our personal
and official responsibility are also governed by the same natural
law, that is, we always stand under the law of love no matter how
its form and our acts in fulfilling it may differ from one situation
to another.[34] It is indeed true that Luther does not think of secular
government as being the same after the fall as it was before the
fall; it now has characteristics which it did not have in its primal
condition before the fall. However, this means nothing more for
Luther than that the one and the same law of responsible love for
the neighbor is applied in various ways.

THE DECALOGUE AND THE "NEW DECALOGUES"

Luther highly praises the law of Moses as the most striking
form of natural law. He calls it "a summary of divine teaching"
that comprehends the entire content of the law. All good works
must have their source here; nothing that is God-pleasing lies outside the sphere of the Ten Commandments. "Therefore we should
prize and value them above all other teachings as the greatest
treasure God has given us."[35]

When Luther praises the decalogue so highly, however, he is
thinking not simply of the decalogue in its historical form (Exodus
20) but of the decalogue as contained in the whole Bible, as
interpreted and fulfilled by the prophets and Christ. He can even

however, makes no distinction between natural law before and after the fall. For
a discussion of Troeltsch's understanding of Luther's concept of natural law and
Holl's refutation of this position, see Wünsch, *Evangelische Ethik des Politischen*,
pp. 126 ff.

[33] Heckel (*Lex charitatis*, pp. 52 ff., 71 ff.) reads this distinction into Luther;
it is not supported by the original texts. Luther does not speak of a twofold
natural law; see Franz Lau, "Leges Charitatis," *Kerygma und Dogma* 2 (1956):
80–84, and Schloemann, *Natürliches und gepredigtes Gesetz*, p. 17.

[34] We shall discuss this further in chapter 4 in connection with Luther's
doctrine of the two kingdoms; see below, pp. 70–74.

[35] The statement is made in the Large Catechism, *WA* 30[I], 179–80, 182; *BC*,
407–408, 410. Heckel takes another position: "In Luther, the law of Moses as
the basic summary of 'physical' life in general is separated from divine law and
restricted to the area of human law." (*Lex charitatis*, p. 80.) There is no
evidence in Luther supporting such an assertion about the decalogue.

say that Christ and the apostles have established "new decalogues."[36] That is, they have gone beyond, supplemented, deep-
ened, and fulfilled the law of Moses through the new insights and
understandings which Christ and his apostles, as moved by the
Spirit of Christ, have brought. "And these decalogues are clearer
than the decalogue of Moses, just as the countenance of Christ is
brighter than the countenance of Moses (2 Corinthians 3:7–
11)."[37] These new decalogues express the intention of God's
commandments better, more completely, and more deeply than
the Mosaic decalogue does.

Christians who are in fellowship with Christ and filled with his
Spirit are also able to establish norms and arrive at right judgments in every case that arises.[38] The Christian is thus called to
make creative decisions and use his own conscience to decide what
God commands here and now.[39] The Christian cannot arrive at
the necessary decision simply by reading the directions given him
in the Bible or by finding applicable statements in the New Testament or even in the sayings of Jesus. None of these are adequate
in terms of a specific situation that is always different from previous situations. Obviously the Christian can also err in this process
and confuse his own fleshly decisions with the guidance of God's
Spirit. Luther therefore admonishes us to abide by the biblical
directives. However, his strong emphasis on the apostolic teaching
does not free us of the need continually to interpret the biblical
directives in new ways. Obviously not all Christians are called to
the same measure of creative interpretation of the scriptural word
—the gifts and the Spirit are given in varying degrees. But
Christianity as such is called on to undertake this task through its
teachers.[40]

This is what Luther himself did. His directions for the Christian
life formally conform to the decalogue—for example, in the
Treatise on Good Works and in the catechisms he interprets the
commandments of the Mosaic decalogue.[41] In substance, however,

---

36 *WA* 39^I, 47; *LW* 34, 112.
37 *WA* 39^I, 47; *LW* 34, 112–13.
38 *WA* 39^I, 47; *LW* 34, 112; *Theology,* 271–72.
39 *WA* 15, 293; *LW* 45, 245.
40 *WA* 39^I, 47; *LW* 34, 113.
41 *WA* 6, 204–76; *LW* 44, 21–114; *WA* 30^I, 132–82, 353–62; *BC*, 365–411,
342–44.

he goes far beyond that decalogue and interprets it very freely in terms of the nature of Christian love. He does not simply repeat the New Testament statements; he updates them on the basis of the whole gospel in order to apply them to contemporary problems in a new way. The Mosaic decalogue and the New Testament directives must repeatedly be reinterpreted as "new decalogues." A man does not recognize God's will for himself independently but only by hearing the Scripture. However, he is also not bound legalistically to a heteronomous word of Scripture, but, as he is moved by the word of Christ's Spirit, he lives in theonomous creativity. The Christian, by virtue of his fellowship with God, is called to freedom of conscience even in his knowledge of God's commandments—for in this fellowship he is justified and certain that God is well pleased with him.[42]

Thus the Christian life is lived under the commandments of God. At every moment of this life, these commandments require us to decide between obedience and disobedience. And yet we cannot forget that Luther also knows an area of the "allowed" which is not determined by a commandment or prohibition of God. Here a man is not bound but has freedom of choice. Luther thinks particularly of choosing food and drink, clothing, and social life.[43]

"NATURAL LAW" AND "CHRISTIAN LAW"

As we have seen, Luther equates natural law with the "law of love."[44] Occasionally, however, he does distinguish "Christian law" from natural law in the sense of the law of love. In his first writing in connection with the Peasants' War (*Admonition to Peace, a Reply to the Twelve Articles of the Peasants in Swabia*) he forbids the peasants to attempt to help themselves by setting themselves up as judges, avenging themselves, and being unwilling to suffer any injustice. He does this in terms not only of "Christian law and the gospel" but also of "natural law and all equity."

---

[42] "Thus a Christian man who lives in this confidence toward God knows all things, can do all things, ventures everything that needs to be done, and does everything gladly and willingly." *WA* 6, 207; *LW* 44, 27.

[43] *WA* 42, 512; *LW* 2, 350.

[44] Luther hopes that in every decision "love and natural law may always prevail." *WA* 11, 279; *LW* 45, 128.

Does the equation of natural law and love compel us to conclude that these are both one and the same norm? Luther's statement seems to presuppose a distinction between them: he says that the peasants' position is "contrary not only to Christian law and the gospel, but also to natural law and all equity."[45] He seems to speak of two norms and to imply that Christian law demands more of us than natural law.[46] What is the additional content of Christian law? What can Luther mean by this? He says it very plainly to the peasants: "Suffering! suffering! Cross! cross! This and nothing else is the Christian law!"[47] Thus Christian law is the law that we as Christians are called to suffer in this world, just as Christ himself suffered. Christian law requires that the Christian man be ready to suffer: it is Luther's theology of the cross which provides the content of his Christian law. "The Christian is a martyr on earth."[48]

One difficulty remains, however. Luther cites in this connection passages of the Sermon on the Mount (such as not defending oneself, not avenging oneself) whose content he elsewhere ascribes to natural law. In writing this pamphlet for the peasants did he perhaps forget and abandon his usual equation of natural law and the commandment of love? Or is it improper to interpret his terminology so exactly? It seems to me that one should at least attempt to see a divergence in substance between the differentiation of these two concepts in this pamphlet written for the peasants and Luther's usual equation of them. The following is to be understood as such an attempt.

The content of natural law is the Golden Rule, which also constitutes the law of love. This is similar to the law of reason, insofar as it alone makes it possible to preserve peace and order in the world.[49] The Golden Rule places men under the law of reciprocity.

---

45 *WA* 18, 304; *LW* 46, 25.

46 "Would to God that the majority of us were good, pious heathen, who kept the natural law, not to mention the Christian law!" *WA* 18, 310; *LW* 46, 29. "Here you see how shamelessly this maxim flies squarely in the face not only of Christian love but also of natural law." *WA* 15, 294; *LW* 45, 247.

47 *WA* 18, 310; *LW* 46, 29.

48 *WA* 18, 328; *LW* 46, 40. For a discussion of Luther's theology of the cross, see *Theology*, 25–34.

49 "Now in all this I have been speaking of the common, divine, and natural law which even the heathen, Turks, and Jews have to keep if there is to be any peace or order in the world." *WA* 18, 307; *LW* 46, 27.

And people fulfill it out of an easily understood interest in peace and in ordering the common life. Rational insight compels a man to keep this law.[50] Such activity substantially corresponds to what love demands; however, it is the kind of thing that can be done and very often is done without any real motive of love, or at least without the love of Christ. As Luther says, even "heathen, Turks, and Jews" must maintain this natural law for the sake of peace and order. It is one thing when natural man fulfills the natural law of love and another thing when the Christian fulfills it. It is one thing when someone does not avenge himself but rather endures injustice according to the Golden Rule, and it is another thing when the Christian acts in this way. For the Christian is determined by more than the insight that he must act in this way for the sake of peace and order; he is moved by the love of Christ and through faith in his Lord's love, and these protect him even when he must suffer.[51]

Thus only the Christian really fulfills the law of love. When he endures injustice without resisting he does so not on the basis of the natural law of reason but on the basis of the law of the cross that holds for Christ and for his Christians: "Cross, cross is the Christian's law." At this point he does something more than preserve peace and order in the world; and at this point we are beyond the realm of reason. For when a Christian endures suffering according to this theology of the cross, then God's glory and kingdom paradoxically enter into this world. And that is more than the natural order of the world. This, I believe, enables us to understand what Luther means when he distinguishes the Christian law as being more than natural law and the law of love.[52]

---

50 "For no one is a Christian merely because he does not undertake to function as his own judge and avenger but leaves this to the authorities and rulers. You would eventually have to do this whether you wanted to or not." *WA* 18, 307; *LW* 46, 27. Cf. Heckel, *Lex charitatis*, pp. 67, 77 n. 552, 82 n. 592, for a discussion of the difference between the spiritual and the physical interpretation of the Golden Rule.

51 *WA* 18, 310; *LW* 46, 29.

52 Wolf raises the question about the relationship between natural law and the law of Christ in Luther. He points out ("Natürliches Gesetz," p. 201) that in one place Luther describes faith as the law of Christ, *WA* 8, 458. However, this is a completely isolated passage. In determining Luther's interpretation of this term, we must focus primarily on Luther's treatment of Galatians 6:2 rather than—as Wolf does—on 1 Corinthians 9:21. Luther's interpretation of Galatians 6:2 clearly says that the law of Christ is nothing else than the law of love.

WA 40^{II}, 145; *LW* 27, 113. In his first commentary on Galatians, Luther says: "Love is the law of Christ." *WA* 2, 604; *LW* 27, 391. This law of love requires, among other things, that we bear one another's burdens. We thus fulfill 1 Corinthians 13:7, and this love in 1 Corinthians 13:7 is explicitly included in the content of the commandment of love. *WA* 40^{II}, 73; *LW* 27, 59. Christ is also described as the example of this love. *WA* 40^{II}, 146; *LW* 27, 114. I agree with Wolf that Luther saw the commandment of love as belonging to and being identical with natural law. However, Luther's basic explanation also indicates that the "law of Christ" is nothing else than this law of love. Wolf contrasts natural law and the law of Christ with each other; for Luther, however, they are one and the same.

3

STATIONS AND VOCATIONS
(THE ORDERS)

THE DECALOGUE and the commandment of love do not give very definite or detailed instructions about what we as individuals ought to do here and now in living together with one another. This commandment of love, valid everywhere and for all people, becomes specific for us as individuals in the context of the station of life in which God has placed us. Through our station in life we are placed into a definite and particular relationship to one another. And our duty to serve one another thereby takes on very specific form.[1]

God has established stations among men—Luther also speaks of orders, institutions, offices, or hierarchies.[2] There are many and various stations in life, for "God is a great lord and has many kinds of servants."[3] Luther sometimes enumerates them—for example, the stations of fathers and mothers, married people, servants and maids, lords and subjects, and pastors, among others.[4] Sometimes Luther summarizes them in three basic stations: ministry, marriage (or the family, including everything related to business and the economy), and secular authority.[5] All those who are associated with the "ministry of the word," and not only with the clergy, have an ecclesiastical station—including administrators of the "community chest," and "sextons and messengers or servants who serve such persons." The station of marriage includes not only parents, children, and servants but also widows and unmarried women. And the station of secular government, according to

---

[1] For a discussion of Luther's teaching on this point, see Werner Elert, *Morphologie des Luthertums,* 2d ed. (Munich: C. H. Beck, 1953), 2:49–65.

[2] *WA* 26, 504; *LW* 37, 364; *WA* 50, 652; *LW* 41, 177; *WA* 31^I, 408; *LW* 13, 368.

[3] *WA* 30^{II}, 570; *LW* 46, 246.

[4] *WA* 31^I, 399; *LW* 13, 358.

[5] *WA* 26, 504; *LW* 37, 364; *WA* 50, 652; *LW* 41, 177; *WA* 43, 30; *LW* 3, 217; *WA* 39^{II}, 42.

Luther's description, includes the "princes and lords, judges, civil officers, state officials, notaries, male and female servants and all who serve such persons, and further, all their obedient subjects."[6] All these are "divine stations and orders" because God has established them in his word, and they are to be honored as holy institutions.[7] Since God has established them jointly and severally and given them to men, they all have the same validity; each station deserves the same honor and respect, and they ought to show this same respect to one another.[8]

God did not simply establish one station and then include everyone in it; rather, he has established a variety of stations with innumerable distinctions and differences between them.[9] Given these differences, the individual stations need one another.[10] All stations have a useful and necessary function in the life of the world. They serve as the means by which God creates (through marriage) and preserves humanity. They establish order, justice, and peace in the world.[11] National legal systems serve this same purpose. However, the stations are not identified with these national systems of law and order because the legal systems change in the course of time but the stations remain basically unchanged in all times—they are stable.[12] God declares that "these stations must remain if the world is to stand."[13]

Luther asserts that the preservation of mankind depends on these stations. He bases this assertion simply on the fact that they are there and that they have endured through the ages. Reason also recognizes that they are necessary and useful for the world—this knowledge is part of the natural law that everyone knows.[14] However, only the Christian knows that these stations have been

---

6 *WA* 26, 504–5; *LW* 37, 364–65.

7 *WA* 31^I, 234; *LW* 14, 15; *WA* 31^I, 409–10; *LW* 13, 369.

8 *WA* 49, 613. "All the estates and works of God are to be praised as highly as they can be and none despised in favor of another." *WA* 30^{II}, 568–69; *LW* 46, 246.

9 "But it is God's will that there be distinctions of ranks." *WA* 44, 440; *LW* 7, 190; *WA* 47, 452. "There must be many stations, and each one has enough to do in his own station." *WA* 49, 606; *LW* 51, 348.

10 *WA* 49, 611; *LW* 51, 351–52.

11 *WA* 30^{II}, 571–72; *LW* 46, 246–48; *WA* 31^I, 399, 409; *LW* 13, 358, 369. "It is God's work to have distinct stations in the world, and that these make for right and righteousness and thus preserve the peace." *WA* 31^I, 410; *LW* 13, 370.

12 *WA* 31^I, 410; *LW* 13, 369.

13 *WA* 31^I, 400; *LW* 13, 358.

14 *WA* 31^I, 410; *LW* 13, 369.

established by God. They are instituted, presupposed, recognized, and honored by the Scripture and are therefore "contained and involved in God's word and commandment."[15] "Christians alone know and teach that these are divine ordinances and institutions. Therefore, they alone can truly give thanks and pray for them in their churches."[16]

These assertions about the stations of life do not mean that Luther adopts an uncritically conservative attitude toward the entire existing order of society or that he glorifies its present form and declares it holy for religious reasons. When Luther says that God intends the stations to "serve God and the world,"[17] or when he says that "the soldier's vocation also springs from the law of love" (that is, that the soldier serves his neighbor),[18] he also gives the criterion for deciding which stations are right and proper and which are not. Luther himself applied this criterion: he recognizes that some stations are "against God" and "sinful" and specifically mentions the ecclesiastical hierarchy and monasticism in this connection insofar as people in these stations are not involved in studying, teaching, or hearing God's word.[19] Thus Luther's teaching about the stations of life is basically open to a thorough criticism of existing social order.

All of human life is comprehended by the stations. In saying this, we must remember that Luther's concept of a station (*Stand*) is quite different from modern concepts of social standing, position, rank, and class. Luther's enumeration of the stations clearly indicates that each person belongs to a variety of stations simultaneously: a prince or lord can also be a husband and father, and hold an ecclesiastical office as well. Every man stands in several relationships to other people. Each one, however, has the duty of serving God and man in his station and fulfilling the law of his station. God's will takes on definite and specific form for a person in the context of the particular station in which he is functioning.[20]

---

15 *WA* 26, 505; *LW* 37, 365.
16 *WA* 31[I], 410; *LW* 13, 370.
17 *WA* 30[II], 578; *LW* 46, 252.
18 *WA* 19, 657; *LW* 46, 131.
19 *WA* 10[I.1], 317; *WA* 12, 132.
20 *WA* 43, 478; *LW* 5, 72; *WA* 50, 652; *LW* 41, 177. For this reason Luther places the "Table of Duties" at the end of his Small Cathechism. This "Table of Duties" consists of individual New Testament passages that describe the special duties of the various stations. *WA* 30[I], 397–98; *BC*, 354–56.

To the extent that each man knows that God has called him to service in his station, he has received his "vocation" (*Beruf*).[21] Before 1522 Luther used *Beruf* in the sense of vocation or calling (*Berufung*). After 1522 he also uses *Beruf* synonymously with station (*Stand*), office or function (*Amt*), and duty (*Befehl*). This broader second usage of *Beruf* was prepared for by its usage in the writings of the German mystics. However, the general adoption of this second broader sense of the German term is due to the decisive influence of Luther's usage.[22] As Karl Holl says, Luther uses vocation as synonymous with station so that "every Christian, insofar as he belongs to a particular station in life, may also feel that he has been called." Luther particularly emphasizes this in discussing completely secular vocations.[23] Even though our modern secularized world commonly uses the word *vocation* in a shallow sense, there is always an echo of its meaning as calling—even though it is frequently only a search for a calling.

God's commandments take on specific form for us in terms of our station and vocation. Our station is the place—although not the only place—where we are to obey God.[24] Our work in this vocation or station is our appropriate service to God. Since God has commanded this work, it certainly pleases him. As a result, Luther rejects any piety that tries to find especially "holy" works. Luther constantly contrasts the works that God commands us to do in our station and vocation with the pious works that we choose for ourselves.[25] Let each "fulfill his duties in his vocation" —then he will have enough and more than enough to do. There is no limit to what our station and vocation require of us. If we take that requirement seriously, we have neither time, nor space, nor energy to seek out special works for ourselves. There is so

---

21 Gustav Wingren, *Luther on Vocation*, trans, Carl Rasmussen (Philadelphia: Muhlenberg, 1957). *WA* 10[I.2], 306 ff.

22 See Karl Holl, "Die Geschichte des Wortes Beruf" (1924), *GA* 3, especially pp. 217–18. For a correction of Holl's position, see Franz Lau, "Beruf III. Christentum und Beruf," in *Die Religion in Geschichte und Gegenwart*, 3d ed. (Tübingen: J. C. B. Mohr, 1957), 1:1078.

23 *WA* 10[I.2], 308–9.

24 *WA* 40[III], 299.

25 *WA* 10[I.1], 307–9. "We ought not to run away from one another and each seek to live for himself; rather, we should stay with one another in all kinds of stations, just as God has joined us together, and each serve the other." *WA* 21, 343 (Cruciger's edition).

much to do "that all our time is too short, all our space too narrow, and all our energies too limited."[26]

There is no special outward characteristic that distinguishes the Christian's activity in his vocation from that of other men. Neither God's word nor faith tell him what to do. Rather, he is directed by reason and the immanent law of his vocation.[27] What he does is Christian because he does it in the certainty that God has called him to serve his neighbor and that God is pleased with what he is doing.

Thus Luther restricts the Christian within the limitations of his station and vocation. Here is the place he ought to serve God with love. Although these limitations are to be taken very seriously in contrast to the works which we might choose for ourselves, they are not intended to limit our whole service to God through the serving of our neighbor simply to the responsibilities of a particular vocation. The "common order of Christian love" stands above the stations. At the same time, only those who are called to a particular vocation are responsible for the special works of that vocation. The same works are not required of everyone; rather, each has different works according to his station and vocation. All, however, are equally called to love in the same way; through love "one serves not only the three orders, but also serves every needy person in general with all kinds of benevolent deeds."[28] Thus the Christian's service of his neighbor goes far beyond the regular duties of his vocation. This is true of those people who are entrusted to an individual in his station—for example, in the rela-

---

[26] *WA* 10[I,1], 309; *WA* 40[II], 71–72; *LW* 27, 56 ff.

[27] "If you are a manual laborer, you find that the Bible has been put into your workshop, into your hand, into your heart. It teaches and preaches how you should treat your neighbor. Just look at your tools—at your needle or thimble, your beer barrel, your goods, your scales or yardstick or measure—and you will read this statement inscribed on them. Everywhere you look, it stares at you. Nothing that you handle every day is so tiny that it does not continually tell you this, if you will only listen. Indeed, there is no shortage of preaching. You have as many preachers as you have transactions, goods, tools, and other equipment in your house and home. All this is continually crying out to you: 'Friend, use me in your relations with your neighbor just as you would want your neighbor to use his property in his relations with you.'" *WA* 32, 495; *LW* 21, 237.

[28] *WA* 26, 505; *LW* 37, 365. Luther (ibid.) gives examples of such "benevolent deeds" as "feeding the hungry, giving drink to the thirsty, forgiving enemies, praying for all men on earth, suffering all kinds of evil on earth, etc." Elsewhere (*WA* 34[II], 313) Luther sees the order of love which stands above all stations as consisting in love of God and of our neighbor.

tionship of parents and children or lords and servants. We are also called to such service by the infinite and unpredictable variety of encounters between one man and another through which God makes them neighbors to each other. Luther's ethics is an ethics of station and vocation, but not in an exclusive sense. Luther consistently emphasizes that God may also require a man to do the extraordinary.[29] However, as long as God does not do that, everyone carries on his work according to the common standard of his vocation.[30]

Since God has established and ordered our vocation, the works which we do in our vocation are, as we have heard, pleasing to him. However, being the kind of people that we are, we cannot fulfill any vocation without being involved in sin. Here again it is very important that all Christian ethos is ethos under justification. This is particularly true of our activity in our vocation, whatever that may be.[31] Thus the work that we do in our vocation cannot be acceptable apart from the certainty that our sins are forgiven. No matter how impossible it is to avoid sins in our station and vocation because of our sinful human nature, however, our station as such remains pure and holy because it is established through God's word.[32] Therefore one should not forsake the station to which God has called him simply because in it he cannot avoid sinning. No matter what we do, we remain sinners as long as we live. And God's forgiveness is greater and more certain if we

---

[29] See Franz Lau, *"Äusserliche Ordnung" und "weltlich Ding" in Luthers Theologie des Politischen* (Göttingen: Vandenhoeck & Ruprecht, 1933), pp. 50 ff.

[30] *WA* 43, 642–43; *LW* 5, 311.

[31] Luther frequently says that no one avoids sin in fulfilling his vocation. He describes this specifically, for example, in relation to the vocations of business and marriage. In discussing this Luther reaches the conclusion that the unavoidable sin of our vocation does not have its source in a man's "wickedness" but in "the very nature and necessity of our occupation." *WA* 15, 297; *LW* 45, 251.

[32] "Show me a station established by God that is without sin. If there were such, I would not have to preach anymore, no servant or maid would have to serve his master, the authorities would never again have to use the sword, and no knight would have to mount his horse. . . . In this life we will never be so pure as to do any good work without sin. We must constantly confess: I believe in the forgiveness of sins. And we must daily pray the Lord's Prayer and say: 'Forgive us our debts.' . . . Now, even though no one fulfills his station without sin, yet God's word is so great that our station remains pure and holy." *WA* 34[I], 71.

remain in our station.[33] This indicates the extent to which Luther is concerned that men serve one another in their stations and thereby preserve order in the world.

---

[33] Speaking of married people, Luther says: "If they are sometimes angry with one another, that is indeed sinful and not right. However, God's forgiveness of their sins will be much greater if only they remain in their station and do not leave it, but rather live in the situation to which God has called them." Ibid.

4

THE TWO KINGDOMS AND
THE TWO GOVERNMENTS^⓵

THE BIBLICAL BASIS

L UTHER DID not base his doctrine of the two kingdoms or the
two governments on his own speculative thinking. He felt
that in this matter too his position was wholly determined by
Scripture. He distinguishes two types of statements. One type is
characterized by Jesus' statements in the Sermon on the Mount ⌐1⌐

---

1 *Temporal Authority: To What Extent It Should Be Obeyed* (1523), *WA*
11, 245–80; *LW* 45, 81–129. *Whether Soldiers, Too, Can be Saved* (1526),
WA 19, 623–62; *LW* 46, 93–137. *The Sermon on the Mount* (1532), *WA* 32,
299–544; *LW* 21, 3–294. See also the sermons on Matthew 5:20–26, the
Gospel for the Sixth Sunday after Trinity, listed in *WA* 22, xlvi–xlvii and a
variety of passages in the sermons on the payment of the tax to Caesar discussed
in Matthew 22:15–22, the Gospel for the Twenty-third Sunday after Trinity,
listed in *WA* 22, lii–liii, for example, *WA* 11, 202; *WA* 17^I, 464, 467; *WA*
29, 598–99; *WA* 32, 178; *WA* 37, 195, 583; *WA* 45, 252. See also Luther's
sermon on Romans 12:17–21 preached in 1531, *WA* 34^I, 120 ff., and his
interpretation of Psalm 101; *WA* 51, 238–39; *LW* 13, 193–99.
  The following literature is also important (for additional material, see Paul
Althaus, "Luthers Lehre von den beiden Reichen im Feuer der Kritik," *Luther-
Jahrbuch* 24 [1957]: 40–68 [reprinted in Paul Althaus, *Um die Wahrheit des
Evangeliums* (Stuttgart: Calwer Verlag, 1962), pp. 263–92]). Franz Lau,
"Äusserliche Ordnung" und "weltlich Ding" in Luthers Theologie des Politischen
(Göttingen: Vandenhoeck & Ruprecht, 1933). Harald Diem, *Luthers Lehre von
den zwei Reichen, untersucht von seinem Verständnis der Bergpredigt aus,*
"Theologische Existenz Heute," Neue Folge, no. 6 (Munich: Chr. Kaiser, 1938).
Ernst Kinder, *Geistliches und weltliches Regiment nach Luther* (Weimar:
Schriftenreihe der Luthergesellschaft, 1940). Gustav Törnvall, *Geistliches und
weltliches Regiment bei Luther* (Munich: Chr. Kaiser, 1947 [orig. 1940]).
Franz Lau, *Luthers Lehre von den beiden Reichen* (Berlin: Lutherisches Verlags-
haus, 1953). Ernst Wolf, "Das Problem der Sozialethik im Luthertum," in
Peregrinatio. Studien zur reformatorischen Theologie und zum Kirchenproblem
(Munich: Chr. Kaiser, 1954), pp. 233 ff. Johannes Heckel, *Lex charitatis. Eine
juristische Untersuchung über das Recht in der Theologie Martin Luthers*
(Munich: Verlag der Bayerischen Akademie der Wissenschaften, 1953). I have
evaluated Heckel's presentation of Luther's doctrine of the two kingdoms in my
article "Die beiden Regimente bei Luther. Bemerkungen zu Johannes Heckels
'Lex charitatis,'" *Theologische Literaturzeitung* 81 (1956), no. 3, cols. 129–36.
Heckel responded to my critique in his book *Im Irrgarten der Zwei-Reiche-
Lehre* (Munich: Chr. Kaiser, 1957). Heinrich Bornkamm, *Luther's Doctrine of
the Two Kingdoms in the Context of His Theology*, trans. Karl H. Hertz
(Philadelphia, Fortress Press, 1966). The most important discussions of the
two kingdoms in relation to political ethics are found in Walter Künneth,
Politik zwischen Dämon und Gott; eine christliche Ethik des Politischen (Berlin:
Lutherisches Verlagshaus, 1954), pp. 72–97, and Helmut Thielicke, *Theological
Ethics*, ed. William H. Lazareth (Philadelphia: Fortress Press), 1 (1966): 371–
82; 2 (1969): 655–56.

and the apostles' statements about the "law of Christ": the disciples of Jesus never use force, do not resist evil, do not avenge themselves, but under all circumstances serve one another in love.[2] These statements of the gospel appear to reject completely the state and the activity of the political authorities.[3] But there is a second type of statement. The same Scripture contains the apostolic affirmation of the state and, as in Romans 13 and 1 Peter 2:13–14, admonishes us to obey the authorities. In addition there are the statements of the Old Testament which institute and establish the "sword" which, as in Genesis 9:6 or Exodus 21:14, 22 ff., includes the death penalty. There is also the conversation between John the Baptist and the soldiers (Luke 3:14) in which John obviously does not in any way condemn the soldiers' station in life but rather recognizes it.[4] Finally, Luther read the Old Testament descriptions of God telling his people to prepare for battle and leading them to war; and he was aware that "all the saints have wielded the sword from the beginning of the world."[5]

Luther was bound to the Scripture and did not teach on the basis of his own willful speculation or in terms of what the political authorities wanted him to say. And the Scripture bound Luther to teach that the secular government, with all that belongs to it, is in the world because God has willed and ordained it. However, Scripture is not alone in asserting this; Scripture agrees with and confirms natural law. It was because these two different and even apparently contradictory types of statements stand side by side in Scripture that Luther was led to his doctrine of the two governments. Franz Lau correctly concludes that it was Scripture itself which led Luther to realize that the Sermon on the Mount did not mean what Enthusiasts like Thomas Müntzer said it did.[6]

---

2 *WA* 11, 248; *LW* 45, 87.

3 "At this point (Matthew 5:25–26), the Gospel can be understood as intending to abrogate the secular sword." *WA* 10^{III}, 251.

4 *WA* 11, 247–48; *LW* 45, 85–87. Luther points out that Peter confirms the military station of Cornelius (Acts 10:34–43), just as John the Baptist confirms the military station of the soldiers with whom he spoke. *WA* 11, 256; *LW* 45, 98.

5 *WA* 11, 255; *LW* 45, 96.

6 One can even say that Luther was led to his doctrine of the two governments on the basis of his correct understanding of the Sermon on the Mount. This is the position of Diem, *Luthers Lehre*, pp. 22 ff., and Lau, *Luthers Lehre von den beiden Reichen*, pp. 21, 24, 35. In many of the sermons which he preached on Matthew 5:20–26, the Gospel for the Sixth Sunday after Trinity,

As we shall see, Luther also includes marriage and the family as well as business in secular government. He sees these—and the laws governing them—as being based in God's creation, that is, in the institution of marriage and in the command to rule over the creatures in Genesis 1 and 2, and therefore as being distinct from the kingdom of Christ.

SPIRITUAL AND WORLDLY GOVERNMENT

God rules the world in a twofold way, at least insofar as his rule is visible to the eyes of faith. But the ruling that is visible does not exhaust God's lordship. As always, Luther distinguishes between the hidden and the revealed God. It is according to his majesty that God works all in all, but this omnipotent lordship— like God's majesty in general—cannot be comprehended by us men.[7] However, here we are not speaking of God's hidden government but of that revealed government which faith can know about. In this context, God has established two governments, the spiritual and the secular, or earthly, temporal, physical.[8] This secular government serves to preserve external secular righteousness; it thus also preserves this physical, earthly, temporal life and thereby preserves the world. The spiritual government helps men to achieve true Christian righteousness and therewith eternal life; it thus serves the redemption of the world.[9] God provides secular government throughout the whole world even among the heathen and the godless; but he gives his spiritual government only to his people.[10]

This spiritual government brings the kingdom of God into being.[11] This is "the kingdom of grace."[12] God's grace is present

---

Luther discusses our actions in fulfillment of an office, especially in government, in terms of the distinction between this type of activity and what Jesus commands in the Sermon on the Mount. In the sermons preached on July 19, 1528, and July 23, 1536, this leads Luther into a discussion of the two kingdoms. *WA* 27, 259; *WA* 41, 638.

[7] *WA* 45, 252.

[8] *WA* 11, 251; *LW* 45, 91; *WA* 17[1], 460; *WA* 19, 629; *LW* 46, 99. Luther contrasts the kingdom of Christ with the kingdom of the emperor. *WA* 27, 259. Luther also uses concepts such as *power, station,* and *office* as well as *government. WA* 32, 387; *LW* 21, 105–6; *WA* 30[II], 206.

[9] *WA* 19, 629; *LW* 46, 99.

[10] *WA* 51, 238; *LW* 13, 193.

[11] For Luther's understanding of the kingdom of God, see especially sermon on Matthew 18:23 ff. preached in 1524. *WA* 15, 724 ff.

[12] *WA* 31[1], 245; *LW* 14, 27.

(5357) in Christ, and so <u>this kingdom is Christ's kingdom</u> and Christ is
its "king and lord."[13] Christ exercises his government by bringing
grace and the gospel to men who are in bondage to sin and death.
This <u>grace includes</u> the <u>forgiveness</u> of sins[14] and therewith the
<u>freedom</u> of the children of God: freedom from the condemning
law, freedom from God's wrath, and at the same time <u>freedom
from all the demonic powers of fate</u> and of this created world.
<u>Christ's government</u> by way of the forgiveness of sins <u>comes to
men through</u> Christianity in the <u>preached word</u>, the <u>sacraments</u>,
and <u>brotherly consolation</u>. Christianity is thus both the place in
which Christ exercises his government and the means by which he
exercises it. The Holy Spirit works through preaching to move men
to faith. When this occurs, the kingdom of God is present for and
powerful in a man. <u>Christ's government is</u> thus nothing else than
the <u>lordship which he exercises in a man's heart through his
Spirit</u>.[15] The <u>only power at work</u> here is the power of the Spirit
which overcomes the heart and brings it to faith. Thus the <u>consti-
tutive element of Christ's lordship is freedom</u>.[16] Force is not used
in this kingdom; rather, everything takes place voluntarily through
the <u>compelling power</u> of the Spirit which is inherent in the word
of the gospel.[17] This power is the "<u>spiritual sword</u>" of God's
word.[18] As a result, the <u>lordship of Christ can never be an institution or an order of this world; it is a completely personal reality</u>.

However, the same God who administers the kingdom of grace
in Christ has also instituted the secular kingdom.[19] <u>Christ does not
participate in this secular kingdom. God—and not Christ—institutes it.</u> It is therefore certainly God's kingdom but it is not
Christ's kingdom. <u>Christ is concerned only with the spiritual kingdom.</u> He concerns himself about secular government as little as
about God's working in nature—as about storms, for example.[20]

---

13 *WA* 11, 249; *LW* 45, 88; *WA* 31I, 238–41; *LW* 14, 19–23.
14 *WA* 15, 724; *WA* 17I, 463.
15 *WA* 11, 252, 258–59; *LW* 45, 93, 100–1; *WA* 45, 669; *LW* 24, 228.
16 *WA* TR 3, no. 3388; *LW* 54, 199.
17 *WA* 31I, 86; *LW* 14, 55.
18 *WA* 11, 258; *LW* 45, 101. It should be noted that this "spiritual sword"
not only works through forgiving of sins but also through retaining them. Cf.
WA TR 6, no. 6672.
19 *WA* 32, 390; *LW* 21, 109; *WA* 36, 385; *WA* 51, 238; *LW* 13, 193.
20 *WA* 11, 202.

At this point Luther clearly distinguishes between the activity of God and the activity of Christ. Not everything that God institutes and works comes from Christ. But Christ, although his kingdom is only the spiritual government, has very explicitly confirmed that this other secular government is also God's will and order.[21] "Thus God himself is the founder, lord, master, protector, and rewarder of both kinds of righteousness."[22]

For Luther, secular government includes much more than political authorities and governments; it includes everything that contributes to the preservation of this earthly life, especially marriage and family, the entire household, as well as property, business, and all the stations and vocations which God has instituted.[23] Luther distinguishes all this from the spiritual reality of grace, of the word of God, and of faith and describes it as an "external matter,"[24] that is, related to our bodies, and also as the "secular sword."[25]

This secular or temporal government is necessary alongside the kingdom of Christ. "For without it [secular government] this life could not endure."[26] Luther's position is based not only—or even primarily—on the fact of sin and the wickedness and licentiousness of men. Luther does indeed emphasize these whenever he speaks of political authority, for only by using the sword can the political authorities restrain that evil which destroys the fabric of society and leads to chaos.[27] But Luther clearly sees that the state does more than use its force and power to restrain evil. The political authorities also exercise the office of a father or of parents insofar as they function in nourishing and taking care of people.[28] It

---

[21] *WA* 10$^{1.2}$, 426. *WA* 11, 258; *LW* 45, 101; *WA* 32, 390; *LW* 21, 109.

[22] *WA* 19, 629; *LW* 46, 100.

[23] *WA* 32, 321; *LW* 21, 29.

[24] "The secular rule has nothing at all to do with the office of Christ but is an external matter, just as all other offices and estates are." *WA* 12, 331; *LW* 30, 76.

[25] *WA* 11, 258; *LW* 45, 101; *WA* 23, 514; *WA* 32, 390; *LW* 21, 109; *WA* 37, 197; *WA* 47, 242; *WA* 30^{II}, 562; *LW* 46, 242. It should be noted, however, that parents also belong to spiritual government, for parents proclaim the gospel to their children. *WA* 10^{II}, 301; *LW* 45, 46. See below, pp. 99–100.

[26] *WA* 32, 390; *LW* 21, 109.

[27] "The presence of the sword shows the nature of the children under it: people who, if they dared, would be desperate scoundrels." *WA* 19, 640; *LW* 46, 112.

[28] *WA* 30^{I}, 152; *BC*, 384; *WA* 32, 153.

would be very difficult to base this function on the fact of sin or
to derive it from the duty of protecting people against violence;
rather, it comprehends all the orders of life. And this is especially
true of the other elements which Luther includes in the secular
government, such as marriage, the household, property, the relationship between master and servant—these do not have their basis
in humanity's fall into sin. They are necessary simply because God
desires to preserve the men whom he has created and these orders
are indispensable for that purpose. For example, anyone who has
an office—beginning with the father of a family who must take
care of his children—needs property. "The world could not endure
if we were all to be beggars and have nothing."[29] In the same way,
earthly life requires relationships in which some are superiors and
others are dependent, in which some give commands and others
obey, in which some rule and others are subjects—and these relationships are not at all restricted to political life in the narrower
sense.[30] Thus everything that Luther understands as secular government has a basis antecedent to the dominion of sin, that is, in
the elementary necessities of this earthly life. This is what Luther
means when he says that secular government was already present
in paradise[31] and that it "was instituted from the beginning of
creation."[32]

Thus secular government existed long before Christ and also
exercised power without him. This indicates that secular government and Christ's kingdom are two distinct entities and that Christ
is not directly involved in secular government.[33]

---

[29] *WA* 32, 307; *LW* 21, 12.

[30] *WA* 6, 252; *LW* 44, 82. Augustine felt that the difference between rulers
and subjects was based on the fact of sin. *The City of God*, book 19, chapter 15.

[31] "God committed secular government to Adam when he said, Genesis 1
[:28]: 'Be fruitful and multiply, and fill the earth and subdue it.'" *WA* 28,
441. Luther thus recognizes that at least some elements of secular government
were present before the fall. *WA* 11, 266; *LW* 45, 111.

[32] *WA* 49, 137, 143. In this passage—from a sermon on John 20:12–23—
Luther makes no reference at all to the fact of sin: "In these words, the Lord
shows what he has done through his resurrection: he has instituted a government that is not concerned with getting and keeping gold and money, or with
this temporal life. For this kingdom was already present, having been instituted
at the beginning of the world and subjected to reason. . . . This is the old
government and it is the concern of the secular authorities who do not need the
Holy Spirit to do their work." Ibid.

[33] *WA* 47, 242.

THE CONCEPTS OF KINGDOM
AND GOVERNMENT

In *Temporal Authority: To What Extent It Should Be Obeyed* (1523), Luther clearly distinguishes between the two "kingdoms" on the one hand and the two "governments" on the other. Because there are two kingdoms, the kingdom of God to which all believers in Christ belong and the kingdom of this world to which all others (that is, nonbelievers) belong, "God has ordained two governments the spiritual . . . and the secular."[34] Later Luther does not maintain this distinction but uses the concepts *kingdom* and *government* in the same sense. He alternates between "spiritual kingdom and secular kingdom" and "spiritual government and secular government," and between "the kingdom of Christ" and "the government of Christ."[35]

"THE WORLD" AND "THE SECULAR"*

Luther uses the concepts *world* and *secular* in the same broad sense that the New Testament does.[36] When he speaks of living "in the world" he frequently refers to people who live in this age of the world or who live "on earth."[37] In this sense the Christian is a "citizen of this world." Luther explicitly says that this secular life and the stations that constitute it are given and instituted by God.[38] "The righteousness of this world," "the outward righteousness before the world" is clearly distinguished from "that principal Christian righteousness by which a person becomes a believer acceptable to God." (Luther understands the statement in Matthew 5:6 about "those who hunger and thirst for righteousness" as referring to this outward righteousness.) Thus this

---

34 *WA* 11, 249–51; *LW* 45, 88–91.

35 See, for example, *WA* 30^{II}, 562; *LW* 46, 242; *WA* 36, 385; *WA* 45, 252; *WA* 49, 137, 143; *WA* 51, 238–39; *LW* 13, 193–94; *WA* TR 6, no. 7026. Luther also speaks of the need "to distinguish properly between the secular and the spiritual stations, between the kingdom of Christ and the kingdom of the world." *WA* 32, 387; *LW* 21, 105—Luther here uses *Stand*, "station," in the same sense as *Regiment*, "government"; see *WA* 37, 602. In George Rörer's notes on Luther's sermons, *regnum* and *regimen* are used in the same sense. *WA* 27, 259–60. The fact that Luther does not continue to distinguish between kingdom and government is related to the change in the structure of his doctrine of the two kingdoms, which is discussed below, pp. 00–00.

36 See Hermann Sasse's "Κόσμος," in Gerhard Kittel et al., *Theological Dictionary of the New Testament*, trans. G. W. Bromiley (Grand Rapids: Eerdmans, 1965), 3:868–95.

37 *WA* 32, 371; *LW* 21, 86.

38 *WA* 39^{II}, 40–41.

* [The terms are *Welt* and *weltlich*. The latter more literally means worldly, but also carries the full sense of secular. I have frequently chosen to translate it as secular rather than worldly.—Trans.]

outward righteousness is indeed considered less valuable than the
true righteousness of the Christian. However, it does have positive
value, for it says "that in his station everyone should do his duty."[39]
If people were seriously concerned about this secular righteousness,
"there would be no rascality or injustice, but sheer righteousness and
blessedness on earth."[40]

On the other hand, Luther, like the New Testament, frequently uses
the word *world* to designate those men who have closed their hearts to
God's word and live in enmity with him or to describe that area in
which sin, Satan, and "the children of Satan" have power.[41] This meaning of world is found in the same contexts in which the other meaning
is found.

Given this breadth of usage, it can happen that Luther, like the New
Testament, combines the various meanings of world and secular in
such a way that both meanings are expressed at once. But that is not
always the case. At times the meanings must be clearly differentiated.
Luther says one thing when he says that marriage is an "external,
worldly matter"[42] and something quite different when he says that the
princes who persecute the gospel are "worldly princes" and live up to
their name and title according to the standards of this world.[43]

Furthermore, Luther's usage of the terms *worldly* or *secular* and
world changes. In *Temporal Authority: To What Extent It Should Be
Obeyed* Luther uses worldly (*weltlich*) or secular in the sense of the
world as God's enemy. Therefore he can describe the princes who are
opposed to the Reformation: "Such tyrants are acting as worldly princes
are supposed to act, and worldly princes they surely are. But the world
is God's enemy; hence they too have to do what is antagonistic to God
and agreeable to the world, that they may not be bereft of honor, but
remain worldly princes."[44] The princes are preserving their worldly
honor. As far as I can see, after 1523 Luther no longer speaks of
worldly princes or of a secular government in this significant theological
sense; rather, worldly is used in the same sense as temporal, earthly,
and bodily. If this observation is correct, it provides evidence for the
development of Luther's thinking about the two kingdoms which I will
now describe: Luther no longer bases his doctrine on the opposition
between the kingdom of God and the kingdom of Satan which originally characterized his doctrine.

---

[39] *WA* 19, 629; *LW* 46, 99–100; *WA* 32, 318–19; *LW* 21, 26.
[40] *WA* 32, 319; *LW* 21, 26.
[41] "These are princes of this world. But the world is God's enemy." *WA* 11,
267; *LW* 45, 113; *WA* 32, 310–12, 314, 318; *LW* 21, 16–17, 19–20, 25;
WA 45, 70.
[42] *WA* 30^III, 205; *LW* 46, 265.
[43] *WA* 11, 267; *LW* 45, 113.
[44] *WA* 11, 267; *LW*·45, 112–13.

CHANGE IN APPROACH AND BASIS

Luther's doctrine of the two kingdoms or governments was involved in a process of change as regards both his approach and the basis of his doctrine. At first the doctrine was developed under the influence of Augustine's theology of history. In 1523, when he wrote *Temporal Authority: To What Extent It Should Be Obeyed, and during the next few years,* Luther asserted that there are two governments: the spiritual and the secular. Luther based this assertion on the basic opposition of the kingdom of God and the kingdom of this world. That is, all true believers in Christ belong to the kingdom of God and all other people belong to the kingdom of this world. In this usage, world means the sinful world under the lordship of Satan. Humanity is also divided into two camps, and those who believe in Christ always remain a small minority.[45] As long as mankind belongs to the kingdom of this world, it stands under the law. The law appears in secular government. This already implies that those who believe in Christ, because they no longer stand under the law, do not need this earthly government, law, and the sword—all this is necessary only for the sake of other people.[46] If all men were Christians, there would be no need of secular government.[47] The relationship between the two governments is thus the relationship between the law and the gospel. It corresponds to the division of mankind into Christians and non-Christians. In this usage, kingdom and government are distinguished: the kingdom of this world is determined by sin; secular government is instituted by God against sin, even though secular government itself may participate in sin.

This doctrine of the two governments is thus closely related to the biblical dualism between the kingdom of God and this world understood as the kingdom of Satan. It is thus also closely related to Augustine's doctrine of the city of God and the city of this

---

[45] *WA* 11, 249–51; *LW* 45, 88–90; *WA* 10^{III}, 252; *WA* 12, 329–30; *LW* 45, 217–19. In 1525 Luther said that God has ordained the sword because of the world, that is, sinful humanity, *WA* 17^{I}, 460. This usage is found as late as 1529. *WA* 28, 281.

[46] *WA* 11, 251; *LW* 45, 91; *WA* 10^{III}, 252.

[47] *WA* 11, 249–50; *LW* 45, 89.

world.[48] Luther thinks of the world primarily in terms of the state, with its office of preventing evil, with its "sword." If secular government is basically represented by the state and particularly by its punitive power, it is obviously easy to approach the whole problem on a dualistic basis—that is, on the basis of the unconditional opposition between the kingdom of God and the kingdom of the sinful world which results in Luther's distinction between two different kinds of government.

However, Luther could maintain this basic understanding of the two governments only as long as he felt that the secular government is basically represented by the state—and particularly by its power of the sword. As soon as Luther began to speak of secular government in a broader sense, including such matters as marriage and property, he could no longer identify the power of evil among men as the basis for secular government in this broader sense. For according to Luther, marriage and property are instituted in paradise and originally have nothing to do with the fall into sin. Thereby, however, the doctrine of the two governments has now been separated from the dualism between the kingdom of God and that kingdom of this world which is in opposition to God. Now the kingdom of this world or the secular kingdom is understood as earthly and as serving to preserve this earthly life. Now Luther no longer needed to distinguish between the terms *kingdom* and *government*; he could use both in the same sense.

After this point, Luther no longer defines the two governments in terms of their relationship to the opposition between the kingdom of God and the kingdom of this world, understood as being in opposition to the kingdom of God. They are now defined as the spiritual government and the secular, or outward, government which affects our physical, earthly life, or as the kingdom of Christ and the kingdom of the emperor. Accordingly, the kingdom of this world is no longer simply identified with being under the law—although that certainly remains true of the authorities' demand for obedience from a subject insofar as he is not a Christian. For Luther now sees that the authorities also express the goodness

---

[48] Ernst Kinder, "Gottesreich und Weltreich bei Augustin und Luther," in *Gedenkschrift für Werner Elert*, Friedrich Hübner et al., eds. (Berlin: Lutherisches Verlagshaus, 1955), pp. 24–42.

of God; and this goodness is even more clearly expressed in other elements of the secular government, such as marriage, property, and all that Luther lists in his explanation of the First Article and the Fourth Petition of the Lord's Prayer in his Small Catechism.[49] The two governments no longer deal with two distinct and different groups, the believers and the unbelievers; rather, both affect the life of the children of God in two different areas of one and the same life. The Christian lives in both governments. He is also a citizen of this world.[50] Therefore, it can no longer be said that Christians do not need secular government for their own persons. And after this time Luther no longer makes this kind of statement.

In all this Luther has not simply and completely abandoned his characterization of the state (that is, of the secular government in its narrow sense) as being necessary because of sin, but this is no longer all that he has to say; this is now valid only for certain functions of the state.

Reinhold Seeberg attempted to combine Luther's doctrine of the two governments with Luther's doctrine of law and gospel in such a way that "the relationship between secular and ecclesiastical government may be understood as a special instance of the relationship between law and gospel." This is not possible.[51] There is more to secular government than the authority to punish. That is, it is not simply characterized by the law, but also by divine goodness and thus also points toward the gospel. The *blessing* of God comes not only through the spiritual government but also through the secular government—even though these are two different blessings. "God has a double blessing, a physical one for this life and a spiritual one for eternal life."[52]

---

49 *WA* 30[I], 363–64, 374; *BC*, 345, 347.

50 "The Christian as a Christian is under the First Table of the law, but outside the kingdom of heaven he is a citizen of this world. Therefore he has two citizenships: he is a subject of Christ through faith and a subject of the emperor through his body." *WA* 39[II], 81.

51 Reinhold Seeberg, *Lehrbuch der Dogmengeschichte*, 4th ed. (Leipzig: Deichert, 1933), 4[1]:368 n. 1 (§84, 11). For a more detailed discussion, see Törnvall, *Geistliches und weltliches Regiment bei Luther*, pp. 53 ff.; Lau, *Luthers Lehre von den beiden Reichen*, pp. 43 ff., and Wilfried Joest, "Das Verhältnis der Unterscheidung der beiden Regimente zu der Unterscheidung von Gesetz und Evangelium," in *Dank an Paul Althaus, eine Festgabe zum 70. Geburtstag*, Walter Künneth and Wilfried Joest, eds. (Gütersloh: Bertelsmann, 1958), pp. 79–97.

52 *WA* 40[I], 395; LW 26, 251. Heckel (*Lex charitatis*, pp. 31 ff.) does not distinguish Luther's development of his doctrine of the two governments in

THE UNITY OF THE TWO GOVERNMENTS

Both governments have been established by one and the same God. Even insofar as secular government exists because of sin, it still does not have its source in sin and is not a city of the devil; rather, it is a divine institution. It is "God's own work, institution, and creation" established in opposition to the devil.[53] The same God stands behind both governments and is effectively present in both; God only works in a different way in each.[54] Luther can even mention in one breath the presence of God in the means of grace of the kingdom of Christ and his presence in the political authorities: "God is in preaching, in baptism, and in government; that is where you can find him." And what Luther says about government naturally applies equally to the household.[55]

We have already said that God rules in both governments with his goodness, love, and mercy. This is no less true of the secular government than of the spiritual government, the kingdom of Christ. It goes without saying that this holds true for the office of parents in dealing with children. However, it is also true of the office of the political authorities and of their use of the "sword," in spite of all misuse. For the political authorities create and maintain law and order, God's good gift, and earthly peace, which is the greatest earthly good and cannot be outweighed by every-

---

Temporal Authority: To What Extent It Should Be Obeyed (1523) and elsewhere in this period from Luther's later thinking on this matter. There is no question that in 1523 and the years immediately following, Luther's doctrine of the two governments is based on the opposition between the kingdom of God and the sinful kingdom of this world, which is ruled by Satan. Heckel however writes as though this were Luther's final position. "Luther's teaching on the governments . . . is first placed in its appropriate context when it is understood in relationship to the two kingdoms" (p. 42). As Heckel understands Luther, he continues to think of the secular government as almost completely overshadowed by the kingdom of this world, which is opposed to God and to his kingdom. Thus he partially distorts Luther's doctrine when he describes it as "Augustinian." See my critical discussion of his position in "Die beiden Regimente bei Luther." The passages from Luther which Heckel cites to support his position require careful examination. In a whole series of instances they do not prove the point that Heckel wishes to establish. See also Martin Schloemann, *Natürliches und gepredigtes Gesetz bei Luther* (Berlin: Töpelmann, 1961), pp. 16–17.

[53] *WA* 11, 251, 257; *LW* 45, 91, 99; *WA* 39[II], 42.

[54] "Thus God himself is the founder, lord, master, protector, and rewarder of both kinds of righteousness. There is no human ordinance or authority in either, but each is a divine thing entirely." *WA* 19, 630; *LW* 46, 100.

[55] *WA* 49, 643.

thing else in the whole world.[56] Through the political authorities, God protects his people from the violent acts of evil men.[57] Therefore Luther can call the authorities "saviors" and place them alongside fathers and mothers and the doctors and lawyers who help us in sickness or in legal matters.[58]

Luther sees a state in which justice prevails as a picture of the kingdom of God, for such a state preserves peace and therewith earthly blessedness: "God wants the government of the world to be a symbol of true salvation and of his kingdom of heaven, like a pantomime or a mask."[59] Thus there is an analogy between secular government and the lordship of Christ, between Christ the Lord and secular lords. In both instances to be a lord means to be a "helping power." When lordship is properly understood and practiced, *lord* is a pleasant, friendly term even in the world. The proper exercise of lordship consists merely in doing good and helpful things. Therefore if the lords of this world wish to be used as helpers and if their subjects wish to use them as such, *trust* must be as much a part of the relationship between lords and subjects as it is part of our relationship to Christ. The fact that someone is my lord means that I may rely on him; there is a correspondence between the lordship of Christ and that of the lords of this world, even though it is only a relative one.[60] Thus Luther establishes a very close relationship between our ethical relationship to political authorities and our relationship to God. Both have a common characteristic.

Admittedly, secular government is also a kingdom of wrath for those who are evil and rebellious.[61] Secular government must use force and punish those who are evil in order to protect the

---

56 *WA* 7, 581; *LW* 21, 335; *WA* 10[I,2], 427.

57 *WA* 37, 49.

58 *WA* 52, 158.

59 *WA* 51, 241; *LW* 13, 197. "Worldly lordship is an image, shadow, or figure of the lordship of Christ." *WA* 30[II], 554; *LW* 46, 237. (In its context, this latter passage emphasizes the difference and the distinctions between the two governments more than their correspondence.)

60 *WA* 37, 49–52.

61 In spite of *WA* 18, 389; *LW* 46, 70–71, Heckel's summary of Luther is one-sided and only half true when he says (*Lex charitatis*, p. 41): "Mankind experiences this kingdom of God [the secular government] as a kingdom of divine wrath"; the same must be said of his assertion (ibid., p. 42) that the secular government is "exercised in the kingdom of divine wrath through government and with the use of the sword of secular authority."

| righteous.[62] Thus wrath also stands in the service of mercy. The situation in the spiritual government is no different. The political authorities cannot repudiate the use of wrath anymore than the parents of a family or a preacher in his pulpit can do so.[63] And just as parents and preachers use "necessary wrath" as a means of love, so it is also a means of God's love when used by the political authorities: "Although the severity and wrath of the world's kingdom seems unmerciful, nevertheless, when we see it rightly, it is not the least of God's mercies."[64]

Our awareness of the unity and the correspondence between these two governments must not, however, prevent us from seeing the thoroughgoing distinction between them.

THE DIFFERENCE BETWEEN THE TWO GOVERNMENTS

First, there is a difference in rank. Although both are instituted by God, the two governments do not have the same rank. In this respect they are related to one another in the same way as true Christian righteousness that counts before God is related to the secular righteousness that counts "before the world."[65] The spiritual government which helps us achieve true righteousness before God has the higher rank, and secular government is subordinate to it. For secular government serves only this earthly life and passes away together with this life;[66] spiritual government, however, stands in the service of eternal life and thus of God's ultimate purpose. In an indirect way, of course, secular government also serves the greatest good: eternal life; for spiritual government— the preaching of the gospel and the life of Christendom—requires earthly peace. However, secular government is never anything more than a means to achieve what is really important for God and men. God administers secular government with his left hand;[67]

---

[62] *WA* 18, 389; *LW* 46, 70–71; *WA* 37, 49.
[63] *WA* 32, 364; *LW* 21, 78.
[64] *WA* 18, 390; *LW* 46, 71.
[65] *WA* 19, 629; *LW* 46, 99.
[66] *WA* 45, 669; *LW* 24, 229.
[67] "This is his kingdom with the left hand. However, the kingdom with his right is wherever he himself reigns." *WA* 36, 385; *WA* 52, 26. Heckel (*Lex charitatis*, p. 41) completely misinterprets Luther's use of the phrase *left hand* as though this referred to a "government at the left hand." Luther, however,

it is really not very important in comparison with the spiritual government which he exercises with his right hand. It is on this latter government that everything depends; it is God's own government, and he has reserved it for himself.[68] "Temporal power is but a very small matter in the sight of God, and too slightly regarded by him for us to resist, disobey, or become quarrelsome on its account, no matter whether the state does right or wrong."[69]

Secular and spiritual government are as definitely and widely separated as heaven and earth.[70] The rule in the kingdom of Christ is that all his people, because of their relationship to him, are one and equal before God.[71] In secular government, however, God has instituted differences between men and made some dependent upon others. He establishes human authority and makes it powerful; the fourth commandment requires us to recognize this authority by obeying it. He calls men into a variety of stations and offices and into corresponding relationships of dependence and of commanding and obeying.[72] Wherever people live together, there is a top and a bottom, there are higher and lower stations.[73] The equality of all Christians before God in faith and love does not abrogate or invalidate natural differences and relationships of dependence and authority among men. The attempt to eliminate these differences would throw human society into chaotic disorder. At the same time, however, the equality is not set aside through

---

does not speak of a government "at the left hand" but rather "with the left hand"! This is the action of divine wrath against the "goats" who stand at the left hand in the Last Judgment.

68 *WA* TR 3, no. 3388; *LW* 54, 199.

69 *WA* 6, 259; *LW* 44, 93. Luther speaks of the "kingdom of this world" as a "filthy and mortal kingdom of the belly" and calls it "a poor and miserable kingdom, indeed, a foul and stinking one." *WA* 32, 467; *LW* 21, 203. In this passage, however, he is not thinking of secular government as such but of the sum total of all earthly goods, or Mammon.

70 *WA* 47, 284.

71 *WA* 32, 316; *LW* 21, 23.

72 *WA* 6, 252; *LW* 44, 82; *WA* 51, 212; *LW* 13, 161; *WA* 49, 606 ff.; *LW* 51, 348 ff.

73 *WA* 11, 202; *WA* 30I, 148; *BC*, 379-80; *WA* 49, 82; *WA* 49, 609-10; *LW* 51, 349-51; *WA* 52, 137; *WA* 51, 212; *LW* 13, 161. Heckel (*Lex charitatis*, p. 36) says that for Luther the inequalities among men in the kingdom of this world are the result of selfishness, but to say this is to read one's own opinion into Luther. The quotations which Heckel cites (*WA* 7, 590, 592; *LW* 21, 344, 346; *WA* 14, 655, 701; *LW* 9, 145, 220; *WA* 40I, 178; cf. *LW* 26, 97-98) do not support his position. All these quotations merely say that the world cannot exist without a "difference between persons and stations." This is also the meaning of *WA* 18, 327; *LW* 46, 39.

the inequality: "God creates one and the same standing within the
great inequalities of many different stations and persons." God
wants every station, especially the higher stations, to recognize this
equality in all inequality and with all humility to refrain from
thinking itself to be more before God than other stations.[74]

The love which Christ commands and exemplifies, rules in the
kingdom of Christ. This love gives and forgives without limit,
does not avenge itself, and uses no other weapon than love itself.
This love is even ready to lose its life for the sake of the brother.[75]
In secular government, at least in the state, justice rules—and
rules with force, for only force is able to preserve law and justice.
The authorities must take the people who do not want to obey
and compel them to obey.[76] In the kingdom of Christ everything
is voluntary. The kingdom of Christ consists in forgiveness; secular
government exercises retribution and punishment.[77] At this point
the kingdom of Christ and secular government are in opposition
to each other.[78] Spiritual government does in fact administer punishment through the office of the Word; however, according to
Matthew 18 this is done only "with God's word," the law. The
political authorities do it quite differently; they exercise outward
force against "open lawlessness."[79] Secular government rules with
the sword; spiritual government rules with the word.[80]

In the kingdom of Christ, Christ rules personally with his
gospel through his Spirit. Secular government has no need of
Christ, his gospel, or the Spirit. Here reason rules.[81] Therefore, in

---

74 *WA* 49, 609–10; *LW* 51, 349–50; *WA* 32, 476; *LW* 21, 214; *WA* 40[I],
178; cf. *LW* 26, 97–98.
75 *WA* 11, 250, 252; *LW* 45, 89, 92; *WA* 32, 390; *LW* 21, 108.
76 *WA* 11, 252; *LW* 45, 92.
77 *WA* 18, 389; *LW* 46, 69–70.
78 *WA* 17[I], 460.
79 *WA* 30[I], 168; *BC*, 398; *WA* 31[I], 130; *LW* 14, 76; *WA* 41, 638.
80 *WA* 28, 281.
81 *WA* 11, 202; *WA* 32, 304; *LW* 21, 9. Concerning business matters, Luther
says: "Now, Christ is not preaching about this. He leaves the division of property and business to the teaching of reason." *WA* 32, 394; *LW* 21, 115. "In
the office of preaching, Christ does the whole thing, by his Spirit, but in the
worldly kingdom men must act on the basis of reason—wherein the laws also
have their origin—for God has subjected temporal rule and all of physical life
to reason (Genesis 2[:15]). He has not sent the Holy Spirit from heaven for
this purpose." *WA* 30[II], 562; *LW* 46, 242; similarly *WA* 45, 669; *LW* 24,
228. "God made the secular government subordinate and subject to reason,
because it is to have no jurisdiction over the welfare of souls or things of
eternal value but only over physical and temporal goods, which God places
under man's dominion, Genesis 2[:8 ff.]." *WA* 51, 242; *LW* 13, 198.

making decisions in the course of fulfilling one's office in the
secular government, one ought not go to Christ for advice but
rather to the law of the land.[82] In this process, positive laws are
always to be tested on the basis of reason, for laws flow out of
reason "as from the spring of justice."[83]

THE TWO GOVERNMENTS
DEPEND ON EACH OTHER

Even though the two governments are different from and essen-
tially independent of each other, they still need each other.

The secular kingdom "can have its own existence without God's
kingdom"; likewise, the spiritual kingdom can exist without the
kingdom of this world.[84] Each government exists independently
and does not need the other government in order to fulfill its own
nature. Even though both governments are so distinct from and
independent of each other, however, they still belong together.[85]
In his doctrine of the stations, or hierarchies, Luther places them
together as stations within the one body of Christendom.[86] They
need each other and exist for each other.

The kingdom of Christ, however, could not exist in this world
apart from the varied functioning of the secular government.[87]
The institution of marriage creates new members for Christendom;
the political authorities create the peace which the congregation of
Christ needs to carry out its task.[88] Christendom does not have the
resources to establish this peace. It has only the gospel. But we

---

82 *WA* 32, 391, 395; *LW* 21, 110, 115.

83 *WA* 11, 280; *LW* 45, 129.

84 *WA* 51, 238–39; *LW* 13, 193–94.

85 *WA* 11, 252; *LW* 45, 92; *WA* 31[I], 50.

86 See above, pp. 36–37. The doctrine of the two kingdoms and the doctrine
of the three hierarchies are not coextensive but complementary. The doctrine of
the three hierarchies is distinguished from the doctrine of the two kingdoms by
the fact that it is completely bound to the particular historical situation and
viewpoint at the time of Luther. As Lau says, Luther was still working with
"a structure of society that, viewed in modern times, comprehends both church
and state; and he considers this intertwining of spiritual and secular government
to be a desirable situation." *Luthers Lehre von den beiden Reichen*, p. 62. Elsewhere Luther points out that the office of the preaching of the word "rests in
the community." Community (*Gemeinde*), as used at this place, refers to a
sociological structure that is both secular and spiritual and was coextensive with
the "congregation." Here both governments are found together with one another
in one totality. *WA* 31[I], 196; *LW* 13, 49.

87 *WA* 11, 258; *LW* 45, 101.

88 *WA* 31[I], 192; *LW* 13, 45.

cannot rule the world according to the gospel in such a way that we could do without secular government and the state.[89] For the gospel does not force people to do anything—and for this reason it does not bring everyone faith.[90] Christians are always a minority; the power of evil continues to exist. And the Christian community will never finish its battle against evil. Rejecting political authority and expecting everything to come from the gospel "would be loosing the ropes and chains of the savage wild beasts."[91]

The secular government needs the spiritual government as much as the spiritual government needs the secular. For no society properly maintains law and order and continues to be blessed if it lacks that knowledge of God and his truth which the spiritual government provides.[92] Only the proclamation of the word permits us to recognize properly and respect secular government and the various stations of society as God's work and will. The office of preaching helps the authorities to preserve peace and order by instructing all stations concerning God's will for them and by teaching "obedience, morals, discipline, and honor."[93] The secular government by itself can indeed force people to behave well outwardly, but it cannot make the heart righteous. Where secular government works by itself, therefore, it produces only hypocrisy and outward obedience without the proper attitude of the heart to God.[94]

However, just as one may not separate these two governments from each other and try to have one without the other, so they may not be mixed.[95] They are and remain two different entities— and precisely for this reason they need each other. Luther says that we cannot have one without the other. And he also says that we should separate them as far from each other as heaven is separated

---

[89] *WA* 11, 251; *LW* 45, 91. "I have often taught that the world ought not and cannot be ruled according to the gospel and Christian love, but by strict laws and with sword and force, because the world is evil. It accepts neither gospel nor love, but lives and acts according to its own will unless compelled by force." *WA* 15, 306; *LW* 45, 264. See also *WA* 15, 302; *LW* 45, 258.

[90] *WA* 11, 260; *LW* 45, 102; *WA* Br 3, 484–85; cf. *S-J* 2, 311. [*S-J* translates the letter but not the accompanying memorandum.—Trans.]

[91] *WA* 11, 251–52; *LW* 45, 91–92; *WA* 17^{I}, 333.

[92] *WA* 31^{I}, 50.

[93] *WA* 30^{II}, 537–38; *LW* 46, 226–27; *WA* 31^{II}, 592.

[94] *WA* 11, 252; *LW* 45, 92; *WA* 30^{II}, 562; *LW* 46, 242.

[95] *WA* 11, 252; *LW* 45, 92; *WA* 32, 387; *LW* 21, 105.

from earth.[96] The Roman papacy has been especially guilty of
mixing the two governments. It has "so jumbled these two together
and confused them with each other that neither one has kept to
its power or force or rights."[97] Through canon law the papacy has
sought to gain control of secular law and make decisions in
secular matters (such as the laws concerning marriage) which are
properly the concern of secular government; thus it has made itself
master over all political authorities.[98] But it is not the function of
the church's ministry to make laws concerning these matters and
to exercise secular government; the ministry is concerned with
secular matters only insofar as they "touch upon consciences." It
is therefore in a position to instruct and comfort consciences.[99]

When the Enthusiasts derive laws for secular government from
the gospel, they confuse the two governments in the same way that
the papacy does.[100] The peasants were making social demands in
the name of the gospel and thus confusing the two kingdoms.[101]
On the other hand, Luther condemns the political authorities and
the secular princes who seek to rule in the church.[102] Thus authorities in both governments misunderstood the distinction between
the kingdoms in two ways, and Luther continually needs to re-
emphasize it.[103]

THE CHRISTIAN IN BOTH GOVERNMENTS

The Christian must live in both kingdoms, and he is a citizen
of the secular kingdom as well as of the spiritual one.[104] Indeed,
he belongs to the kingdom of this world even before he belongs

---

[96] *WA* TR 6, no. 6672.

[97] *WA* 30^III, 206; *LW* 46, 266. In opposition to this, Luther maintains "that
the two authorities or realms, the temporal and the spiritual, are kept distinct
and separate from each other and that each is specifically instructed and restricted to its own task." Ibid. See also *WA* 30^II, 112; *LW* 46, 166.

[98] *WA* 30^II, 112; *LW* 46, 166; *WA* 30^III, 205; *LW* 46, 265–66.

[99] *WA* 30^III, 205; *LW* 46, 265. "Let whoever is supposed to rule or wants to
rule be the ruler; I want to instruct and console consciences, and advise them
as much as I can." *WA* 30^III, 206; *LW* 46, 267.

[100] *WA* 51, 239; *LW* 13, 194.

[101] *WA* 18, 327; *LW* 46, 39; *WA* 41, 538.

[102] *WA* 51, 239; *LW* 13, 194.

[103] "Constantly I must pound in and squeeze in and drive in and wedge in
this difference between the two kingdoms, even though it is written and said
so often that it becomes tedious. The devil never stops cooking and brewing
these two kingdoms into each other." *WA* 51, 239; *LW* 13, 194.

[104] *WA* 32, 390; *LW* 21, 109; *WA* 39^II, 40, 81.

to the kingdom of God, for he was born even before he became a Christian. Therefore he stands under both governments. He has two lords: one in the earthly kingdom and one in the spiritual kingdom. He is obligated to the emperor and to Christ at the same time; to the emperor for his outward life, to Christ inwardly with his conscience and in faith.[105] How can the Christian live this sort of double existence? Are not his attitudes and his activities tragically and hopelessly fragmented?

Luther posed these questions very seriously and with complete clarity. The meaning of Christ's lordship over men is clarified by Jesus' strict statements concerning the attitude of men in the kingdom of God as these statements are collected in the Sermon on the Mount and adopted and interpreted by the apostles.

THE INTERPRETATION OF THE SERMON ON THE MOUNT[106]

All Jesus' statements in the Sermon on the Mount have a twofold meaning. Jesus calls his disciples to *freedom* and to *love*. The disciples of Jesus are to be free in their relationship to the world and to its goods: Jesus warns them against bondage to Mammon and to worry. In their relationship to people, the disciples of Jesus live purely and exclusively out of love. This love gives and forgives without limits; it suffers injustice without resisting; it does not repay others what they have coming. Love always responds with and defends itself with love. Thus this love is completely opposed to the style of life typical of this world, in which those who are mighty rule—whereas love itself knows no other lordship than in service. How is it possible to live in this way and at the same time live in a world that is characterized by property and profit, by law, by economics, by the state, and by politics—for example, to be a property owner who has to administer his estate, a judge, a statesman, or a soldier?

Luther asks this question in all its sharpness because he does not

---

105 *WA* 32, 187; *WA* 32, 390, 393; *LW* 21, 109, 113.
106 Georg Wünsch, *Die Bergpredigt bei Luther. Eine Studie zum Verhältnis vom Christentum und Welt* (Tübingen: J. C. B. Mohr, 1920). Wünsch's description of Luther's position is strongly influenced by Ernst Troeltsch. For my criticism of this position, see my review of this book in *Theologisches Literaturblatt* 43 (1922), col. 81–89.

weaken either side of the question. He takes Jesus' statements very seriously. And he is very realistic about the task of living in this world as a citizen subject to secular laws.

When Luther interpreted the statements of Jesus which we summarize under the name of the Sermon on the Mount, he was confronted by two opposing opinions.[107] On the one side was the official Roman Catholic interpretation of the Sermon on the Mount at the time of the Reformation. According to this interpretation, no one can fulfill the Sermon on the Mount while living in the midst of this world. Its strictest requirements can only be fulfilled by small groups who withdraw from life as much as possible and form a Christian elite—for example, a monastic community. In any case, the most sharply formulated statements of Jesus and his most difficult demands are not intended as unconditional *commandments* for everyone but only as *counsels* for those who wish to achieve perfection. Alongside this, there is room for a secular Christianity which follows only the commandments but not the counsels. Consequently, there are two stages of discipleship.[108] The ascetic ideal proclaimed by Jesus is valid only for a select group; it is moderated for most Christians.

On the other side Luther was confronted by the Enthusiasts'— for example, the Anabaptists'—interpretation and application of the Sermon on the Mount. They too assert that the Sermon on the Mount and life in this world as it now is are in irresolvable contradiction to each other. If Christians really want to obey their Master, then they must leave this world. They neither may nor can participate in the institutions of this world, such as property, law, oath-taking, the exercise of authority, affairs of state, police work, the penal system, any kind of use of power, and war. Tolstoi asserted that true disciples of Jesus may not even participate in marriage, and similar opinions were current at the time of Luther. Another form of Enthusiasm concludes from Jesus' statements that the world must be basically reformed through a Christian revolution and made to conform to the "evangelical law." In this way it can become a thoroughly Christian world and take on

---

107 *WA* 32, 299 ff.; *LW* 21, 3–6.
108 *WA* 11, 249, 259; *LW* 45, 88, 101–102; *WA* 28, 279; *WA* 30^{II}, 110; *LW* 46, 164; *WA* 32, 299, 361; *LW* 21, 3, 74.

the shape of the kingdom of God on earth—this is the activistic
form of Enthusiasm. As passive Enthusiasm asserts that we must
radically withdraw from the world, so active Enthusiasm asserts
that we must radically reform and reshape the world.

Luther opposes both the Roman Catholic and the Enthusiast
viewpoints. He begins by rejecting their common presupposition
that the statements of Jesus cannot be fulfilled by living in this
world as it is. Luther thereby does not in any way weaken the
Sermon on the Mount. He takes it absolutely seriously. Even those
statements of Jesus which are most strict and which natural man
and his reason consider to be "impossible" are "precepts binding
on all Christians alike" and not "mere counsels for the perfect."[109]
Luther thus rejects the Catholic interpretation because it fails to
grasp the difficult but utterly serious demands of the Sermon on
the Mount.

At the same time, Luther asserts that the Christian may not
leave this world. He ought to use the world and not refuse to
accept the offices and responsibilities that are necessary for the life
of this world.[110] In every situation, he is to act as a Christian in
obedience to Jesus—there is no interruption or moratorium in such
obedience—and at the same time regularly take his place as a
citizen of this world, which may include possessing property, acting as a judge, a prince, or a soldier. Is it possible to realize both
of these at the same time? How can the Christian who lives in
the world, uses it, and participates in it preserve the freedom and
the love to which Jesus calls him?

Luther recognizes—as Clement of Alexandria did earlier[111]—
that the freedom from the world of which Jesus speaks does not
consist of outward but of inner distance. Freedom from the service
of Mammon means "not setting our confidence, comfort, and trust
on temporal goods," "being spiritually poor in our hearts," and
"spiritually forsaking everything." Freedom is thus a matter of

---

109 *WA* 11, 245, 249; *LW* 45, 82, 88; *WA* 28, 282; *WA* 32, 299; *LW* 21,
3; *WA* 39[II], 189.

110 "Christians all belong to the imperial government, which Christ has no
intention of overthrowing. Nor does he teach us to escape from it or to desert
the world and our office and station, but to make use of this rule and established
order." *WA* 32, 393; *LW* 21, 113.

111 [For example, see "The Rich Man's Salvation," in George W. Forell, *Christian Social Teachings* (New York: Doubleday Anchor, 1966), pp. 54–57.—Trans.]

the heart and of our inner attitude. We cannot all be poor in an economic sense and have no possessions. What is important, however, is that even when we have possessions, our soul remains free of them. "While we live here, we should use all temporal goods and physical necessities, the way a guest does who spends the night in a strange place and leaves in the morning." At every hour of our life, we should be prepared to lose everything and surrender it for the sake of God and "always keep our hearts set on the kingdom of heaven." Even a man who is outwardly poor can, when viewed in terms of his inner attitude, be a "rich belly," a servant of Mammon. On the other hand, many saints have possessed much and have still been poor in the sense that Jesus intended. "The gospel looks into the heart." Luther recognized that Jesus never speaks of a restructuring or reordering of this world but rather only of the personal attitude of his disciples toward the goods of this world.[112]

This inner freedom—which Paul describes "as having nothing, and yet possessing everything," 2 Corinthians 6:10—is expressed in action whenever the situation demands it. There are times when the disciple of Jesus can and should give—perhaps even give away everything and let everything be taken from him. In theses prepared for an academic disputation in 1539, Luther explains that we must be able to abandon everything for God's sake whenever our obedience to the first commandment, our confession of faith in God and the gospel, is at stake. Then Jesus' demand must be fulfilled literally and in actuality; we must joyfully abandon everything for the sake of the pearl of great price. Here Luther does not diminish any of the strictness of Jesus' admonition.[113]

However, the situation which requires us to abandon all earthly property and goods is not created by man but by God alone. Abandoning everything can never be an achievement that we choose for ourselves but only simple obedience to God's leading of our lives. The hour that requires such a sacrifice is indeed not an infrequent hour, but it nevertheless remains an extraordinary hour—a borderline and emergency situation. It cannot therefore call into question the principle which governs the ordinary situa-

---

112 Quotations in this paragraph are found in *WA* 32, 307–8; *LW* 21, 13–15.
113 *WA* 39[II], 40.

tion. Rather, this extraordinary admonition to abandon everything presupposes the ordinary possession of earthly goods and personal property and its use to maintain our life, to earn our living, and to engage in business as God's good institution.[114] Jesus speaks of a basic inner freedom that can act at any time and must be ready to do so. One of Luther's statements about private property shows just how seriously he takes this readiness: "Anything left over that is not used to help our neighbor is possessed unjustly; it is stolen in God's sight, for in God's sight we ought to give and lend and let things be taken away from us."[115] Any of our property that is not necessary for the preservation of our own life belongs to our neighbor. In a certain sense Luther anticipated the socialist slogan "Property is theft," that is, property *can become* theft when the excess which we do not need for our own person is not used for the welfare of our neighbor.

Luther is thus able to show a way in which we can live in the world in harmony with the Sermon on the Mount, because he understands Jesus' statements in terms of our personal attitude and readiness. We have seen that this does not simply mean an ethics of attitudes or only of inner disposition. There is no doubt that Luther has interpreted Jesus' statement as the Master himself intended it. For even our Lord did not require all his disciples to abandon their possessions; he did, however, require them to be prepared to do so anytime God specifically called them to abandon everything.

Luther interprets the love commanded by Jesus—like the freedom from the world—as an attitude which can constantly be lived out while we are participating in the orders and institutions of this world.

TWO AREAS AND FORMS OF ACTIVITY

Viewed in terms of his activity, a Christian man is indeed a double person functioning in a twofold office and living under a twofold law.[116] His activity has a twofold form. These two cannot be harmonized, since even God's government is not a unit but

---

114 *WA* 39[II], 39.
115 *WA* 10[III], 275.
116 *WA* 32, 390; *LW* 21, 109.

appears in the double form of spiritual and secular kingdoms or governments. The Christian stands in two areas of activity.

Luther expressed the fact that the Christian man lives in two areas in various ways. Sometimes he describes "the two persons or the two types of office that are combined in one man" by distinguishing the "Christian" and the "secular person."[117] Elsewhere he distinguishes between "a person acting in his own behalf" and "a person acting in behalf of others, whose duty it is to serve them"; or between the "private person" and the "public person"; or between life and activity "when you are the only person affected" and life and activity when you are "a Christian-in-relation" who is "bound in this life to other persons." Since we are persons for others when we are fulfilling our office, Luther distinguishes between "person" and "office," or between "Christians as individuals who are not involved in an office and government" and Christians who "occupy a public office." He also distinguishes between "what each of us, acting in his own behalf, should do to others" and our duties "within secular government." He thus distinguishes our private relationships to people from our official relationships to people. Luther also distinguishes between "the natural person," according to which we are all equal to one another, and the "person according to his station," according to which we are unequal. Occasionally Luther distinguishes the two areas as "inward" and "outward"; but it would be a misunderstanding to interpret his use of "inward" as referring only to our attitude and not to our activity.[118]

The phrase "Christian-in-relation" might be taken to imply that as "private" Christians we are not constantly related to other people and our lives not bound together with theirs, but this is not what Luther intends to say. This phrase—like another that he uses, "Christians as they live for their own person"—does not describe activity that is related exclusively to our own person with-

---

117 *WA* 32, 316, 390; *LW* 21, 23, 109; *WA* 34[I], 121–22. In referring to Luther's sermons on Matthew 5–7, one must take into account that individual phrases may not come from Luther himself but from the editors. (See *WA* 32, p. lxxvi; *LW* 21, xiv–xv.) However, the basic picture of Luther's distinction between two persons in one Christian is clear.

118 For the above paragraph, see *WA* 19, 648; *LW* 46, 122; *WA* 32, 316, 334, 368, 390–93; *LW* 21, 23, 44, 83, 109–13; *WA* TR 3, no. 2911a; cf. *LW* 54, 180–81.

out regard to our neighbor. According to Luther, we are never
without a relationship to others; we are continually bound to our
neighbors. When he nonetheless speaks of life-in-relationship as
something special, what he has in mind is our commitment to
others insofar as it is governed "by secular law," that is, in a
station which makes me responsible for protecting or serving
someone else in a particular way (for example, as a parent or as
a prince).[119] Luther thus distinguishes a purely private relationship
to my neighbor from one that is given by virtue of my "station."[120]
He also distinguishes between what affects our own person and
what affects someone who has been entrusted to us. Luther's usage
of all such individual sets of contrasting terms must be understood
in such a way that they clarify one another.

(1)   Taken together, all these terms imply that a distinction must be
made between acting (and suffering) in my own behalf in a
private relationship with my neighbor on the one hand, and acting
(2)   (and suffering) in my office, that is, in the responsibility for
others inherent in my station.[121]

In these two areas one and the same Christian person now has
to do things that are quite different, even diametrically opposed.
It is as though there really were two persons, one here and another
there, with the result that the Christian must do something in one
area that he may not do in the other.[122] Luther here establishes a
sharp opposition between what the Christian does as a private
person and Christian and what he does and has to do in fulfilling

---

119 *WA* 32, 391; *LW* 21, 110; *WA* 30[I], 172; *BC*, 402.

120 *WA* 32, 316; *LW* 21, 23; *WA* 30[I], 157; *BC*, 389.

121 What is involved here is our responsibility within secular government.
Being there as a Christian for others is also a constant factor in a private relationship, but not the same way as when an office is involved. Even as a brother,
sister, or friend I can be put into a situation in which my responsibility as a
fellow Christian requires me to make my neighbor aware of the evil he is doing
and correct him, and thus in this sense "punish" him. This private Christian
responsibility is not to be confused with the public responsibility which a secular
office or station lays upon us: I may and must correct my fellow Christian, but
I am forbidden to sit in judgment and condemn him "in my own behalf"
without having any office of secular responsibility. "Likewise, although no one
has in his own person the right to judge and condemn anyone, yet if they whose
duty it is fail to do so, they sin as much as those who take the law into their
own hands without such commission." *WA* 30[I], 172; *BC*, 402.

122 In speaking of the fifth commandment, "You shall not kill," Luther says:
"Therefore neither God nor the government is included in this commandment,
yet their right to take human life is not abrogated. . . . Therefore, what is forbidden here applies to private individuals, not to governments." *WA* 30[I], 157;
BC, 389.

the responsibility of his office in behalf of those who have been
entrusted to his care. As a Christian, when his own personal welfare is involved, he seeks to do nothing else than serve his neighbor, even if his neighbor is his enemy. He is prepared to suffer
injustice without protecting himself and resisting evil, without
calling upon the authorities and their judicial power for help,
without avenging himself—all this in accordance with the statements of Jesus and the apostles.[123] However, as a secular person,
fulfilling his office of protecting those entrusted to his care and
acting in matters that affect the welfare of his neighbor, he must
under all conditions fulfill his duty to protect them, to oppose evil,
block it, punish it, and use force in resisting it. "A Christian
should not resist any evil; but within the limits of his office, a
secular person should oppose every evil."[124] It is not appropriate
for the authorities to be meek and mild; that would run counter
to the task which God has given them.[125] The governing authorities cannot justify such a lenient attitude toward evil on the basis
that Jesus says we should not demand justice and retribution, for
these statements are not at all concerned with secular government
and cannot be established as a rule governing it. Rather, they are
concerned with the Christian's <u>attitude</u> in his heart.[126] They are
binding on the Christian not in terms of what he does in his
office as a secular person but only in his personal relationship to
his neighbor.[127] They are not intended to regulate secular affairs
and thus serve to preserve this earthly life; rather, they show the
way to eternal life.[128]

---

123 *WA* 11, 259–60; *LW* 45, 101–103.
124 *WA* 32, 393; *LW* 21, 113.
125 *WA* 32, 316; *LW* 21, 23. "The rule in the kingdom of Christ is the
toleration of everything, forgiveness, and the recompense of evil with good. On
the other hand, in the realm of the emperor, there should be no tolerance
shown toward any injustice, but rather a defense against wrong and a punishment of it, and an effort to defend and maintain the right, according to what
each one's office or station may require." *WA* 32, 394; *LW* 21, 113.
126 *WA* 28, 282.
127 *WA* 10III, 251. "Christ is not giving lessons in the use of the fist or of
the sword, or in the control of life and property. He is teaching about the heart
and the conscience before God. Therefore we must not drag his words into the
law books or into the secular government." *WA* 32, 374; *LW* 21, 90. "Christ
has no intention here of interfering in the order of the secular realm, or of
depriving the government of anything. All he is preaching about is how individual Christians should behave in their everyday life." *WA* 32, 382; *LW* 21,
99; *WA* 32, 307, 389, 395; *LW* 21, 12, 108, 115; *WA* 37, 482.
128 *WA* 32, 304; *LW* 21, 9.

UNITY IN LOVE

Such completely different attitudes and activities in the two
areas of life are nonetheless compatible with each other. The personal unity of an individual Christian and the unequivocal character of his ethos are not destroyed in the sense of a double morality
or an ethical dualism between "personal morality and official
morality," as Ernst Troeltsch claimed.[129] On the contrary, a deep
and basic unity prevails in the midst of the difference and opposition. Admittedly, it is not apparent in the *form* of activity in both
areas—that is markedly different. This unity is apparent however
in the *meaning* of the action and the personal attitude which is
expressed in our activity in each area. The office of which Luther
speaks and which he distinguishes from the activity which I carry
out in my own behalf is really the same as God's mandate to serve
others. God in his mercy has given me the task of serving and
protecting others, and that is an office of love.[130] It is precisely as
forms of service to men, as stations of service, that the offices are
"divine stations" and thus conform to God's nature as love. They
are therefore also sanctified as God's word.[131] Thus when Christians act to fulfill the functions of the offices in which they serve,
they do not fall out of the love which Jesus commands and gives.
Luther can say that when Christ exhorts us to give the emperor
what belongs to the emperor (Matthew 22:21) he is thinking of
love.[132] Thus in the Christian's activity the distinction, in terms of
whether he is acting as a private person or an official person, is
made within the activity of love itself. There is a great difference
between direct service to our neighbor and the administration of
an office which protects his life and serves him as the official
authorities do. However, this concerns only the form of the activity
and describes the broad variety that is possible. The meaning of
this activity—including the corresponding personal attitude—is
the same in both cases: serving the life of the other person. The
only difference is that in one case service occurs in direct personal

---

129 *The Social Teaching of the Christian Churches,* trans. Olive Wyon (New
York: Harper Torchbook, 1960), 2:508–509, 550–76.
130 *WA* 32, 314; *LW* 21, 20; *WA* 11, 274; *LW* 45, 121.
131 *WA* 32, 316; *LW,* 21, 23.
132 *WA* 11, 202.

encounters) between people and in the other case through the structures and orders which support the life of society and through which the Christian serves his brothers. Such official activity is also *ministry*; it is ministerial activity in the original sense of the word, that is, it is the readiness to serve and to help.

Because the offices, particularly the political offices, have been instituted by God as the indispensable form of serving our fellow-man, Luther encourages Christians to make themselves available) for such offices wherever there is a lack of people to administer) them properly.[133] Christians ought always to be available whenever they have the opportunity to serve others, no matter what form such service may actually take. They should not selfishly ask whether a particular service is important in the eyes of the world or attractive to them personally, but only how necessary it is.[134] Christians should be especially ready to fill the political offices as a special service to God.[135] Christians are also needed in these offices because political and judicial offices, like all kinds of power, may be so easily misused by someone with a selfish attitude. They then no longer serve but tyrannize and carry out their own arbi-trary and vindictive purposes. Christ purifies the hearts of his people and enables them to administer their offices singlemindedly according to God's own purpose, that is, in order actually to serve.[136] In all this Luther stands much closer to Jesus and the New Testament than did Tolstoi, who felt that service in govern-ment could not be reconciled with being a disciple of Jesus.

Luther repeatedly refers to the distinction between private and official activity in his discussion of Jesus' prohibition of anger in Jesus' interpretation of the fifth commandment, Matthew 5:20 ff. Jesus forbids private anger in matters that affect our own person.

---

133 *WA* 11, 255; *LW* 45, 95.
134 "Love of neighbor is not concerned about its own; it considers not how great or humble, but how profitable and needful the works are for neighbor or community." *WA* 11, 261; *LW* 45, 103–104. See also *WA* 11, 256; *LW* 45, 98.
135 "For the sword and authority, as a particular service of God, belong more appropriately to Christians than to any other men on earth." *WA* 11, 258; *LW* 45, 100. See also *WA* 11, 254; *LW* 45, 94.
136 *WA* 11, 274; *LW* 45, 122. "A Christian may carry on all sorts of secular business with impunity—not as a Christian but as a secular person—while his heart remains pure in his Christianity, as Christ demands. This the world cannot do; but contrary to God's command, it misuses every secular ordinance and law, indeed every creature." *WA* 32, 393; *LW* 21, 113.

However, it is something quite different when we are angry and
punish with the authority that is given us by our office, when we
act as judges or rulers or even as parents, as fathers or mothers.
Such official anger is not only not forbidden but is even commanded by God. It is good, a "necessary and divine wrath"—
God's own anger which he expresses through his representatives.[137]
This is also true of spiritual offices. The preacher must also be
angry and condemn people when God's honor is involved; indeed,
as biblical examples indicate, he must sometimes even curse.[138]
Thus the distinction between private and official activity does not
coincide with the distinction between spiritual and secular government. The spiritual government also has offices and therefore also
has official activity. However, official anger and condemnation have
nothing to do with our private concerns or with the passions of
vindictiveness and hatred: it is impersonal wrath and impersonal
condemnation administered because of our office, that is, because
of our responsibility for justice, for God's commandments, and
for God's *honor*. This is anger without hatred of our neighbor.[139]
"Then wrath is not wrathful."[140] For the officeholder serves not
his own personal anger but God's wrath. Woe to anyone who
allows his subjective, personal, passionate feelings of personal
hatred to enter into his official wrath and condemnation.[141] Such
a man misuses his office and dishonors God's name; he thus breaks
the second commandment. But because of original sin and the
temptation of the devil, people do this repeatedly.[142] Christians
must struggle to keep from confusing their personal anger with
God's wrath. It even happens that honorable people convince their
consciences that their personal anger and hatred are a righteous
expression of their official responsibility. Thus they identify what
is a sin in God's eyes with their own personal ideas of virtue.[143]
If the judge sentences the lawbreaker on the basis of his own

---

[137] *WA* 20, 455; *WA* 32, 364; *LW* 21, 78; *WA* 34[II], 6–8, 10; *WA* 37,
383, 385, 482–83; *WA* 41, 638.
[138] *WA* 20, 456; *WA* 34[II], 8; *WA* 37, 384; *WA* 40[I], 309; *LW* 26, 186;
WA 41, 638.
[139] *WA* 37, 115; *WA* 45, 112.
[140] *WA* 41, 638.
[141] *WA* 20, 456.
[142] *WA* 37, 383–84; *WA* 41, 636–38; *WA* 45, 111–12.
[143] *WA* 32, 366–68; *LW* 21, 81–83.

subjective anger, the judge himself becomes a murderer.[144]

The impersonal objectivity with which the Christian serves God's purpose of preserving the world through political offices shows itself in the fact that even when his office requires him to be angry with someone and to administer the law very strictly, as a judge sometimes must, he still loves this person as his brother before God.[145] The brotherly relationship of Christians to other people is neither excluded nor interrupted by our official relationship to them; rather, both have their place alongside each other. The Christian opposes his fellowman only in his office, not with his heart. If his office as prosecutor or as judge requires him to condemn or punish someone, "he keeps a Christian heart. He does not intend anyone any harm, and it grieves him that his neighbor must suffer grief."[146] It pains him that he must condemn and punish someone in the name of justice. All judicial activity must necessarily be characterized by anger and by deadly seriousness. However, this is only the outward form within which punishment takes place. The heart of the Christian who must sit in judgment does not share in this anger. On the contrary, the harder the action which he must take against his brother man, the more love burns in his heart, the more he feels pity and compassion for him.[147]

There is more to Christian love than what is expressed in an administrative office; love always addresses itself to our neighbor

---

[144] *WA* 20, 456.

[145] *WA* 10[III], 252. "Here an official should properly not feel anger in his heart, even though he must express anger; let his voice be sharp and his fist be rough, but he should keep his heart sweet and friendly, free of any malice." *WA* 32, 362; *LW* 21, 76; *WA* 32, 392; *LW* 21, 111.

[146] *WA* 32, 393; *LW* 21, 113; *WA* 20, 456.

[147] "We see that a godly judge painfully passes sentence upon the criminal and regrets the death penalty which the law imposes. In this case the act has every appearance of anger and disfavor. Meekness is so thoroughly good that it remains even in such wrathful works. In fact, the heart is most tormented when it has to be angry and severe. . . . I must not regard my own possessions, my own honor, my own injury, or get angry on their account; but we must defend God's honor and commandments, as well as prevent injury or injustice to our neighbor. The temporal authorities do this with the sword; the rest of us by reproof and rebuke. But it is to be done with pity for those who have earned punishment." *WA* 6, 267; *LW* 44, 103. See also *WA* 27, 267. "For example, a pious judge gets angry with a criminal, even though personally he wishes him no harm and would rather let him off without punishment. His anger comes out of a heart where there is nothing but love toward his neighbor. Only the evil deed is punishable and must bear the anger." *WA* 32, 368; *LW* 21, 83.

in direct ways as well. However, Luther criticizes the administration of justice under the papacy for the reason that people hesitated to condemn a man to death "because they were unable to distinguish between the private and the public person." Luther rejects the common custom of the time which required the executioner to do penance and to request the condemned man to forgive him for executing the death sentence—as though the condemnation and execution were also sin, even though he was merely fulfilling the office to which God had called him.[148] Thus official and personal activity may neither be confused nor separated from each other.

Furthermore, the distinction between what we do out of concern for our own person and what we do because we are responsible for others is not Luther's final word. Something that affects my own person may have a significance that extends beyond my personal life and is relevant to the whole community. An injustice that is done to me is an injustice in and of itself and endangers the whole order of justice within which all others in the community must also live. Under these circumstances it can happen— and Luther considers this case both in *Temporal Authority: To What Extent It Should Be Obeyed* and in his sermons on the Sermon on the Mount—that a Christian calls upon secular government for justice in his own behalf and brings his case to court. The Christian may do so as long as his purpose is to preserve law and justice and to guard against injustice—that is, as long as he does not act primarily for his own benefit but because he loves righteousness, not from selfish vindictiveness but "out of a true Christian heart." We ought not to give in to every kind of violence, keep quiet about it, and do nothing at all—what would that lead to! If we did that, all order would be destroyed. If the preservation of law and justice is involved, Luther can even say that we are commanded to go to court and defend ourselves against the injustice that we have experienced.[149]

We may, however, seek justice in this way only if we are at the same time completely prepared to suffer injustice and violence and to follow the example of Jesus before the high priest. When

---

[148] *WA* TR 3, no. 2910B; *LW* 54, 179.
[149] *WA* 11, 261; *LW* 45, 104; *WA* 32, 388, 392; *LW* 21, 107, 111.

the high priest's servant struck Jesus, he condemned the unjust act with his words but, here and throughout his whole passion, endured being beaten without defending himself.[150] Luther feels that since we are the kind of people we are, it would be a miracle if someone were to seek justice for himself with such inner freedom and complete objectivity. It does not happen very often, and this is a dangerous road to follow. We very much like to conceal our deepest personal interest under the cover of selfless objectivity. A special grace is needed here, the grace of a pure heart motivated by God's Spirit.[151] Such an action is properly understood in terms of a person's office, that is, his responsibility for the common life. Thus Luther continues to apply his basic distinction between concern for our own person and concern for our service to other people—only now the distinction must be applied in matters which themselves concern our own person. They are a matter of personal concern and I must be prepared to suffer; at the same time, they may also be a public matter that requires me to protect myself. Thus readiness to suffer and the determination to fight to preserve justice can exist side by side. As Luther sees it, they are not contradictory.

In later discussions of the question of resisting injustice, Luther replaces the distinction between matters that affect our own person and matters that affect our office with a distinction between matters that concern the Second Table of the law and matters that concern the First Table. This is a distinction between matters which affect us as citizens of this world and matters which affect our faith and confession. The distinction is made in the disputation on Matthew 19:21 (1539),[152] but it also occurs as early as Luther's sermons on Matthew 5–7 (1530–1532).[153] This means that whenever a Christian is threatened and attacked as a Christian (that is, for the sake of the gospel and thus for the sake of Christ), he does not defend himself; rather, he is ready to suffer injustice and violence without resisting and to abandon joyfully all that he has—even his body and his life. But in secular matters, when his suffering is not for the sake of the gospel, he may turn to the authorities for help and demand justice and protection. If his request is not granted, then he must suffer in the secular matter too.

---

150 *WA* 28, 282–83; *WA* 32, 393; *LW* 21, 112.
151 *WA* 11, 261; *LW* 45, 104; *WA* 32, 392; *LW* 21, 111.
152 *WA* 39^{II}, 39 ff., especially theses 21 ff.
153 *WA* 32, 395; *LW* 21, 116.

This corresponds to Luther's opinion of self-defense.[154] If the authorities persecute the Christian because of his faith (that is, in matters related to the First Table of the law), he does not resist but instead suffers everything, including death.[155] If a thief or robber uses violence against him, however, the Christian as a "citizen of this world" ought to defend himself. The secular authorities require him to do so, and they themselves must resist the evil.[156] If a highway robber wants to take his life, he ought to meet violence with violence. In such a case he is protected by the secular authority, and he represents the authorities to whom he is subject. He acts as these authorities themselves would act and ought to act in fulfilling their responsibility to protect their citizens. Such violent self-defense is required of me, and therefore permitted, only when my life itself is threatened and not in opposition to some other injustice. If my life is not threatened, any private exercise of force is forbidden, since in such cases we ought to wait for the authorities to act.[157] Luther thus establishes my right to defend myself when my life is under attack by asserting that it is no longer a private action for my own personal benefit but an official action of the authorities which I perform in an extraordinary way, that is, as a substitute for the official authority.

All this applies not only to the relationship of the Christian to his own government but also to every relationship in which one man is subject to and ought to obey another, wherever the Christian may stand within the orders of this world. There is basically no conflict between obeying God and obeying human officials. For God also gives us his commands through the offices which he has instituted, from parents to lords and princes. Therefore, when I obey the men who have been set in authority over me, I do so "for God's sake," that is, I obey God himself.

However, just as obedience to God forms the basis for my obedience to men, so it also limits it. My duty to obey God far exceeds any duty to obey earthly authorities. In fact, it requires me to disobey the authorities if they command me to do anything that is specifically contrary to God's command. In such a case the Christian—because it is God who commanded us to obey men if the first place—is at the same time also free of men. The Christian's direct relationship to God and God's direct relationship to

154 *WA* 18, 647; *LW* 46, 120.
155 *WA* 39[II], 41; *WA* TR 2, no. 1815.
156 *WA* 39[II], 41, 80; *WA* TR 2, no. 1815, 2666a, 2727a.
157 *WA* 39[II], 41.

him in faith does not exclude but rather includes the relationships mediated through human authority. These two are never identical, however, and our relationship to God is never circumscribed by our relationship to human authority; our relationship to God both transcends and is (completely independent of) our relationship to human authority. God's command and our obedience to him can indeed be immanent in the commandments of men and our obedience to them, but at the same time the former always transcends the latter. This is shown in the fact that these two can in fact be in conflict with each other.[158]

The tension between our personal attitude and our objective activity for the sake of justice, between love in our hearts and the severity of our administration of justice, is great indeed.[159] However, the Christian must not be destroyed by this tension anymore than God himself is. For, as Luther shows, the same deep tension is found in God himself. God administers justice but is at the same time nothing else than love itself. God must use force against those who rebel against him, and yet his heart burns with love for them. God's love appears in our evil world also in the broken form of his wrath—as his "strange work." Thus the ethical paradox in which the Christian finds himself when he administers his office justly is no more difficult to bear than the theological paradox of God's own activity. Indeed, Luther feels that the first paradox is based on the second. This clearly shows that his solution of the problem of the Christian in political office is not based on a compromise. The basis of Luther's solution lies deep in his knowledge of God.[160]

Luther thus illustrates the unity of the Christian's attitude and activity in the two realms in relationship to both the Sermon on the Mount and the Bible's affirmation of law and the state.[161] The Christian acts in one way in matters that affect only his own

---

[158] For a further discussion of this, see our treatment of the authority of parents and of political authorities below, pp. 100, 124–32.

[159] Luther finds this tension in the Bible, for example, in Moses, Paul, David, and others in the Old Testament. He says that "they used the sword energetically in fulfilling their office and executed people like chickens—but at the same time they were no less meek, mild, and friendly in their hearts." *WA* 10[III], 252–53.

[160] *WA* 36, 427.

[161] "Thus the word of Christ is now reconciled, I believe, with the passages which established the sword." *WA* 11, 260; *LW* 45, 103.

person and in another way when he fulfills his official responsibility in behalf of others. However, it is one and the same love
that works in both realms; and it must act differently, precisely
because it is love. The same gospel commands both types of
activity. Luther thus sees the gospel's commandment of love as
being very closely related to our life within the orders of this
world. The gospel is not opposed to our service of government
under law but requires it, as a service of our neighbor in love.[162]

Thus the two governments do not exclude each other—presup-
posing that each remains within the limits of its own area. Luther
establishes that a Christian may also be, for example, a prince and
that a prince may remain a Christian; he also points out that a
Christian may be a subject of both Christ and the emperor.[163]
This demonstrates once again that the relationship between the
two governments is completely different from the relationship
between the kingdom of God and the kingdom of Satan. These
latter kingdoms completely exclude each other. "You cannot serve
God and mammon" (Matthew 6:24). According to Luther, however, one can serve both God and the emperor. For God himself
has instituted the emperor and his imperial office and is effectively
present in him; God is hidden behind the earthly lord. When we
obey the emperor, we are basically obeying God himself. We are
here involved not with "two masters," as in Jesus' statement about
Mammon, but with one God; the only distinction is that we at
one time obey him directly and at another time indirectly.[164]

---

162 "In this way the two propositions are brought into harmony with one
another: at one and the same time you satisfy God's kingdom inwardly and the
kingdom of the world outwardly. You suffer evil and injustice, and yet at the
same time you punish evil and injustice; you do not resist evil, and yet at the
same time, you do resist it. In the one case, you consider yourself and what
is yours; in the other, you consider your neighbor and what is his. In what
concerns you and yours, you govern yourself by the gospel and suffer injustice
toward yourself as a true Christian; in what concerns the person or property of
others, you govern yourself according to love and tolerate no injustice toward
your neighbor. The gospel does not forbid this; in fact, in other places it
actually commands it." *WA* 11, 255; *LW* 45, 96. When Luther speaks of gospel
in this statement he is thinking first of all of the Sermon on the Mount and
second, of statements such as "Render therefore to Caesar the things that are
Caesar's" (Matthew 22:21). Luther understands this latter statement as an
exhortation to love by serving others through the state. *WA* 11, 202.
163 *WA* 11, 246, 273; *LW* 45, 83, 121; *WA* 19, 629; *LW* 46, 99; *WA* 32,
393; *LW* 21, 113; *WA* 39^II, 81.
164 Luther comments on Jesus' statement "No one can serve two masters" in
Matthew 6:24: "He is referring to two masters that are opposed to each other,
not to those that govern together. There is no contradiction involved if I serve

RESPONSE TO THE CRITICISM
OF LUTHER'S DOCTRINE OF THE
TWO GOVERNMENTS

Luther's doctrine of the two kingdoms or governments is frequently criticized.[165] There are two basic objections. First, Luther's doctrine limits the claim of Jesus Christ to be lord of all areas of life and of the world. Luther derives only the new attitude of the Christian in the world from the gospel; however, he does not describe the task and responsibility of the Christian in the renewal of the world and in the transformation of its orders to conform with the kingdom of Christ. The Enthusiasts—so we are told—properly identified an inadequacy in Luther's theology at this point. The second objection is that Luther differs from the New Testament insofar as he disregards the eschatological tension between the two kingdoms and instead thinks of the two governments as simply standing alongside each other in static coexistence, rather than as being at war with one another.

The response to the first objection is that Luther too intends to view secular life, insofar as Christians participate in it, as being under the lordship of Christ. In fact he does not claim that Christ is lord within the *orders* as such but only in the *men* who act within these orders.[166] Thus the secular kingdom does not stand under the lordship of Christ in the same way that the kingdom of Christ or Christendom does.[167] On this, Jesus and the New Testament agree with Luther.[168] The New Testament itself speaks of the lordship of Christ only as his lordship in persons, that is, in their faith.[169] Such Christians will, in fact, work in the world so

---

both God and my prince or emperor at the same time; if I obey the lower one, I am obeying the highest one as well, since my obedience moves in an orderly fashion from the one to the other." *WA* 32, 453; *LW* 45, 186.

165 For a detailed summary of this criticism, see Althaus, "Luthers Lehre von den beiden Reichen im Feuer der Kritik," pp. 40–68.

166 *WA* 11, 246; *LW* 45, 83.

167 Erwin Mülhaupt, "Herrschaft Christi bei Luther," *Neue Zeischrift für systematische Theologie* 1 (1958): 165–84.

168 This is also the conclusion of Lau, *Luthers Lehre von den beiden Reichen,* p. 88.

169 In faith, the Christian knows that Christ is the lord of all things, even of money, and lives accordingly. "There are many people who believe that Christ is the lord, but they do not believe that he is the lord of all things, such as money, and do not trust him to feed them; rather, they live as though they had to scratch out a living for themselves—and when they are touched by poverty, they become very worried." *WA* 12, 459.

that the orders and relationships which God has established to
serve human life may be reestablished and set free from misuse
and distortions. Even though this is true, however, this goal cannot be defined in terms of "Christ's lordship in the orders"—as
though there were a Christocracy. According to the New Testament there will continue to be two governments of God as long
as this world endures. The lordship of Christ is to be understood
in the context of the theology of the cross. It is still hidden under
the "form of this world."[170] The fact that the orders do not stand
under the lordship of Christ, but are to be formed and shaped
according to reason, does not mean that they are not subject to
the will and commandment of God. For reason is obliged to shape
the orders in order to fulfill God's strict demands that life be
preserved. Luther constantly reasserted this, not only in general
statements but also by making very specific criticisms and by giving directions for specific activities.

The second objection presupposes that Luther's doctrine is to
be evaluated in terms of the New Testament's teaching of the
two aeons and the conflict between the kingdom of God and the
demonic kingdom of Satan and sin. It overlooks the fact that—
in spite of Luther's earlier approach to this doctrine, which he did
not later maintain[171]—Luther is speaking about an entirely different problem. He is well aware of what the New Testament says
about the world and about the biblical contrast between the kingdom of God and the kingdom of Satan. Wherever he looks in
history, or in the administration of the orders, or in every human
heart, he sees the battle going on between these two kingdoms,
and he therefore also knows something about the eschatological
tension.[172] And Luther summons Christians to join in the battle
against the demonic powers. However, this battle and conflict may
under no circumstances be confused or identified with the relationship between the two governments in Luther's theology. For
God has instituted both governments; and he has specifically in-

---

[170] "Therefore the kingdom of Christ is and remains a secret kingdom, con-
cealed from this world, maintained in Word and faith until the time of its
revelation." *WA* 31^I, 248; *LW* 14, 30. See *Theology*, 31–32.
[171] See above, pp. 51–53.
[172] *Theology*, 404–405.

stituted the secular government *against* the kingdom of this world, if the kingdom of this world is understood in the absolute theological sense of the power and kingdom of Satan.[173]

Admittedly, the kingdom of this world, Satan, and evil continually reassert themselves in the actual administration of secular government; but this is a misuse of secular government and contrary to God's intention for it. This is equally true of the church and of Christendom, that is, in the area of spiritual government. Satan constantly roams about *in both governments* and rages against them in order to corrupt them, contrary to God's intention for them.[174] God and Satan struggle with each other in both governments. Indeed, Satan is a far greater danger in the spiritual government. For this reason an office in the spiritual government is far more dangerous and difficult than an office in the secular government,[175] and the failure of people who hold spiritual offices is far more dangerous for the people they are intended to serve. Thus the line of battle between the kingdom of God and the kingdom of Satan cuts through the middle of both governments. For this reason, it is absolutely impossible to equate Luther's doctrine of the two governments or kingdoms with the absolute opposition between the kingdoms of God and Satan; it is also impossible to correlate the two sets of concepts. It is therefore not appropriate to evaluate and criticize Luther's theology of the secular government on the basis of the biblical statements about the kingdom of this world as opposed to God.

We cannot discuss here the question of the theological and ecclesiastical development of Luther's doctrine in later generations or consider the purposes for which it was used or perhaps misused. Our concern at this point is simply to present the actual teaching of the Reformer. Later misuse of this teaching to set government and politics free from the norms of morality is not based on Luther's doctrine itself, and we cannot hold Luther responsible for it. In his own specific application of this doctrine,

---

[173] Luther explains that the kingdom of this world would be the kingdom of Satan if there were no secular government. *WA* 17¹, 467.
[174] *WA* 23, 514. See Törnvall, *Geistliches und weltliches Regiment,* pp. 185 ff.
[175] *WA* 37, 602.

Luther does indeed reveal the influence of his historical situation.[176] Our world is different from the world in which Luther lived. And Luther's ideas must be reinterpreted and applied in terms of this new situation. However, their basic structure continues to demonstrate its truth.[177] Luther's doctrine of the two kingdoms is one of the most valuable and enduring treasures of his theology.

Luther never abandons the political world to autonomous self-administration; rather, he constantly struggles against the self-glorification of the princes and their misuse of the secular government. He clearly admonishes the consciences of politicians to conform to the will of God. The emancipation of political governments from any moral concern does not have its source in Martin Luther but in the Renaissance, a movement which swept across the entire expanse of European politics, invading Roman Catholic countries earlier than Lutheran areas but with equal force. Lutheranism itself stood in opposition to this development for a long time.[178] That it did so was the result of Luther's theology.

---

[176] On this point, see Paul Althaus: *Religiöser Sozialismus. Grundfragen der christlichen Sozialethik* (Gütersloh: Bertelsmann, 1921), pp. 91–92; idem, *Obrigkeit und Führertum* (Gütersloh: Bertelsmann, 1936) p. 55; idem, "Luthers Lehre von den beiden Reichen im Feuer der Kritik," pp. 67–68.

[177] "We live in a world in which Christ has not yet established his lordship but which is still controlled by other powers. Luther's doctrine of the two kingdoms remains the best available help to live a Christian life in such a world. A more adequate or clearer interpretation of the biblical understanding of Christian existence in a world which must guarantee its own existence by means of force has not yet been given us." Lau, *Luthers Lehre von den beiden Reichen*, p. 95.

[178] Althaus, "Luthers Lehre von den beiden Reichen im Feuer der Kritik," pp. 62 ff.

5

LOVE, MARRIAGE, PARENTHOOD[1]

SEXUALITY AND LOVE

LUTHER WITHOUT exception considers sexuality as part of God's good creation; he bases this position on Genesis 1:27 and Genesis 2:18.[2] The fact that human beings are male and female and that the sexes differ is God's good will and work. Both sexes are God's good work. Therefore, one sex ought not to despise or humiliate the other but honor it as "a divine and good creation that pleases God himself."[3] Whether I am a man or a woman, God has created me to be what I am, and I have no choice or power in this matter.[4] God has made people in such a way that men and women cannot exist independently of one another. And God makes men and women in such a way that they are attracted to and desire each other. Of sexual love in its most physical and sensual manifestation, and of the drive to physical intercourse and conception, Luther says: All this is God's work.[5] God himself works through his creating word in this characteristic human drive. Luther points out that we are created through God's word and that God has said that we should "be fruitful and multi-

---

[1] *A Sermon on the Estate of Marriage* (1519), *WA* 2, 166–71; *LW* 44, 7–14. *The Estate of Marriage* (1522), *WA* 10[II], 275–304; *LW* 45, 17–49. *Commentary on the Seventh Chapter of St. Paul's Letter to the Corinthians* (1523), *WA* 12, 92–142. *The Order of Marriage for Common Pastors* (1529), *WA* 30[III], 74–80; *LW* 53, 111–15. *On Marriage Matters* (1530), *WA*[III], 205–48; *LW* 46, 265–320. *A Marriage Sermon on Hebrews 13:4* (1531), *WA* 34[I], 50–75. *Lecture on Psalm 128* (1532/1533), *WA* 40[III], 269–309.
Reinhold Seeberg, "Luthers Anschauung von dem Geschlechtsleben und der Ehe und ihre geschichtliche Stellung," *Luther-Jahrbuch* 7 (1925): 77–122. Olavi Lähteenmäki, *Sexus und Ehe bei Luther* (Turku: Schriften der Luther-Agricola Gesellschaft, 1955).
[2] *WA* TR 1, 320.
[3] *WA* 10[II], 275, 293; *LW* 45, 17–18, 37; *WA* 40[III], 274.
[4] "For it is not a matter of free choice or decision but a natural and necessary thing, that whatever is a man must have a woman and whatever is a woman must have a man." *WA* 10[II], 276; *LW* 45, 18.
[5] *WA* 32, 373; *LW* 21, 89.

ply" (Genesis 1:28). This word still controls us; and we cannot separate ourselves from it. Through the power of this creative word of God—and Luther is not thinking of a word which was spoken once for all at the time of creation but of a word which God continues to speak today—"procreative seed is planted in man's body and a natural, ardent desire for woman is kindled and kept alive."[6]

Luther gives high praise to love between the sexes. Among all the forms of earthly love it is "the greatest and the purest." He not only ranks it above "false love," which is selfish, but also above natural love between parents and children and brothers and sisters. "But over and above all these is married love, that is, a bride's love, which glows like a fire and desires nothing but the husband. She says, 'It is you I want, not what is yours. I want neither your silver nor your gold; I want neither. I want only you. I want you in your entirety, or not at all.' All other kinds of love seek something other than the loved one: this kind wants only to have the beloved's own self completely. If Adam had not fallen, the love of bride and groom would have been the loveliest thing."[7]

Adam did fall, however, and mankind is now subject to sin. This also affects the love between the sexes. Now it is no longer pure, no longer simple surrender of the self to the other, "but each seeks to satisfy his desire with the other." The physical joy of marriage has become lustful.[8] "In paradise, where to lice as no such ardor and raging passion, marriage must ha ds marria pleasant. Flesh and blood were different then.' But they he will of been so infected with original sin that th au us pecially Conception is no longer a pure act, therefore us.ness outside of fall into sin, but has been corrupted by the

As a result, Psalm now applies to all brought forth in iniquity, did my On this basis, Luther asserts that it was n be conceived naturally by a man and a wo virgin. At this point Luther is still caug

planted within us. Go, proclaim that it is now ng passion or married cannot do it without grace proclaims it to be our nature." (See also union was ordained by and unclean that takes nness and yet maintain *WA* 43, 454; *LW* 5,

---

6 *WA* 18, 275; *LCC* 18, 273.
7 *WA* 2, 167; *LW* 44, 9.
8 Ibid.
9 *WA* TR 4, no. 3508; *LW* 54,

marriage.[18] Only in marriage is sexuality not a destructive force.[19] Therefore, knowledge of the problems and sinfulness of our sexual life should lead everyone to enter into marriage.

There are, of course, exceptions and God himself makes them. First, some people are personally not capable of marriage. Second, God has given some the great and supernatural gift of continence, which enables them to remain chaste without being married.[20] Luther did not forget what Matthew 19:12 and 1 Corinthians 7:1 say about those who are called to celibacy. Luther interprets Matthew 19:12, "There are eunuchs who have made themselves eunuchs for the sake of the kingdom of heaven," to mean that there are people who say: "I could marry if I wish; I am capable of it. But it does not attract me. I would rather work at the kingdom of heaven, that is, the gospel, and beget spiritual children." Such persons, says Luther, are "rare, not one in a thousand, for they are a special miracle of God."[21] The Roman Church has not adequately considered that such celibacy is a very rare and extraordinary gift of God's grace; therefore it has made celibacy a law for the priests. If God has given this gift to a person, he ought to thank God for it.[22] But no one ought to trust himself to be continent and attempt to live without getting married unless God has "specially called" him to celibacy as he did Jeremiah (16:2), or unless he feels God's gracious gift of continence as a powerful force within him.[23] Anyone who attempts to remain celibate without having this special gift of God will be involved in "great whoredom and all sorts of fleshly impurity"; even if he does not become involved in these sins outwardly and physically, he will still become involved inwardly and spiritually—"he will have his heart filled with thoughts of women day and night."[24]

Luther thus leaves room for the possibility of celibacy and

---

18 Anyone who chooses to "live alone undertakes an impossible task . . counter to God's word and the nature that God has given and preserves in him. . . . Such persons revel in whoredom and all sorts of uncleanness of the flesh while they are drowned in their own vices and driven to despair." *WA* 18, 276, *LCC* 18, 273.

19 *WA* 30^I, 162; *BC*, 393; *WA* TR 1, no. 233; *LW* 54, 31.

20 *WA* 30^I, 162; *BC*, 393; *WA* 40^{III}, 285, 289.

21 *WA* 10^{II}, 279; *LW* 45, 21.

22 *WA* TR 4, no. 4138.

23 *WA* 12, 105; *WA* 40^{III}, 277.

24 *WA* 12, 98.

emphasizes its special responsibility and value. In the Old Testament it was sinful to live without a wife and child, but not in the New Testament.[25] And Luther agrees with Paul (1 Corinthians 7:32–35) that celibacy is better insofar as an unmarried man "may better be able to preach and care for God's word. . . . It is God's word and the preaching which make celibacy—such as that of Christ and of Paul—better than the estate of marriage. In itself, however, the celibate life is far inferior."[26] However, no station in life is morally superior to marriage. God even uses the problems which he lays upon married people to help them mortify the old man; and through these problems, they learn the difficult art of patiently subjecting themselves to God's will. Marriage presents innumerable opportunities for demonstrating love and patience that are not available to the celibate.[27] And not least important, marriage is as a rule given to everyone as a universal gift, whereas the ability to live a continent life is an unusually rare gift that is given to very few people.[28]

Since this is the case, we ought to encourage and urge people to get married. "Stop thinking about it and go to it right merrily. Your body demands it. God wills it and drives you to it."[29] Indeed, we ought to marry and stay married with joy because we know that God is well pleased with marriage and with married people. Marriage is "adorned and sanctified" by God's word.[30] Knowing this gives us joy in marriage in spite of all of its troubles, problems, and disappointments. This knowledge gives "peace in grief, joy in the midst of bitterness, happiness in the midst of tribulations."[31] "Seeing marriage in the light of God's word is a great art, and it alone is able to make the estate of marriage and married people lovable."[32]

Thus God considers marriage to be very holy and a "divine and blessed station (estate)."[33] For it has "God's word in its favor

---

[25] *WA* 12, 99.
[26] *WA* 10[II], 301; *LW* 45, 47; *WA* 12, 105.
[27] *WA* 40[III], 283.
[28] *WA* 12, 105.
[29] *WA* 18, 276; *LCC* 18, 274.
[30] *WA* 30[I], 162; *BC*, 393.
[31] *WA* 10[II], 295; *LW* 45, 39; *WA* 40[III], 282.
[32] *WA* 34[I], 67.
[33] *WA* 30[I], 161; *BC*, 393.

and was not invented or instituted by men."[34] Luther explicitly rejects a secularistic view of marriage which treats marriage as though it were "nothing more than a purely human and secular state, with which God has nothing to do."[35] On the contrary, marriage has been created and ordered by God. God's will and word make it a holy station of life.[36] This station of marriage is made holy for us, however, when we live in it in the knowledge that it has been instituted by God, that is, when we live in it in faith.

Luther does not in any way contradict his description of marriage as a holy and spiritual station when he also refers to it as an outward physical, secular, or worldly station, and speaks of the marriage ceremony as a secular affair.[37] This means that marriage belongs to the natural order of creation and not to the order of redemption through Christ. It is not a sacrament, as the Roman Church has asserted on the basis of an incorrect understanding of Ephesians 5:32. Marriage is indeed a picture of the intimate love of Christ for the church,[38] and we can fully live in it as it was intended to be lived only through the power of the love of Christ; in spite of this, however, it is not a "spiritual matter" in the sense of the Roman division between spiritual and secular. It is a holy station even among non-Christians. Luther does not use the terms *worldly* or *secular* and *holy* or *divine* in contradiction to one another. When he emphasizes that marriage and the marriage ceremony are a secular matter, he rejects the claim of Roman clericalism that the church is responsible for the legal aspects of marriage. Marriage is not subject to canon law and is to be regulated not by the ecclesiastical courts but by the officials of the

---

[34] *WA* 30III, 75; *LW* 53, 112.
[35] *WA* 32, 378; *LW* 21, 95.
[36] *WA* 30I, 162–63; *BC*, 393–94; *WA* 36, 503.
[37] "For marriage is a rather secular and outward thing, having to do with wife and children, house and home, and with other matters that belong to the realm of the government, all of which have been completely subjected to reason." *WA* 32, 376; *LW* 21, 93; *WA* 30III, 74–75; *LW* 53, 111–12; *WA* 30III, 205; *LW* 46, 265. Johannes Heckel's assertion that Luther understands marriage as an outward physical matter only as a result of sin has no basis in Luther's writings and contradicts his basic approach. *Lex charitatis. Eine juristische Untersuchung über das Recht in der Theologie Martin Luthers* (Munich: Verlag der Bayerischen Akademie der Wissenschaften, 1953) p. 101.
[38] *WA* 6, 552; *LW* 36, 95.

government, that is, by the lawyers and not by the theologians.[39]

Luther thus wishes to distinguish clearly the two governments of God in all matters related to marriage.[40] The church has no business establishing laws about this natural order of God, just as Christ and the apostles did not establish such laws except when matters of conscience were involved.[41] This is still a valid exception. There are situations and questions related to marriage which involve our conscience: our conscience becomes uncertain and confused and we need advice. In such cases pastors should fulfill their office, advise and when necessary comfort such consciences, particularly when someone has entered into marriage contrary to the proper order of marriage.[42] Luther did this himself, even though as a minister of the word, he in principle wanted nothing to do with marital matters and considered them completely within the competence of the secular authorities. Still, upon request he gave his opinion, even to the authorities; for example, in 1530 he published a treatise, *On Marriage Matters*, in which he discusses a whole series of specific questions in great detail.[43] However, Luther considers that the church's proper responsibility is to proclaim God's will for marriage and to preach the gospel to people who are entering into or living in marriage. The church thus makes available the power of faith and of love without which we cannot properly live the married life.

Accordingly, Luther did not restrict participation in the marriage rite to the clergy. He continues the traditional division of the rite into two parts: the actual marriage before the door of the church —that is, the uniting of the couple in marriage—and the spiritual action at the altar of the church during which God's word was proclaimed over this marriage, the blessing of God announced, and intercessory prayers offered by the congregation for the young couple.[44] Otto Albrecht points out that the marriage ceremony before the door of the church "basically remained an extra-

---

[39] *WA* 30^{III}, 74; *LW* 53, 111; *WA* 30^{III}, 246; *LW* 46, 318; *WA* 32, 377; *LW* 21, 93.
[40] *WA* 30^{III}, 206, 243; *LW* 46, 266, 314.
[41] *WA* 30^{III}, 205; *LW* 46, 265; *WA* 32, 377; *LW* 21, 93.
[42] *WA* 30^{III}, 246; *LW* 46, 318.
[43] *WA* 30^{III}, 205–48; *LW* 46, 265–320.
[44] *The Order of Marriage for Common Pastors* (1529), *WA* 30^{III}, 74–80; *LW* 53.

ecclesiastical act, a kind of legal act, even though it took place in religious form." Earlier this act was also administered by laymen.[45] Luther summarizes both actions at once when he describes the activity of the minister: "In blessing the bride and bridegroom, the minister confirms their marriage and testifies that they have previously joined themselves together in marriage and have made this a matter of public record."[46] Here the spiritual and the legal aspects are parallel.[47] Because of the great value which God places on marriage, Luther felt that the marriage ceremony should be as festive and solemn as possible.[48]

Under all circumstances divine law[49] requires that the marriage ceremony be a public event. For the basic nature of marriage requires that it be a matter of public record. It is a public station in life and therefore ought also to be entered into publicly with witnesses before the congregation.[50] There is nothing certain about secret vows, and the testimony of the couple themselves is not an adequate basis for recognizing their marriage.[51] It is particularly important that people ought not to marry without the knowledge and consent of their parents. People who get married without the consent of their parents act contrary to the fourth commandment and its injunction of obedience. We cannot say that such marriages have been joined together by God; rather, they are contrary to God and his word.[52] On the other hand, parents ought not to compel their children to enter into a loveless marriage against their will; and when young people love each other, parents ought not to forbid them to marry.[53]

---

45 *WA* 30[III], 60.

46 *WA* 53, 257.

47 Otto Albrecht, in another connection, reminds us that although Luther "distinguished in principle between the spiritual and secular, he still regarded the civil and religious communities as an actual unit." *WA* 30[III], 74 n. 4.

48 *WA* TR 4, no. 4138; *WA* 30[III], 75; *LW* 53, 112.

49 *WA* 30[III], 297.

50 "Because marriage is a public station which is to be entered into and recognized publicly before the church, it is fitting that it should also be established and begun publicly with witnesses who can testify to it." *WA* 30[III], 207; *LW* 46, 268.

51 Ibid.

52 *WA* 30[III], 207, 213–14; *LW* 46, 269, 277–78; *WA* 15, 167; *LW* 45, 389.

53 In 1524 Luther wrote a brief pamphlet: *That Parents Should neither Compel nor Hinder the Marriage of Their Children, and That Children Should Not Become Engaged without Their Parents' Consent.* The two parts of the pamphlet correspond to the two themes of the title. *WA* 15, 163–69; *LW* 45, 385–93; *WA* TR 5, no. 5541; *LW* 54, 450–51.

THE TWOFOLD MEANING OF MARRIAGE

What, then, is the deep divine meaning which Luther finds in
marriage? To what extent is it really a service of God which brings
its own joy? In discussing these questions, Luther always refers to
two things: the relationship of husband and wife to each other
and the work of conceiving and raising children. Although he
places great emphasis on the latter, it is by no means the only
source of the meaning and goodness of marriage.

First of all, husband and wife are created for each other.
Marital happiness results when "husband and wife cherish each
other, become one, and serve each other."[54] Sensual love and the
physical relationship do not create this. "There must be harmony
with respect to patterns of life and ways of thinking."[55] The
spouses serve each other in every need, beginning with their
physical relationship. "The station of marriage is comprehended
in the law of love."[56] The relationship between husband and wife
is governed by the same commandment that applies to all Christians: "For the love among Christians should be the same kind of
love as that of every member of the body for every other one,
. . . each one accepting the faults of the other, sympathizing with
them, bearing and removing them, and doing everything possible
to help him."[57]

Marital love is characterized by faithfulness. It is "a covenant
of fidelity. The whole basis and essence of marriage is that each
gives himself or herself to the other, and they promise to remain
faithful to each other and not give themselves to any other. By
binding themselves to each other, and surrendering themselves to
each other, the way is barred to the body of anyone else, and they
content themselves in the marriage bed with their one companion."[58] Within this covenant of fidelity, sexual desire and the
physical relationship are different from what they are outside
marriage. In a marriage properly lived under "the law of love"

---

54 *WA* 10[II], 299; *LW* 45, 43. "For marital chastity, it is above all essential
that husband and wife live together in love and harmony, cherishing each other
wholeheartedly and with perfect fidelity." *WA* 30[I], 163; *BC*, 394.
55 *WA* TR 5, no. 5524; *LW* 54, 444.
56 *WA* 12, 101.
57 *WA* 32, 381; *LW* 21, 98.
58 *WA* 2, 168; *LW* 44, 10–11.

the sexual relationship is not—as in prostitution—determined by
the selfish desire for pleasure but through the will to serve the
other with one's own body, as Paul says, 1 Corinthians 7:3. This
law of love (together with one's own capacity to abstain) also
determines the periods of abstention. Luther refers to Paul's
authority in rejecting any other regulations of such abstention.[59]
The frequency of sexual intercourse therefore need not be limited
to what is necessary for the conception of children. God permits
married people to use intercourse as an expression and realization
of marital love. "However, one must still discipline himself to
moderation and not turn marriage into a filthy pigpen."

Marital love and faithfulness are particularly tested when we
are disappointed in our spouse and when there are conflicts because the other is hard to live with or malicious. Luther has a
very sober view of marriage. Married people do not live in paradise before the fall into sin; rather, they live in this world, which
is characterized by original sin, and "in the midst of demons."[60]
If we attempt to live in marriage solely on the basis of our own
strength, therefore, our marriage is always in danger. Our natural
selfish feeling is that a marriage which brings only disappointment
is a disaster. However, the Christian looks at things differently
through the eyes of faith. We may not measure our situation
according to our selfish superficial desire for happiness but ought
to be concerned with God's will.[61] Then we will be able to see,
even in an unhappy marriage, how God is at work to save us.
Through such a marriage God intends to purify us and mature
us for his kingdom. "Now, if one of the parties were endowed
with Christian fortitude and could endure the other's ill behavior,
that would doubtless be a wonderfully blessed cross and a right
way to heaven."[62] Admittedly, not everyone has the strength to
endure this.

Luther evaluates in the same way the situation when one spouse
is ill. Should there be a divorce? "By no means. Let him serve the
Lord in the person of the invalid and await his [God's] good

---

[59] *WA* 12, 101–102; *WA* 10^{II}, 292; *LW* 45, 35–36.
[60] *WA* 40^{III}, 275.
[61] *WA* 10^{II}, 295; *LW* 45, 39.
[62] *WA* 10^{II}, 291; *LW* 45, 34.

pleasure. Consider that in this invalid God has provided your household with a healing balm by which you are to gain heaven. Blessed and twice blessed are you when you recognize such a gift of grace and therefore serve your invalid wife for God's sake." If we serve our spouse with such trust in God's gracious will, then we may also trust that he will be faithful and will not give us more to bear than we are able to bear. God will certainly respond to such faithful service by giving the power to live continently.[63]

Thus everything depends on whether one enters into and lives in marriage with God or does so with the self-confidence that he can manage it without God, without fear of God, and without asking for God's blessing.[64] Are we able to see God's will at work in our own marriage, with all its disappointments and troubles, or do we view everything with selfish eyes?[65] This determines which of two statements will be true of a marriage: "Oh, what a truly noble, important, and blessed condition the estate of marriage is if it is properly regarded! Oh, what a truly pitiable, horrible, and dangerous condition it is if it is not properly regarded!"[66] It is simply impossible to build a marriage on the flames of the first, "intoxicating" love that people feel for each other. This first fire burns only a short time. "It's easy enough to get a wife, but to love her with constancy is difficult. A man who can do this has reason to thank our Lord God for it."[67]

The devil makes us bored with each other and gives us eyes for someone else.[68] "At first everything goes all right, so that, as the saying goes, they are ready to eat each other up for love. But when their curiosity has been satisfied, then the devil comes along to create boredom in you, to rob you of your desire in this direction, and to excite it unduly in another direction."[69] "Good God, we

---

63 *WA* 10[II], 291–92; *LW* 45, 35.
64 *WA* 32, 378; *LW* 21, 95; *WA* 40[III], 273 ff.; *WA* TR 1, no. 185; *LW* 54, 25–26; *WA* TR 4, no. 4016.
65 *WA* 12, 106.
66 *WA* 2, 170; *LW* 44, 13–14.
67 *WA* TR 5, no. 5524; *LW* 54, 444; *WA* TR 3, no. 3530; *LW* 54, 223.
68 *WA* 32, 372; *LW* 21, 87–88; *WA* 40[III], 275.
69 *WA* 32, 374; *LW* 21, 89. For this reason, Luther expresses concern about early marriage for young people. When the first flame is past and desire has been satiated, the marriage does not hold together. One should wait until he is older and more mature. *WA* TR 3, no. 3615; *WA* TR 5, no. 5264. Luther recommends marriage at age twenty for men and fifteen to eighteen for girls. *WA* 10[II], 303–304; *LW* 45, 48.

see daily how much trouble it takes to remain in marriage and keep conjugal fidelity."[70] The devil can so thoroughly destroy a marriage "that hate is never so bitter as there."[71] This happens because so many enter into marriage in blind self-confidence, without fearing God or praying to him. God punishes them with failure of their marriage.[72]

We must remember that marriage is always in danger among us sinners. We ought to defend ourselves against this danger by beginning and directing our marriage under God's eyes with prayers for God's help against such great danger. In this way we will also be able to master the temptation to be bored with our spouse and to desire someone else. Then we will be able to view our spouse according to God's word and recognize that God has brought us into this relationship to this particular person.[73] This is "the dearest treasure and the loveliest ornament you can find in a man or a woman."[74] Luther knows that even a Christian can sometimes think that another woman is more attractive or desirable than his own wife.[75] In response to such thoughts I can say to myself: "In my wife at home I have a lovelier adornment, one that God has given me and has adorned with his word beyond the others, even though she may not have a beautiful body or may have other failings. Though I may look over all the women in the world, I cannot find any about whom I can boast with a joyful conscience as I can about mine: 'This is the one whom God has granted to me and put into my arms.' I know that he and all the angels are heartily pleased if I cling to her lovingly and faithfully. Then why should I despise this precious gift of God and take up with someone else, where I can find no such treasure or adornment?"[76]

---

[70] *WA* 18, 277; *LCC* 18, 275.

[71] *WA* TR 1, no. 185; *LW* 54, 25; *WA* 32, 374; *LW* 21, 89.

[72] *WA* 32, 379; *LW* 21, 95; *WA* 40[III], 274.

[73] *WA* 32, 371; *LW* 21, 87. God has not only instituted marriage in general but, through his word which joined a couple together, has also instituted a specific marriage. "God's word joins them together and they ought not desert each other, but stay together as God wills and commands." *WA* 36, 503.

[74] *WA* 32, 372; *LW* 21, 87.

[75] *WA* 31[I], 65.

[76] *WA* 32, 372; *LW* 21, 87. "The word will make you fearful and shy of other women, even make you detest them—and it will so adorn your wife, no matter how mean and hateful, independent, and impatient she may be, that she will be more attractive to you because of God's word. She will be more pleasing

According to God's word and will, the second focal point of marriage is fertility. "The greatest good in married life, that which makes all suffering and labor worthwhile, is that God grants off-spring and commands that they be brought up to worship and serve him. In all the world this is the noblest and most precious work." For God likes nothing better than that people be brought to him through the gospel and thus be saved.[77] And he calls parents to fulfill this wonderful function in the lives of their children. Parents thus have the opportunity of doing "all Christian works." They are "apostles, bishops, and priests to their children."[78] They have a very honorable and richly fulfilling life. This is especially true for the wife who is a mother. Even though as the weaker vessel and the one less able to do heavy work she may seem to be inferior to her husband, still she has the highest honor of motherhood.[79] As a mother she is permitted to fulfill God's loving will for his creatures. In all that she does she has the honor of being an instrument in God's hand.[80] This is true even of being pregnant and giving birth—with all its troubles and dangers. Even though childbirth may cost a mother her life, she dies doing "a noble deed and in subservience to God."[81] A woman is really healthy when she is a mother. This is true even though she is physically exhausted by many pregnancies and dies earlier than she might have otherwise.[82]

---

to you than someone else adorned with gold." *WA* 34[I], 71. See the discussion of divorce below, pp. 97–99.

[77] *WA* 10[II], 301; *LW* 45, 46. "Married life is no matter for jest or idle curiosity, but it is a glorious institution and an object of God's serious concern. For it is of the highest importance to him that persons be brought up to serve the world, promote knowledge of God, godly living, and all virtues, and fight against wickedness and the devil." *WA* 30[I], 161; *BC*, 393.

[78] *WA* 10[II], 301; *LW* 45, 46.

[79] *WA* TR 4, no. 4138.

[80] *WA* 10[II], 296; *LW* 45, 40.

[81] Ibid.

[82] "And even if they bear themselves weary—or ultimately bear themselves out—that does not hurt. Let them bear themselves out. This is the purpose for which they exist. It is better to have a brief life with good health than a long life in ill health." *WA* 10[II], 301; *LW* 45, 46. Luther is drawing a comparison between women who have children and women who remain barren. He occasionally suggested that misformed infants, or "changelings," should be drowned. He believed that such a changeling was not created by God, but was made by the devil and had no soul—or even that the devil himself was in them as their soul. *WA* TR 5, no. 5207; *LW* 45, 396–97. Cf. *WA* TR 2, no. 2528–29; *WA* TR 3, no. 3676; *WA* TR 4, no. 4513. Luther here is under the influence of a massive primitive dualism and a mythological concept of the devil. It makes no

The services that a mother performs for her children are for the most part small and coarse and hardly noble. However, Christian faith "opens its eyes, looks upon all these insignificant, distasteful, and despised duties in the Spirit, and is aware that they are all adorned with divine approval as with the costliest gold and jewels."[83] For they are the means whereby God "graciously cares for us like a kind and loving mother."[84] Faith recognizes that what seems to natural man to be nothing but trouble and a burdensome limitation is instead a unique calling to serve God's gracious will and to express our faith and love. If we recognize that, we "will find delight, love, and joy without end" in the midst of the "bitterness, drudgery, and anguish."[85]

The greatness of the task, and all the troubles which marriage lays upon us, drive us especially to trust in God, to believe, and to exercise our faith. For this reason it is really a spiritual station. For what is more spiritual than faith, trusting only in God's word, and everything that calls and compels us to believe?

DIVORCE

Luther—in contrast to the law of Moses—asserts that God wills marriage to be indissoluble.[86] He does this on the basis of Jesus' statement: "What therefore God has joined together, let no man put asunder" (Matthew 19:6).[87] People who want to be Christians do not get divorces. People want divorces because marriage has failed. Marriages fail because people do not recognize that the marriage estate is created and ordered by God and do not observe his purpose in instituting marriage. As a result, when their marriage is unhappy they become impatient and are not ready to forgive each other. But patience and forgiveness are the most effective defense against the thoughts of divorce.[88]

---

sense for modern advocates of euthanasia to cite such statements by Luther in support of their position—as has been done in the popular press. For those who make such statements do not have the slightest intention of sharing Luther's idea that such children have been produced by the devil. Rather, they use a weakness of the Reformer for their own profit.
83 *WA* 10[II], 295; *LW* 45, 39.
84 *WA* 10[II], 298; *LW* 45, 43.
85 *WA* 10[II], 294; *LW* 45, 38.
86 *WA* 10[II], 288; *LW* 45, 31; *WA* 30[I], 175; *BC*, 404.
87 *WA* 6, 555; *LW* 36, 92; *WA* 32, 378; *LW* 21, 94.
88 *WA* 32, 378–81; *LW* 21, 94–98.

On the basis of Jesus' statement (Matthew 5:32 and 19:9),
Luther recognizes adultery as the only basis for the dissolution of
a marriage.[89] Adultery is "the greatest robbery and theft that is
possible on earth."[90] The adulterer has already dissolved the marriage. As a result, the betrayed spouse is no longer bound to this
marriage unless he or she should assert the desire to continue it in
spite of everything.[91] Thus on one hand, Luther permits the
political authorities to grant a divorce with a good conscience
when a marriage has already been destroyed through adultery. On
the other hand, he advises those who "wish to be Christians" to
follow the way of reconciliation even in the case of adultery (as
long as the guilty party humbly confesses and seeks to improve
himself). The partner who seeks reconciliation will respond with
Christian love and forgive as long as there is hope that the guilty
party will improve and will not misuse this forgiveness.[92] What
is possible in a single case of adultery, however, is not a valid
response to a continuing sin against marriage. "For one oversight
is still pardonable, but a sin that takes mercy and forgiveness for
granted is intolerable." Similarly, no one can be forced "to take
back a public prostitute or an adulterer if he does not want to do
so or is so disgusted that he cannot do so."[93]

In *The Babylonian Captivity of the Church* (1520) and in
The Estate of Marriage (1522) Luther refers to other grounds
for divorce: impotence, the refusal of sexual intercourse, and
incompatibility. Except in cases of impotence, 1 Corinthians 7:10–
11 remains the rule: people divorced under these circumstances may
not enter into a new marriage. Furthermore, married people ought
not to separate on their own initiative: divorce, like marriage, must
take place publicly through the judgment and decision of the secular
authorities and "with the knowledge of the community."[94]

---

89 *WA* 6, 559; *LW* 36, 105.

90 *WA* 12, 101.

91 *WA* 32, 379; *LW* 21, 96. Luther can also argue that since according to
the law of Moses an adulterer deserves death, he is already dead before God.
And death dissolves the marriage.

92 Luther raises no objection if the spouse who has been betrayed through
adultery feels free to enter a new marriage, but it would be much better if the
partners in the marriage would reconcile themselves with one another and
preserve the marriage. *WA* 30III, 241; *LW* 46, 311.

93 *WA* 32, 380; *LW* 21, 96.

94 *WA* 6, 557–58; *LW* 36, 102–105; *WA* 10II, 287–91; *LW* 45, 30–34;
WA 30III, 241; *LW* 46, 311.

Characteristically, Luther's instructions in these matters distinguish between what must take place for the sake of public
order—and therefore also applies to non-Christians—and what is
to be expected of Christians. Luther does not require all to conform to the latter standard, but he appeals to Christians to do so.
The secular authorities must permit divorce in order to prevent
greater evil. However, more is expected of those who wish to be
Christians: love and patience which can bear the burdens in
marriage that others find unbearable. Jesus' statement about the
indissolubility of marriage is not laid upon all as a law, neither
are average people exempted; rather, it continues to stand as an
appeal to Christians.[95] For Christians, the rule of Christ stands
above the legal order administered by the secular authorities.

PARENTS AND CHILDREN

Luther particularly emphasizes the authority of parents. Parents
stand "in the place of God." They have the highest authority on
earth. All other human authority—for example, the authority of
the secular government—is derived from parental authority.[96]
Parental authority is uniquely different from all other authority
because it functions in both governments. Parents not only exercise
authority over their children in the secular government, but they
also proclaim the gospel to their children. Thus they are at one
and the same time secular authorities and, through the universal
priesthood, spiritual authorities for their children.[97]

The spiritual function which parents exercise in relationship to
their children requires them not only to love their children "according to the flesh," and educate them to live in secular society
and achieve outward success, but also to be concerned about the

---

[95] "This same thing might even be advisable nowadays, if the secular government prescribed it, that certain queer, stubborn, and obstinate people, who have
no capacity for toleration and are not suited for married life at all, should be
permitted to get a divorce. Since people are as evil as they are, any other way
of governing is impossible. Frequently something must be tolerated even though
it is not a good thing to do, to prevent something even worse from happening."
WA 32, 377; *LW* 21, 94.

[96] *WA* 30[I], 147, 150, 152; *BC*, 379, 382, 384.

[97] "Most certainly father and mother are apostles, bishops, and priests to
their children, for it is they who make them acquainted with the gospel. In
short, there is no greater or nobler authority on earth than that of parents over
their children, for this authority is both spiritual and temporal." *WA* 10[II], 301;
LW 45, 46.

spiritual life of their children. "Oh, how perilous it is to be a father or mother, where only flesh and blood are supreme!" By the way they raise their children parents can attain salvation, but they can also earn hell.[98]

Since God has instituted parents as his representatives, children should see their parents as acting on behalf of God. This means, as Luther emphasizes in the Large Catechism, that children should honor their parents. "For it is a much greater thing to honor than to love."[99] Honoring our parents, like honoring God, includes fearing as well as loving them. There ought to be no love without fear, but there also should be no fear without love. Rather, there should be "fear mingled with love." A hidden majesty dwells in parents. It deserves to be feared—and Luther understands this fear to be more than what we call reverence.[100] We honor our parents primarily by obeying them. This obedience is limited only when parents wish to train and educate their children contrary to God's commandment. In such a situation, children ought not to obey. "According to the first three commandments, God is to be more highly regarded than parents."[101]

---

98 *WA* 6, 251, 253–54; *LW* 44, 82–83, 85–86.
99 *WA* 30¹, 147; *BC*, 379.
100 "Honor includes not only love but also deference, humility, and modesty, directed (so to speak) toward a majesty hidden within them." Ibid.
101 *WA* 6, 251–53; *LW* 44, 81–84.

6

WORK

AS THE SITUATION required, Luther specifically discussed a
number of topics and questions related to the Christian
life: marriage, secular authority, the military, war, and business.
Other topics are not discussed comprehensively but only within the
context of the interpretation of related Bible passages. One such
topic is work. Luther speaks about work when a particular passage
of Scripture offers the opportunity. He does so particularly in his
interpretation of Psalm 127 and Psalm 128.[1]

God has commanded work. The fact that men work is based on
God's will to create and to preserve his creation. All men know
that a married man must work in order to support his wife and
children, and this knowledge belongs to natural law.[2] Work is
part of God's created order not only as a result of sin but already
was so before the fall: even in paradise God gave Adam "work to
do, that is, [to] plant the garden, cultivate, and look after it."[3]
Work is the "mask" behind which the hidden God himself does
everything and gives men what they need to live.[4] Our work in
and of itself does not produce the goods that are necessary for
life. God himself must add his blessing to our work. However,
he has ordered work and commanded us to work as the means by
which he blesses us. In this respect work is very honorable; it is
a most holy thing and, as the means through which God blesses
us, is itself a blessing.[5]

Admittedly, work is also a tiring burden and is accompanied by
tension, worry, and disappointment. It stands under the curse
which God placed on the soil after the fall into sin. Luther, bound
as he is to the biblical story of the fall into sin, does not reduce

---

1 *WA* 40^{III}, 202 ff., 278 ff.
2 *WA* 40^{III}, 278.
3 *WA* 7, 31; *RW* 1, 371; cf. *LW* 31, 360.
4 *WA* 31^I, 437; *LW* 14, 115; *Theology*, 107–108.
5 *WA* 40^{III}, 278, 280.

this in any way. However, his perspective on work goes far beyond that. The world only sees the troublesome and heavy burden of work and therefore flees and hates it. To do that, however, means to look at work with the "eyes of the flesh," which can only see the toil and trouble of work—and the flesh ought not to have anything else.[6]

However, Christians see work with the eyes of the Holy Spirit— Scripture does this in Psalm 128:1–2 when it blesses the man who works industriously. He is blessed because in the midst of all the toil and bitterness of work, the believer may know that his work obeys God and therefore stands under God's approval. God accepts it as a sacrifice of worship and praise and uses it to bless us. God has sweetened the sourness of work with the honey of his good pleasure and the promise of his blessing. Because the Christian views work in this way, it is precious to him. He can easily bear the burden and do it with joy and courage.[7] Thus work is indeed under a curse, but it also stands under God's blessing.

Luther also interprets the meaning of work in terms of the apostolic admonitions in 1 Thessalonians 4:11–12, 2 Thessalonians 3:8, 12, and Ephesians 4:28: work makes a man independent of others and enables him to give to someone who is in need. Whoever does not work is a thief and robs his neighbor in two ways. First, he permits others to work for him and nourishes himself from their "blood and sweat." Second, he withholds what he ought to give his neighbor.[8]

Quite apart from anything it produces, work in and of itself— and more specifically work as toil—is beneficial. It disciplines a man, helps him to deal strictly with his flesh and its desires, and assists him in exercising and maintaining patience. It is precisely for this reason that work done by the sweat of our brow pleases God.[9] In view of these statements we can properly ask whether anything of the curse is left, since the toil itself has become a means of discipline and pleases God. Does Luther refer to the curse only because of Genesis 3?

---

[6] *WA* 40^{III}, 279–81; *WA* 42, 152 ff.; 259; *LW* 1, 203 ff., 352–53.

[7] *WA* 40^{III}, 281–83. "Should not the heart leap and melt with joy when it can go to work and do what is commanded?" *WA* 30^{I}, 149; *BC*, 381.

[8] *WA* 15, 302; *LW* 45, 258–59; *WA* 22, 322.

[9] *WA* 40^{III}, 279, 281, 283.

Luther's evaluation of work has frequently been characterized on the basis of his translation of Psalm 90:10: "What is best in life is trouble and work [*Arbeit*]." Otto Scheel has distinguished this "courageous and joyful affirmation of the value of work" from the "tired" view of life of the Old Testament psalmist.[10] Scheel asserts that work is the best part of a long life, as if Luther had said: "Life is best when it is work and trouble." However, Scheel's type of interpretation completely distorts the meaning of Luther's translation.[11] In his commentary on Psalm 128:2, Luther himself emphasizes that the Hebrew word for work or toil used by the biblical authors in this verse conveys a broader sense than the German word *Arbeit*. That is, the biblical word is used not only to describe our active work but also to describe the difficulties and bitternesses that we experience in our calling—the Bible speaks of work where we would speak of toil and trouble.[12] On this basis, Luther himself used the German word both in the narrower and in the broader sense, a possibility that was open on the basis of German usage. For just as *labor* has a double meaning in Latin, so in early German *Arbeit* is used to describe work in the modern sense as well as toil and trouble. Indeed, the latter is the basic meaning of the word. Luther uses it in this sense, for example, in Isaiah 3:11 when he translates the Hebrew referring to "the travail of his soul" into German by "because his soul worked," (*gearbeitet hat*), that is, because his soul bore and suffered. Likewise, in Revelation 14:13 the Greek for "They shall rest from their troubles" was literally "They shall rest from their work [*Arbeit*]." A similar parallel is to be found in Luther's translation of Isaiah 43:24: "You have burdened me [*mir Arbeit gemacht*] with your sins. . . ." Again, in Genesis 5:29 and throughout his translation of the Bible, Luther uses the phrase *Mühe und Arbeit,* which means toil and work in modern German as a translation for toil and trouble. Luther's lectures on Genesis[13] clearly indicate that he understands toil and trouble as a general designation of the difficulties of this life; the same is true in his translation of Psalm 55:10 and Sirach 51:30 (German: Psalm 55:11 and Sirach 51:35).

Thus Luther's translation of Psalm 90:10 does not speak of work in our sense of the word and most certainly does not refer to it as desirable; rather, it says that work even at its height and lived at its best is toil and trouble. There is no trace here of the hymn in praise of work which liberal Protestantism thought to find. This passage may not be used in determining Luther's evaluation of work.

---

10 "Evangelium Kirche und Volk bei Luther," *Schriften des Vereins für Reformationsgeschichte* 51 (1934), no. 156: 46–47.
11 See Paul Althaus, "Und wenn es köstlich gewesen ist," in *Theologische Aufsätze* (Gütersloh: Bertelsmann, 1935), 2:151 ff.
12 *WA* 40III, 281–82.
13 *WA* 42, 259; *LW* 1, 354.

Since Luther's evaluation of work is based on God's commandment, this commandment also establishes the limits of work. For
God limits his commandment to work by commanding us to rest.
Together with work, God has also commanded the Sabbath. Therefore the worship of God, which work signifies, is not exhausted in
work. In a letter of May 12, 1530, Luther exhorts Melanchthon:
"We worship God also when we rest; indeed, there is no greater
worship of God than this."[14] How is it possible for us to worship
God more when we rest than when we work? At this point we
once again stand at the center of Luther's theology: God is God
and he alone is the creator. We can worship God by resting; indeed, in resting we can worship him better than in any other way
because it is when we really relax our body and soul that we cast
our care on God. We thus honor God as the one whose blessing
rests upon and surrounds all our work, and who keeps on working
for us even when we rest and sleep. The capacity truly to rest from
our cares with our body and soul is a special confirmation of our
faith and is related to justifying faith. The high value which
Luther puts on resting protects him from any idolization of work.
He interprets this as one of the basic meanings of the third commandment. And in his hymn on the Ten Commandments, he interprets the third commandment in this sense: "From thine own work
thou must be free, that God his work have in thee."[15]

---

[14] Luther continues: "For this reason he wishes the Sabbath commandment
to be observed more rigidly than the others." *WA* Br 5, 317. Johannes.
Mathesius reports, in his twelfth sermon on Luther's life, that when Luther and
Melanchthon stopped to visit Spalatin on their return from Coburg, Melanchthon
kept working on the *Apology* even when they were eating. Then Luther got up,
took the pen out of his hand, and spoke almost the same words as are quoted
in the text above. *Ausgewählte Werke,* ed. Georg Loesche (Prague: J. G.
Calve'sche, 1898), 3:299–300.
[15] *WA* 35, 427; *LW* 53, 279.

7

PROPERTY, BUSINESS,
AND ECONOMICS[1]

LUTHER BASES the right of private property on the fact that
every man must have something to use in performing the
service which he owes his neighbor. Every Christian is called to
give to his neighbor. Whoever wishes to give must have. And
whoever does not have anything that belongs to him is not able
to give anything. Personal property is thus based on the norm of
love.[2]

This is particularly true of those who are officials in the secular
government. These officials must fulfill their duties if the world
is to continue to exist. The officials must have money and property
available, however, to use in carrying out their duties. Officials of

---

[1] *The Short Sermon on Usury* (1519), *WA* 6, 3–8. *The Long Sermon on
Usury* (1520), *WA* 6, 36–60; *LW* 45, 273–308. *To the Christian Nobility of
the German Nation concerning the Reform of the Christian State* (1520), *WA*
6, 465–66; *LW* 44, 212–14. *Trade and Usury* (1524), *WA* 15, 293–313,
321–22; *LW* 45, 245–310. (The second section of this treatise is a reprinting of
The Long Sermon on Usury of 1520.) *Letter to the City Council of Danzig*
(1525), *WA* Br 3, 484 ff.; *S-J* 2, 310–11. (Only the covering letter is translated.) *Admonition to Pastors to Preach against Usury* (1540), *WA* 51, 331–
424.
Karl Holl, "Der Neubau der Sittlichkeit" (1919), *GA* 1, 257–58, 273 ff.
Werner Elert, *Morphologie des Luthertums*, 2d ed. (Munich: C. H. Beck,
1953), 2:466–91. Georg Wünsch, *Evangelische Wirtschaftsethik* (Tübingen:
Mohr, 1927), pp. 315 ff. Heinz Reymann, *Glaube und Wirtschaft bei Luther*
(Gütersloh: Bertelsmann, 1934). Hermann Barge, *Luther und der Frühkapitalismus* (Gütersloh: Bertelsmann, 1951).
[2] "If a Christian is to give something, he must already have it. Whoever has
nothing gives nothing. And since he is to give tomorrow, the day after tomorrow
and a year from now (for Christ tells me to give as long as I live), he cannot
give everything away today. Therefore, since our Lord Christ commands us to
give, he commands those who have something and are able to give it." *WA* 51,
384. Luther also demonstrates this on the basis of Jesus' admonition, "Sell what
you have, . . ." asserting that this presupposes private property. For Jesus does
not say that we should give it away or that we should give it back, as though
it were stolen property that he possessed unjustly; rather, he says to sell it,
and that implies that the person to whom he is speaking legally possesses the
property. In the same way, the commandment forbidding us to steal also
recognizes private property. *WA* 39[II], 39.

government such as lords and princes need this, but so do fathers who have families.[3] Luther consistently bases his position on private property on the fact that having something is the necessary presupposition of serving our neighbor.

Accordingly, Luther rejects the communism which the Enthusiasts and the peasants sometimes advocated. Love does indeed require the Christian to make himself and his property available to his neighbor in his need. In the face of my neighbor's need, love removes the boundary between mine and yours, even though the law must establish this boundary for the sake of love itself. When my neighbor is in need, however, then my property is no longer mine but is set aside for my service of my neighbor. Similarly, love can lead individuals to contribute their property in a common effort to care for their neighbors. The sharing of possessions among the early Christians was such a work of love. On one hand, such sharing is possible only if people have private property.[4] On the other hand, we dare not make such a voluntary act—which is appropriate under some circumstances—a general principle or systematize it as though this were what the gospel always intended.[5]

The Christian may not be inseparably bound to his personal property or to anything else in this world. Here too he is free for God's sake. He must at any time be prepared to sacrifice joyfully or lose his possessions in conflict and in persecution for the sake of the gospel.[6] In relationship to his property the Christian is also free for God's sake when he needs it to help his neighbor. God has given him possessions so that he can use them to serve his neighbor and help him in need. This is the meaning of pos-

---

[3] "Having money, property, honor, power, land, and servants belongs to the secular realm; without these it could not endure. Therefore, a lord or prince should not and cannot be poor, because for his office and station he must have all sorts of goods like these. This does not mean, therefore, that one must be poor in the sense of having nothing at all of his own. The world could not endure if we were all to be beggars and to have nothing. The head of a household could not support his household and servants if he himself had nothing at all." *WA* 32, 307; *LW* 21, 12.

[4] *WA* 39[II], 63, 68–69.

[5] "And the gospel does not make goods common, except in the case of those who, of their own free will, do what the apostles and disciples did in Acts 4." *WA* 18, 359; *LW* 46, 51.

[6] *WA* 39[II], 40.

sessions. Possessions cease to be "goods" when they are merely
piled up.[7] Thus we are to use possessions first of all to preserve
our own life and the life of our families. However, what is left
over after meeting this need belongs to our neighbor. Otherwise
it is "unrighteous Mammon."[8]

Luther also takes the Sermon on the Mount very seriously at
this point. Following Jesus' example (Matthew 5:40 ff.), Luther
repeatedly distinguishes three ways of using my worldly goods in
relationship to my neighbor. He calls them three grades or steps;
the first is the highest and the third is the lowest.[9] (1) The
Christian allows his possessions to be taken from him or allows
himself to be deceived and cheated in business in the certainty that
his heavenly Father will keep his promise and give daily bread to
his people. The Christian knows that he has a treasure in heaven
that no one can steal from him. (2) With the same confidence the
Christian voluntarily gives to those who are in need. (3) The
Christian lends to his neighbor according to Luke 6:34, without
charging interest and without expecting repayment; thus he risks
being uncertain as to whether he will get his money back or not.

All three steps are outlined in the Sermon on the Mount; they
may not be regarded as merely a counsel for those who wish to
achieve a higher level of perfection. Rather, the Sermon on the
Mount must be strictly interpreted as the Lord's commandment
for everyone. We are really free to act in this way only if we do
not keep count but believe. This means that we depend not on
anything that we are going to receive on this earth but solely and
completely on God. We then consciously accept the risk that we
will lose our money when we lend it (Luther speaks of risk in this

---

[7] "This is a comforting difference among possessions. Not only are the possessions of the wicked perishable and transitory, but they are evil and damnable
possessions, because they have only been heaped up and have not been distrib-
uted to those in need. This violates the nature of possessions." *WA* 19, 561;
LW 14, 219. [The word used by Luther for possessions is *Güter*. It is a word
which can be translated either as "possessions" or as "goods."—Trans.]

[8] "Thus Mammon may also be used for evil purposes, and Jesus then calls it
unrighteous Mammon. In God's sight everything which a man has left over and
does not use to help his neighbor is an illegal and stolen possession; for before
God one ought to give, to lend, and to let everything be taken away from him.
Therefore the popular proverb says that 'the biggest big shots are the biggest
thieves,' for they have the most left over and give the least." *WA* 10[III], 275.

[9] *WA* 6, 3; *WA* 6, 36; *LW* 45, 273; *WA* 15, 300 ff.; *LW* 45, 256–57; *WA*
19, 231; *WA* 32, 395; *LW* 21, 115; *WA* 51, 377; *WA* 10[III], 227.

connection), and we risk the loss knowing that God will pay us far more than any amount involved.[10]

Luther rejects charging interest on loans as unchristian. Whoever lends and demands more in return than he has given is a usurer. Luther not only cites the Sermon on the Mount and Deuteronomy at this point but also knows that he is in agreement with the Church Fathers generally.[11] The Christian who possesses more than is required to meet his own needs and the needs of his family ought to lend without interest or (preferably) give to those who are in need.[12] Only when the Christian does not have anything extra available to lend is he permitted to accept interest. Then, however, the interest ought to be limited—to approximately four percent—and the creditor should share in the risk. This should be done by arranging a rate of interest that can be adjusted according to the income of the debtor. Such an arrangement can be helpful to both parties.[13]

All this holds true for Christians. However, the fact that they do this in the freedom of love does not make secular laws regulating these matters unnecessary. Christians permit someone who wants to rob them to take their possessions from them. But the secular authorities ought not to take this into account in protecting property, they ought to prevent theft, robbery, and stealing. If they do not, peace, business, and commerce will be destroyed. Christians do not require the return of what they have lent; however, the authorities must require people to return what they have borrowed. Christian love thus does not replace the law which the secular authorities are responsible for administering.[14]

We must thus distinguish between the actions of Christians, which in their very nature are completely voluntary, and the order of secular life, (in which Christians are always a small minority.) Luther does not in any way weaken Jesus' statement forbidding

---

[10] *WA* 15, 302; *LW* 45, 257–59.

[11] *WA* 6, 47; *LW* 45, 287–88. On the attitude of the early and medieval church toward interest, see Barge, *Luther und der Frühkapitalismus,* pp. 7 ff.

[12] *WA* 15, 303; *LW* 45, 259–60.

[13] *WA* 6, 57; *LW* 45, 303.

[14] *WA* 15, 302; *LW* 45, 258. "Otherwise, if only love were applied, everyone would eat, drink, and live at ease at someone else's expense, and no one would work. Indeed, everyone would take from another what was his, and we would have such a state of affairs that no one could live because of the others." *WA* 15, 306; *LW* 45, 264.

Christians to take interest. However, as he points out in his *Letter to the City Council of Danzig* (May 1525), interest should not simply be abolished in this world. It has in fact become the ordinary arrangement, and it ought not to be simply done away with (see 1 Peter 2:13) but so shaped and "set right" that it would correspond to "natural equity" and to "love and equity." At the same time, Christians still remain free to follow Jesus' word and to reject the interest which they have coming to them according to secular law.[15]

Luther also rejects taking interest on mortgages as it was practiced during his life. The custom in Luther's time was to lend money on unnamed real estate—instead of the earlier custom of specifying exactly what property was involved. Luther says that the "devil invented this practice." But Luther was willing to discuss the former practice of taking interest on mortgages.[16] Luther makes suggestions for practicing this business with love and equity. Thus a difference remains between what Jesus' disciples do freely and what is required by the order of secular life.

Luther also expresses his opinions on matters of business such as buying and selling. Christ has not given us any instruction on these matters but has left the regulation of this area to reason.[17] In spite of this, Luther makes some suggestions in this area, primarily for Christians, since questions of business not only involve reason but also the conscience.[18] In connection with this he discusses the then current methods of doing business, and earnestly exhorts and warns and makes very sharp judgments and very pointed suggestions. As he sees it, all business is dominated by an unlimited selfish desire for profit. Businessmen sell their merchandise for the highest possible price and thus use the need and trouble of their customers for their own profit, in violation of both natural law and the gospel.[19] Luther shows that there is a way of arriving at a reasonable price and rate of profit in terms of the cost of doing business, the cost of the raw materials, and the

---

[15] *WA* Br 3, 485–86.
[16] *WA* 6, 466; *LW* 44, 213; *WA* 6, 51; *LW* 45, 295.
[17] *WA* 32, 395; *LW* 21, 115. Accordingly, Luther can comment in 1522 that buying and selling are completely secular matters and that he does not wish to get involved in the business of the secular government. *WA* 10[III], 227.
[18] *WA* 15, 294; *LW* 45, 247.
[19] *WA* 15, 295; *LW* 45, 247.

risks taken by the businessman rather than according to the law of supply and demand.[20] Luther's proposal was given serious consideration by economists from time to time.[21]

Luther was extremely critical of the contemporary rise of capitalism and world trade. He objects to the practices of the trading companies and their monopolies.[22] The whole new economy based on money seems to him to be unjust and corrupt. "How is it possible in the lifetime of one man to accumulate such great possessions, worthy of a king, legally and according to God's will?"[23] "How could it ever be right and according to God's will that a man should in a short time grow so rich that he could buy out kings and emperors?"[24] Luther particularly aims his comments at Jakob Fugger: "In this connection, we must put a bit in the mouth of the Fuggers and similar companies."[25] The investment of capital in order to gain profit without work seems to Luther to be, with certain exceptions, immoral. The exceptions basically involve people who are not able to work, such as widows and orphans. In such cases love and natural equity indicate that we should permit them to earn interest on their capital.[26] In his treatise *To the Christian Nobility* . . . Luther argues against the extension of trade to distant countries, the excessive foreign imports which drained so much money out of the country, completely unnecessary refinements in the style of life, and the luxurious innovations found among the nobility and the rich.[27] Since so much land was still uncultivated, Luther felt that agriculture was more important than trade and commerce.[28]

20 *WA* 15, 296; *LW* 45, 248.
21 Gustav Schmoller describes Luther's proposal as "very significant and insightful"; he also says that Luther here demonstrates "an awareness of national economic problems that is unusual for his time." "Zur Geschichte der national-ökonomische Ansichten in Deutschland während der Reformationszeit," *Zeitschrift für die Gesammte Staatswissenschaft* 16 (1860): 495.
22 *WA* 15, 305, 312; *LW* 45, 261–62, 270.
23 *WA* 6, 466; *LW* 44, 213.
24 This quotation continues: "They have brought things to such a pass that everybody else has to do business at the risk of loss, winning this year and losing next year, while they always win, making up their losses by increased profits. It is no wonder that they quickly appropriate the wealth of the whole world." *WA* 15, 312; *LW* 45, 271.
25 *WA* 6, 466; *LW* 44, 213.
26 *WA* Br 3, 485; *WA* 51, 371.
27 *WA* 6, 465; *LW* 44, 212.
28 *WA* 6, 466; *LW* 44, 214.

Thus Luther seriously warned against the economic developments of his time. He was not able to halt the economic trends. Today we live under the laws of world trade and capitalism and cannot undo that development. And yet here too we can still learn much from what Luther says. However we may evaluate his individual judgments, the seriousness with which he criticizes economic life on the basis of love and equity remains a valid example. Just as he did not recognize any Machiavellian autonomy in politics, so he recognized no mammonistic autonomy in business. The danger of materialistic distortion of our economic system is always present. Christians must be on the watch against it. For this reason it is good for us again to hear and consider what Luther says about property and business.[29]

---

[29] It is not possible to discuss here individual details of Luther's business ethics. For such discussions, see the literature cited in note 1, particularly Holl, "Der Neubau der Sittlichkeit," and Barge, *Luther und der Frühkapitalismus*.

8

THE STATE[1]

POLITICAL AUTHORITY
AS GOD'S CREATION AND ORDER

RULERS AND people—Luther also speaks of the people ruled as "the community"—belong together and are attached to one another. Both are God's creation and order. Luther explicitly asserts that this is also true of a people in the sense of a national group (*Volk*). He does not feel that the development and continued existence of such a people can be taken for granted or that it happens accidentally; rather, it is the mystery of God's creating and preserving work. "Mad reason, in its shrewdness," knows nothing of this; it considers it to be a mere accident "that people hold together and live side by side." Scripture proclaims and faith knows, however, that "God has made, and makes, all communities. He still brings them together, feeds them, lets them grow, blesses and preserves them."[2] All nations have received their historical

---

[1] In addition to the political writings of 1523–1526 (see chapter 4, n. 1), many of which are translated in *LW* 45 and 46, especially *Temporal Authority: To What Extent It Should Be Obeyed* (1523), *WA* 11, 245–80; *LW* 45, 81–129, see Luther's *Commentary on Psalm 82* (1530), *WA* 31I, 189–218; *LW* 13, 41–72; his *Commentary on Psalm 127* (1532/1533, but not published until 1540), *WA* 40III, 202–69; his *Commentary on Psalm 101* (1534/1535), *WA* 51, 200–64; *LW* 13, 145–224; and his *Commentary on the Song of Solomon* (1530/1531), *WA* 31II, 586–769.
  Hermann Jordan, *Luthers Staatsauffassung, ein Beitrag zu der Frage des Verhältnisses von Religion und Politik* (Munich: Müller and Fröhlich, 1917), traces the various stages in the development of Luther's understanding of the state. Karl Holl, "Der Neubau der Sittlichkeit," *GA* 1, 252–57, 265–81. Theodor Pauls, *Luthers Auffassung von Staat und Volk* (Bonn: K. Schroeder, 1925). Werner Elert, *Morphologie des Luthertums*, 2d ed. (Munich: C. H. Beck, 1953), 2:313–34. Georg Wünsch, *Evangelische Ethik des Politischen* (Tübingen: Mohr/Siebeck, 1936), pp. 150 ff. Gunnar Hillerdal, *Gehorsam gegen Gott und Menschen. Luthers Lehre von der Obrigkeit und die moderne evangelische Staatsethik* (Göttingen: Vandenhoeck & Ruprecht, 1954), pp. 17–119.
[2] *WA* 31I, 193; *LW* 13, 46. The fact that Luther at this place in his *Commentary on Psalm 82* speaks of people and community in a synonymous sense is determined by his translation of Psalm 82:1: "God stands in the midst of the congregation. . . ." In using these terms Luther does not make the distinction which we ordinarily make today between the political and the Christian congregation or community, but sees both in the one community. Cf. *WA* 31I, 196; *LW* 13, 49, where Luther says that God has "appointed priests and preachers" in "his congregation." [Luther's word *Gemeine* could be translated either as "community" or as "congregation."—Trans.]

sphere of authority from God.[3] Thus a people is an order of God's creation.[4] In faith I know that God loves my people.[5] Luther calls us to rejoice because we are permitted to belong to a people that has been created and preserved by God.[6] The people belong to God. Rulers ought never to forget this and treat the people as though they were their own property. They must view the people "in the fear of God and in humility."[7]

The people ought to view their rulers in the same way. Here too "the fear of God and humility" are in order. For the political authorities are also an order created by God.[8] Luther bases his position on Scripture, particularly Genesis 9:6, Romans 13, 1 Peter 2:13–17, and Jesus' statement on the payment of tax, Matthew 22:21.[9] Government is thus "instituted by God's word." God himself establishes and preserves all government; therefore it is a "divine thing," a "divine order," and those who hold office in government are—according to Luther's interpretation—called "gods" in Psalm 82.[10] For all the offices of government, from the highest to the lowest, are orders created by God, and like everything else that he has created are good.[11] He has not only instituted them but he himself is effectively present in them: he himself rules, speaks, and administers justice through them. "He has placed the law into the hearts of those who rule."[12]

Those who govern sit in God's place.[13] Therefore disobedience and rebellion against the government are disobedience and rebellion against God himself.[14] When governments punish, God's own

---

[3] "God himself created and established them [kings and nations], and divided up the world for them to rule." *WA* 31^I, 234; *LW* 14, 14.

[4] *WA* 31^I, 193; *LW* 13, 46.

[5] *WA* 31^{II}, 595.

[6] *WA* 31^I, 194; *LW* 13, 47.

[7] Ibid.

[8] *WA* 11, 247; *LW* 45, 85; *WA* 30^{II}, 556; *LW* 46, 237; and frequently elsewhere.

[9] *WA* 11, 247; *LW* 45, 85–86; *WA* 31^I, 195; *LW* 13, 48; *WA* 24, 203; *WA* 42, 360–62; *LW* 2, 139–42. In this passage, Luther asserts on the basis of Genesis 9:6 that "here God establishes government and gives it the sword."

[10] *WA* 31^I, 191–92; *LW* 13, 44.

[11] *WA* 11, 257; *LW* 45, 99; *WA* 31^I, 191; *LW* 13, 44.

[12] *WA* 41, 639. "For the hand that wields this sword and kills with it is not man's hand, but God's; and it is not man, but God, who hangs, tortures, beheads, kills, and fights. All these are God's works and judgments." *WA* 19, 626; *LW* 46, 96.

[13] *WA* 10^I, 2, 426; *WA* 10^{III}, 252; *WA* 30^I, 157; *BC*, 389; *WA* 31^I, 192; *LW* 13, 44; *WA* 41, 639.

[14] *WA* 20, 455; *WA* 32, 316; *LW* 21, 23; *WA* 37, 383.

wrath is at work.[15] This is the case even though officials are often "knaves and rascals" who misuse their office, act arbitrarily, and perpetrate injustice.[16] This certainly raises some questions which Luther must deal with. But such questions do not call into question his basic position on government: God wishes rulers to be treated as "high and glorious."[17] In all this, Luther feels that the re-discovery of the gospel, with its awareness of the difference between the two governments, has restored the honor to the "secular sword"—the state—which it lost after it was devalued by the medieval clerical system.[18]

In instituting government, God has given it a specific task. It is to protect the people committed to its care against exploitation by the brutal selfishness and violence of their fellowmen. The government does this by making laws and using its power to enforce them. It preserves law and order by using the power of the sword to punish the criminal who breaks them.[19] Without this power of the sword, laws are useless and justice is powerless. Law is a vital force only when government has power and uses it.[20]

Luther feels that no one's life would be secure if the government were to permit the great masses, the non-Christians, to have their way and get control of the situation.[21] "It is the function and honor of worldly government to make men out of wild beasts and to prevent men from becoming wild beasts."[22] Thus government preserves the precious gift of peace. "Where peace is, there is half a heaven."[23] Without peace, human life cannot exist. And it is

---

15 *WA* TR 3, no. 2911B.

16 *WA* 30[II], 521.

17 *WA* 31[I], 192; *LW* 13, 44.

18 *WA* 19, 625; *LW* 46, 95; *WA* 30[II], 110; *LW* 46, 163; *WA* 31[I], 190; *LW* 13, 42; *WA* 31[II], 600; *WA* 38, 112; *WA* 51, 246; *LW* 13, 202.

19 *WA* 6, 258; *LW* 44, 92; *WA* 30[II], 125, 131; *LW* 46, 180, 188.

20 *WA* 14, 665; *LW* 9, 161. For Luther, all the state's power and might are to be used to preserve law, order, and peace. Ernst Troeltsch says that Luther's teaching "glorifies power for its own sake, which in fallen humanity has become the essence of law; it therefore glorifies whatever authority may happen to be dominant at any given time." *The Social Teaching of the Christian Churches*, trans. Olive Wyon (New York: Harper Torchbook, 1960), 2:529. There is no trace of such an attitude in Luther, even though Troeltsch imputes it to Luther. The following is typical of Luther's position: "Even in temporal affairs force can be used only after the wrong has been legally condemned." *WA* 11, 269; *LW* 45, 114.

21 *WA* 12, 330.

22 *WA* 30[II], 555; *LW* 46, 237.

23 *WA* 31[I], 202; *LW* 13, 55. "Peace [is] the greatest of earthly goods, in which all other temporal goods are comprised." *WA* 30[II], 538; *LW* 46, 226.

precisely because God wills to create and preserve peace among
men that he has instituted governments. "For where there is
no government, or where government is not held in honor, there
can be no peace."[24] Therefore, we can no more dispense with
the office of government "than with life itself."[25]

However, the function of government, according to Luther, is
not limited simply to preserving peace and order. All authority is
based on paternal authority. And parenthood is the basic and
original pattern of earthly authority and responsibility; all other
authority and responsibility are derived from it. Thus the government also stands "in the place of parents" and derives its authority
to rule from the office of parenthood. For this reason we, like the
Scripture, still speak of our rulers as "fathers" or as "fathers of
our country." Thus rulers "act in the capacity of fathers and ought
to have fatherly hearts toward their people."[26] They also have the
responsibility to care for their people. In doing this, they fulfill
paternal functions.[27]

All this makes government "the most precious treasure and jewel
on earth."[28] Admittedly, secular government does not have the
rank and value of the lordship of Christ and the office of the
ministry—the relationship between these two is that between
eternal and temporal life. To the extent that eternal life stands
above this temporal life, the office of the ministry also ranks incomparably far above secular government. The latter can be described as only a shadow, while the former is comparable to the
body itself.[29] God still preserves the world only so that the gospel
can be preached.[30] The secular government exists, not least of all,
in order to provide a situation in which the gospel can be preached.

---

[24] *WA* 31ᴵ, 192; *LW* 13, 44–45.

[25] *WA* 30ᴵᴵ, 556; *LW* 46, 238.

[26] *WA* 30ᴵ, 152–53; *BC*, 384–85. "Out of the authority of parents all other
authority is derived and developed. . . . All who are called masters stand in the
place of parents and derive from them their power and authority to govern."
Ibid.

[27] "By the administration of just laws, he supports all his subjects as a father
supports his children." *WA* 31ᴵ, 205; *LW* 13, 58. This passage makes it clear
that the paternal office of the ruler is not a second office in addition to the
preservation of law and peace but rather that it manifests itself therein.

[28] *WA* 30ᴵ, 153; *BC*, 396.

[29] *WA* 30ᴵᴵ, 554; *LW* 46, 237; *WA* 51, 258; *LW* 13, 217.

[30] "Indeed, it is only because of the spiritual estate that the world stands and
abides at all; if it were not for this estate, the world would long since have
gone down to destruction." *WA* 30ᴵᴵ, 527; *LW* 46, 220.

After the office of the preaching of the gospel, however, secular government is the most useful and most necessary function on earth, the highest worship of God, the highest good—Luther cannot find words adequate to describe the high position and value of the secular government.[31] It is the *grace* of God that gives government to men. It is God's gift; no man can create it by himself.[32] Even though many princes misuse secular government and exploit it for their own selfish purposes without fearing God, it remains God's good gift in and of itself.[33]

Secular government is a gift of God's goodness. This remains true even when the political rulers fulfill their God-given task of making those who violate the law and break the peace feel the wrath of God (Romans 13:4). In relationship to evil, secular government is "a kingdom of wrath and severity." However, the secular government does not administer such severe punishment simply for the sake of punishment itself; it does so because punishment is, in this evil world, the indispensable means of protecting the righteous and preserving the very precious gifts of peace and security. It is, therefore, despite all appearances to the contrary, rightly viewed as a work of divine mercy. This is how Scripture teaches us to view it.[34]

The sword which the secular government bears "is not a foxtail with which to tickle people"[35]—this is Luther's paraphrase of Paul's assertion that the government "does not bear the sword in

---

31 *WA* 31[I], 198; *LW* 13, 51. "In a word, after the gospel or the ministry, there is on earth no better jewel, no greater treasure, no richer alms, no fairer endowment, no finer possession than a ruler who makes and preserves just laws." *WA* 31[I], 201; *LW* 13, 54.
32 "Temporal government is purely and solely God's gracious gift, which no man can establish or maintain by his own wisdom or strength." *WA* 31[I], 82; *LW* 14, 54.
33 *WA* 31[I], 88; *LW* 14, 56.
34 *WA* 18, 389; *LW* 46, 70. "Although the severity and wrath of the world's kingdom seems unmerciful, nevertheless, when we see it rightly, it is not the least of God's mercies." *WA* 18, 389; *LW* 46, 71. "The Scriptures, therefore, have good, clear eyes and see the temporal sword aright. They see that out of great mercy, it must be unmerciful, and from utter kindliness, it must exercise wrath and severity. . . . It looks upon the righteous with mercy, and so that they may not suffer, it guards, bites, stabs, cuts, hews, and slays, as God has commanded. . . . The merciless punishment of the wicked is not being carried out just to punish the wicked and make them atone for the evil desires that are in their blood, but to protect the righteous and to maintain peace and safety. And beyond all doubt these are precious works of mercy, love, and kindness." *WA* 18, 391; *LW* 46, 73.
35 *WA* 19, 628; *LW* 46, 99; *WA* 20, 456.

vain" (Romans 13:4). God has given secular government power over life and death; Luther proves this by referring to a number of pertinent passages of the Old and New Testaments.[36] Thus Luther has no difficulty in asserting that the state has the right and duty to impose the death penalty as well as to wage defensive war. In both activities, the government protects against violence all the people who are its subjects. In this sense Luther can even understand war as a work of Christian love. "Thus it is also a work of Christian love to protect and defend a whole community with the sword and not to let the people be abused."[37]

All this holds true of the government and of the state, whatever else must also be said about specific states and governments in any concrete historical situation. Luther's attitude toward the historical manifestations of the state was extremely sober and unromantic. The great states have ordinarily been established through violence and injustice.[38] This can be illustrated by Nimrod, whom Luther calls the "first prince on earth." Luther points out that Scripture calls him "a mighty hunter before the Lord" (Genesis 10:8–9), and thus directs our attention to the violence on which his kingdom was founded and maintained. He has become the model for all states.[39] Luther frequently quotes Augustine's statement that the great states are great robbers.[40] And Luther himself agrees that it is not possible, or at best very difficult, for a prince not to be part robber; furthermore, the greater the prince, the greater a robber he will be.[41]

Luther's opinion of the average prince is very sharp and bitter.[42] And yet in spite of all the evil that men use them for, government and the state do not cease to be God's institution and order, the

---

36 For example, Genesis 9:6; Exodus 21:14, 23–25; and Matthew 26:52. *WA* 11, 247 ff.; *LW* 45, 84 ff.; *WA* 24, 203.

37 *WA* 12, 330; *LW* 30, 76.

38 "An empire seldom has come into being except by robbery, force, and wrong; or, at the very least, it is often seized and possessed by wicked people without any justice." *WA* 30[II], 123; *LW* 46, 178.

39 *WA* 10[II], 233; *WA* 14, 210; *WA* 30[II], 123; *LW* 46, 178.

40 *WA* 30[II], 123; *LW* 46, 178. Augustine, *The City of God*, 4:4.

41 *WA* Br 2, 380; *LW* 48, 294.

42 *WA* 6, 73; *LW* 39, 19. "You must know that since the beginning of the world a wise prince is a mighty rare bird, and an upright prince even rarer. They are generally the biggest fools or the worst scoundrels on earth; therefore, one must constantly expect the worst from them and look for little good, especially in divine matters which concern the salvation of souls." *WA* 11, 267; *LW* 45, 113; *WA* 11, 265, 270; *LW* 45, 109, 116.

tools through which he works.[43] God is still able to rule and to
preserve peace and order even through a thoroughly bad government.[44] However a government may have come into existence and
however it may conduct its affairs, its all too human nature sustains
God's order. This must be seen in a twofold perspective. First,
God gives us a government in order to place a tool of responsible
service into our hands; this is true no matter how much human
injustice may have been at work in the history of a particular
government. Second, it is still God who entrusts this government
to us today through the hands of men: "It does not matter to God
where an empire comes from; his will is that it be governed."[45]
We must guard against confusing these two perspectives on the
state. We may neither derive a theory of the historical legitimacy
of a government from the fact that it is now ordained by God, nor
conceal the fact that it is now ordained by God behind the obvious
illegitimacy and revolutionary character of a government's history.
God works in history even in and through human injustice.[46]

Similarly, Luther's theological evaluation of government is in no
way restricted to a particular form of government. It is true that
he thinks primarily in terms of the German principalities and the
empire, and therefore conceives of the state primarily in patriarchal
terms. But Luther also asserts that the ancient republics and the
governments of the free cities of his time are governments instituted by God.[47]

THE CHRISTIAN'S ATTITUDE
TOWARD THE STATE

In recognizing the state as God's will and work, the Christian
has already made the basic decision about the state.

---

[43] "It is also true that in the second group, the temporal rulers, the majority
use that which has been entrusted to them for pride, vanity, pleasure, mischief,
and all manner of wantonness, without any awe or fear of God. Nevertheless,
government remains God's good and useful gift and is a blessing in itself."
WA 31[1], 88; *LW* 14, 56. "There are some who abuse this office. . . . But that
is the fault of the persons, not of the office." *WA* 19, 627; *LW* 46, 97.

[44] *WA* 44, 800; *LW* 8, 301.

[45] *WA* 6, 464; *LW* 44, 209.

[46] For a critique of Legitimism as it was represented, for example, by Prussian
conservatives in the nineteenth century, see my essay *Obrigkeit und Führertum*
(Gütersloh: Bertelsmann, 1936), pp. 29 ff. The Lutheran theological faculty at
the University of Erlangen represented the Lutheran position in that controversy
and rejected the Legitimism of Fr. J. Stahl.

[47] *WA* 40[III], 219.

The Christian ought to be particularly thankful to God for the gift of government, through which he graciously preserves human life.[48] Government is part of "daily bread" and ought also be "received with thanksgiving."[49] Along with thanks goes respect. In his Small Catechism, Luther places rulers—that is, government—alongside parents, and therewith includes them in the commandment to honor our parents.[50] We honor our parents by serving and obeying them; similarly, we show our respect for the government by obedience, by the subordination which Paul commands in Romans 13—as though we were obeying God himself.

According to 1 Peter 2:13, we obey the government for the sake of God, who has established and preserves government and uses it as a means for caring for human life.[51] Even though the Christian does not need the state for himself, he still honors and supports it for the sake of his neighbor who needs the state and benefits from it—that is, because he loves his neighbor. The Christian who becomes an anarchist and rejects the state acts contrary to love. Although he is basically defenseless and not concerned about protecting his own rights in matters affecting his personal welfare, the Christian affirms the juridical power of the state for the sake of the others: subjecting oneself to the state is also a "work of love."[52]

Even when the Christian has no need of the government, the government still needs him. "Although you do not need to have your enemy punished, your afflicted neighbor does. You should help him that he may have peace and that his enemy may be curbed, but this is not possible unless the governing authority is honored and feared." Therefore, the Christian "does all he can to assist the governing authority, that it may continue to function and be held in honor and fear."[53] Because the Christian honors and supports the government, he also does not become involved

---

48 *WA* 31I, 78; *LW* 14, 52.

49 *WA* 30I, 253; *BC*, 347.

50 "It is our duty to honor and magnify them as the most precious treasure and jewel on earth." *WA* 30I, 152–53; *BC*, 385–86.

51 *WA* 12, 328; *LW* 30, 74; *WA* 31I, 192; *LW* 13, 44. Christians who are captured and enslaved by the Turk ought to obey even him as their master, according to the admonitions to slaves by Paul and Peter. *WA* 30II, 192–93.

52 *WA* 11, 253–54; *LW* 45, 94.

53 *WA* 11, 253–54; *LW* 45, 94–95. (The first quotation above follows the second in Luther's text.)

in the complaints about the government which are so popular
among the people of this world, that is, he avoids the "secret
backbiting" and the evil slanders which people use to arouse
opposition to the government. Criticism of the government is the
concern of those whose office requires it of them. And it is their
task to express their criticism "openly and publicly." However,
God has forbidden those who are not called to exercise this office
to comment on these matters. Nothing is easier than discovering
the mistakes and errors of those who administer their office in full
view of the public. Such critics however need to be reminded of
the saying about the mote and the beam (Matthew 7:1–5). The
irresponsible and inappropriate nature of their comments is evident
when their concern to depose the government leads them to ignore
the merits of the governing authorities and permits them to speak
only of their mistakes.[54]

Since the Christian ought to obey the governing authorities
"only for the sake of God," that is, because God has instituted
their offices and they stand in the place of God, he ought to obey
whether the government acts justly or unjustly. If the goverment
acts unjustly toward me, exploits me, and takes away my property,
I must endure that patiently without resistance or seeking revenge,
"for God's sake." The fact that the government is misusing its
power does not concern me; the governing authorities will meet
their judge soon enough.[55]

The Christian also recognizes, honors, and supports the state by
being ready to accept an office in the government and thus take

---

[54] "The lords sit in high places, and everyone sees their sins and faults most
of all. And because men see them most of all, no sin is more prevalent than
speaking evil of lords. Everyone loves to do it, for in so doing he forgets his
own unrighteousness. Even though their lord had every virtue, and they could
discover in him only one vice as small as a mote, while they themselves were
full of vices as large as beams (Matthew 7:3–5), yet they see the mote in high
places before they see the virtues, and they do not see the beams in the depths
of all vices." *WA* 31^I, 196–97; *LW* 13, 50.

[55] "Thus we must endure the power of the prince. If the prince misuses his
authority, I ought not for that reason avoid him, take vengeance on him, or do
something to punish him. I must obey him for God's sake, for he stands in the
place of God. No matter how oppressive their taxes, I must obey them and
endure everything patiently for God's sake. Whether they act justly or unjustly
will all be worked out at its proper time. Therefore, if the government takes
away your possessions, your body, your life, and everything you have, then say:
'I am glad to give it to you because I recognize you as my lord. I am happy to
obey you. Whether or not you use the power God has given you for good or for
evil is a matter for you to be concerned about.'" *WA* 10^{I,1}, 426.

an active part in secular government. Christians ought to be moved
to do this simply by thankfulness for the benefits which God gives
through the government. Participating in government by accepting
a political office is "the finest thank-offering, the highest service
of God."[56] We serve God whenever we help to preserve any of
the orders, including secular government, through which he wishes
to preserve the world.[57] It is indeed true that a non-Christian can
administer the affairs of secular government as well as a Christian
can.[58] However, Christians think of themselves as being more
obligated to serve God in this way than others do.[59] Christians are
more obligated because they stand before God and know that
political service is service of God, and because they are less likely
to seek their own selfish goals in fulfilling their office and more
likely to devote themselves to serving people.[60]

Political office provides the opportunity for the noblest kind of
helping activity.[61] It also carries with it great dangers, however.
The greatest danger is that the ruler, instead of serving the people
as God intended in giving him his office, will use his subjects to
achieve his own selfish purposes and exploit his might and power
for personal gain.[62] Not only is natural, unredeemed humanity
itself corrupt, but also it corrupts and misuses all God's gifts and
offices.[63] This is particularly true of political offices. There is a far
greater temptation for those who have great power than for lower
officials.[64]

As a result, it is quite unusual for a prince both to be a Christian
and to administer his office according to God's intention.[65] His
station is far more dangerous than that of his subjects. And his
heart must be incomparably more secure and better defended.

---

56 *WA* 30[II], 561; *LW* 46, 241.
57 *WA* 30[II], 564; *LW* 46, 243.
58 *WA* 12, 331; *LW* 30, 76.
59 *WA* 11, 258; *LW* 45, 100.
60 *WA* 11, 274; *LW* 45, 122.
61 *WA* 31[I], 198–200; *LW* 13, 51–53.
62 *WA* 11, 261, 273; *LW* 45, 103, 120.
63 "The world is perverse and perverts all God's gifts and blessings. This is
what it does with these divine offices, too." *WA* 31[I], 206; *LW* 13, 59.
64 "In short, someone in a higher station, in all that he does, is always in
greater danger than someone in a lower station, and where the lower station has
to fear once, the higher station has to fear ten times over." *WA* 6, 70; *LW* 39,
16.
65 *WA* 11, 273; *LW* 45, 121; *WA* 19, 648; *LW* 46, 122.

"Dear friend, that takes a heart with the strength of nine hearts, and fidelity that goes beyond all fidelity."[66] On the basis of the Wisdom of Solomon 6:8–9, Luther asserts that God's judgment will fall heavily on the mighty.[67] The irresponsible government official will be accused and condemned by his very office when he stands in God's judgment.[68] Luther was thinking particularly of princes when he made this strong condemnation: "Cursed and condemned is every sort of life lived and sought for the benefit and good of self; cursed are all works not done in love."[69]

However, government officials can also act in love. They then resist the temptation to "dominate people by force" and seek the welfare of their subjects rather than their own benefit. In this sense, Luther calls the princes to follow Jesus by emptying themselves of their power. "In such manner should a prince in his heart empty himself of his power and authority, and take unto himself the needs of his subjects, dealing with them as though they were his own needs. For this is what Christ did to us [Philippians 2:7]; and these are the proper works of Christian love."[70] The prince ought to give up his power and authority "in his heart." This does not mean that he should actually abandon them and thus cease to be the prince, the one who bears power. However, he should administer this power as a means of serving his subjects instead of using it to do anything he wants to for his own benefit.[71] His power is given him to provide the base for responsible action, not to fulfill his own selfish desires.

Political power is constantly tempted. It easily falls into the temptation of exceeding the limits which God has set for it. Establishing itself as an absolute, it assumes the place of God and says: "We will be our own God."[72] More will be said about this

---

66 *WA* 31[I], 205; *LW* 13, 58.

67 *WA* 6, 70; *LW* 39, 16.

68 "What an awful responsibility it is to rule and sit in high places. . . . His very authority will condemn him." *WA* 6, 467; *LW* 44, 215.

69 *WA* 11, 272; *LW* 45, 118.

70 *WA* 11, 273; *LW* 45, 120.

71 "He must give consideration and attention to his subjects, and really devote himself to it. This he does when he directs his every thought to making himself useful and beneficial to them; when instead of thinking, 'the land and people belong to me; I will do what best pleases me,' he thinks rather, 'I belong to the land and the people; I shall do what is useful and good for them. My concern will be not how to lord it over them and dominate them, but how to protect and maintain them in peace and plenty.'" *WA* 11, 273; *LW* 45, 120.

72 *WA* 47, 564.

in connection with our discussion of the relationship between state and church. It ought not to be forgotten, however, that Luther feels that ecclesiastical authorities are in danger of committing the same sin as secular authorities. Both must constantly be reminded of humility.[73]

In view of all this, it is very important for the prosperity of a state that the ruling prince be a Christian, to whom we can appeal on the basis of his faith. "Would to God they were all Christians, or that no one could be a prince unless he were a Christian!"[74] Luther clearly recognized that good government can be found even outside Christendom—for example, among the Turks: "We see very well that God distributes secular dominions or kingdoms among the godless in the grandest and most wonderful way."[75] And he explicitly declared that it is not necessary to have a Christian as head of state in order to have a proper form of government.[76] For building a state, making laws, and preserving order in the community are matters subject to human reason, and we do not need the Holy Spirit to accomplish them. Reason has been given to all men. And political reason can be found outside Christianity as well as within it. Indeed, Luther concludes that heathen states are often better in terms of both their laws and their rulers than those that have been established among the people of God.[77]

And yet Luther wishes that all rulers were Christians. What do non-Christians lack? What advantage do Christian princes have over them? In his *Commentary on Psalm 127* Luther answers such questions by comparing the doctrine of the state in the world of classical antiquity to the biblical view of the state and politics. He asserts that a difference in the *theory* of the state corresponds to a decisive difference in the *administration* of the state.[78] The doctrine of the state in classical antiquity, as in any natural or philosophical understanding of the state, views the state in terms of a purely immanent and humanistic definition of its source and

---

[73] *WA* 42, 382; *LW* 2, 171. See below, pp. 150–51.

[74] Luther makes this statement with particular reference to the conduct of the war against the Turks. *WA* 30[II], 112; *LW* 46, 166. However, he also makes the same statement more generally: "It would even be fine and fitting if all princes were good, true Christians." *WA* 11, 257; *LW* 45, 100.

[75] *WA* 51, 238; *LW* 13, 193.

[76] *WA* 27, 418; *WA* 6, 318; *LW* 39, 97; *WA* 12, 331; *LW* 30, 76.

[77] *WA* 40[III], 204; *WA* 51, 242; *LW* 13, 198.

[78] *WA* 40[III], 202 ff.

124   *The Ethics of Martin Luther*

goal. Reason is therefore the best guide for ruling a political community insofar as it is concerned with technical matters of administration and establishing a code of laws. However, reason of itself does not know what the true source and the real goal of the state are; for as long as reason is without faith it does not know about God.[79] Faith sees the state as God's work: "Unless the Lord builds the house, those who build it labor in vain" (Psalms 127:1). And faith knows and reflects on the fact that God uses men with their reason only as tools of his own activity in history. Faith thus remembers that the prosperity of the state does not lie in the hands of men but that everything depends on God's blessing. Whether a politician trusts entirely in himself and in his own reason and depends on his own works without reference to God, or whether he stands under God is of decisive significance for the spirit of a state and for the ethos of its administration—even though the technique of administration is unchanged.[80]

Faith in God thus preserved the statesman from both being proud and thinking that his success is so much his own work that he neither thanks the giver of all good gifts nor requests his blessing. It also saves him from the despair that comes when success cannot be achieved. Such pride and despair are part of every man's inheritance since the fall into sin.[81] Thus faith is of great significance for political activity. Furthermore, the Christian who holds a political office is bound by his Lord and is really motivated to devote his power and his person to serve the welfare of the people entrusted to his care. It is therefore desirable that a ruler be a Christian.[82]

THE LIMITS OF THE AUTHORITY OF GOVERNMENT AND OF OBEDIENCE

Definite limits have been placed on the authority of government. Government is concerned with regulating this physical, temporal life but not with men's conscience and soul. Its authority to issue orders extends only over bodies and property. The soul belongs to

---

[79] *WA* 40[III], 202. See *Theology*, 10.
[80] *WA* 40[III], 203, 209–10, 219.
[81] *WA* 40[III], 223.
[82] "You have no right to assume that somebody else will take as deep an interest in you and your land as you do yourself, unless he be a good Christian filled with the Spirit. The natural man will not." *WA* 11, 274; *LW* 45, 122.

God alone, and only God gives it orders.[83] "God cannot and will
not permit anyone but himself to rule over the soul. Therefore,
where the temporal authority presumes to prescribe laws for the
soul, it encroaches upon God's government and only misleads souls
and destroys them." By so doing, the secular government leads the
soul into hypocrisy.[84] In matters of faith, therefore, the state must
not permit any compulsion or maintain a reign of terror. Luther
thus asserts the right of freedom of faith and of conscience—not
only for Christians who have the true faith but also for heretics.[85]
True faith and heresy are both matters of the conscience and of
the spirit, and the government may not deal with them by using
force.

God himself works faith in the heart, and we neither can nor
may try to compel someone else to believe.[86] This is also why we
cannot overcome and eliminate heresy by force. For it too is a
spiritual matter. Against heresy, only the word of God is powerful.[87] Using force only increases the inner strength of the persecuted faith or the heresy—and betrays the inner weakness of one's
own position. Using force implies that one is not able to deal with
opponents on the basis of God's word but only by violence.[88]

All this, however, clearly presupposes that the other faith or
the heresy does not openly advocate anarchy and radical communism, and thus undermine the basic structures and authority of
government as such. It also presupposes that no one publicly opposes the common Christian teaching. When either of these occurs,
the state's toleration has reached its limit and the authorities must
intervene.[89] Luther cites Romans 13 as evidence that the govern-

---

[83] *WA* 29, 603.

[84] *WA* 11, 262, 264; *LW* 45, 105, 108.

[85] "No ruler ought to prevent anyone from teaching or believing what he
pleases, whether it is the gospel or lies. It is enough if he prevents the teaching
of sedition and rebellion." *WA* 18, 298–99; *LW* 46, 22.

[86] "For faith is a free act, to which no one can be forced. Indeed, it is a work
of God in the spirit, not something which outward authority should compel or
create." *WA* 11, 264; *LW* 45, 108.

[87] *WA* 11, 268, 270; *LW* 45, 114, 117; *WA* 17[II], 125.

[88] *WA* 11, 268; *LW* 45, 114.

[89] *WA* 18, 299; *LW* 46, 22. "Some heretics are seditious and teach openly
that no rulers are to be tolerated. . . . They are not only heretics but also rebels,
who are attacking the rulers and their government, just as a thief attacks another's goods, a murderer another's body, and an adulterer another's wife; and
this is not to be tolerated." Those who "teach doctrines contradicting an article
of faith clearly grounded in Scripture and believed throughout the world by all

ment should intervene against public propaganda for anarchism and communism. He also thinks the government should intervene against a public attack on the scriptural and common Christian articles of faith because such a public attack is blasphemy, and the government ought to punish blasphemy. However, Luther still preserves freedom of faith and of conscience. Only public teaching against the Christian faith is forbidden and threatened with punishment.[90] Luther's position is also influenced by the consideration that is is not good to have contradictory doctrines proclaimed simultaneously. When that is done, division and tensions are created even in secular life.[91] There is, of course, a great difference between Luther's ideas and our understanding of our situation in a pluralistic society.

The limits placed on the government's authority and use of force also indicate the limits of obedience for subjects. And Luther indicates the limits of obedience sharply and clearly in describing the subject's duty to obey the government as though he were obeying God himself. When the government exceeds the limits of its authority and seeks to compel us to act contrary to God and his word—for example, to deny or to oppose the truth of the gospel—then Luther asserts on the basis of Acts 5:29 that our duty to obey has come to an end.[92] Christians are obligated to obey the government only in terms of the government's assignment to care for this physical life, not in matters relating to the word of God and of faith. A government which demands obedience in these matters has therewith ceased to be a government established by God.[93]

Christendom . . . are not mere heretics but open blasphemers." *WA* 31[I], 207–8; *LW* 13, 61.

[90] "By this procedure no one is compelled to believe, for he can still believe what he will; but he is forbidden to teach and to blaspheme. For by so doing he would take from God and the Christians their doctrine and word, and he would do them this injury under their own protection and by means of the things all have in common. Let him go someplace where there are no Christians." *WA* 31[I], 208; *LW* 13, 62.

[91] *WA* 31[I], 209; *LW* 13, 62–63.

[92] *WA* 6, 265; *LW* 44, 100; *WA* 11, 266; *LW* 45, 111.

[93] "We should obey God more than men. Thus God has not given any ruler the kind of authority over his subjects that authorizes him to fight and struggle against God and his word. And if any ruler tries to do that, no subject is obligated to obey him in any way. Indeed, he then no longer has any authority at all. For subjects are only obligated to serve their government as best they can with their bodies so that peace may be preserved upon earth and this earthly life may be lived in security and order." *WA* 30[II], 197.

For Luther, God's word is the basis of all authority and all obedience in the orders of this life. However, God's word also sets limits for both authority and obedience. If obeying any earthly authorities— whether father or mother, secular government, or the church—involves us in disobeying God, we do the devil's work. Luther thus also indicates the limits of our duty to obey the fourth commandment.[94]

This also means that oaths to obey human authorities are binding only if nothing has been promised that is "contrary to God, for one can promise nothing against God." This limitation holds whether explicitly stated in the oath or not. All vows and oaths of obedience are limited by the promise made to God in our baptism. "And if my later vows deviate a hairbreadth from my first promise, then I shall trample them underfoot in order not to deny my God or despise his grace."[95] Vows and oaths are not all equally binding. They are not valid and binding in and of themselves, or because of their form. Their validity is determined by their content: Can they be fulfilled without disobeying God?

Luther specifically applied this principle to soldiers. In a case where a prince has begun an obviously unjust war, that is, a war that is not defensive, Luther calls on the soldiers to refuse to obey their prince, desert their stations, and save their souls. No one must—and indeed no one may—keep his oath of obedience when he thereby falls into the danger of being guilty and condemned by God. Whoever fights to achieve an obviously evil goal shares in the guilt.[96] But if the subjects are uncertain as to whether or not their prince's cause is just or unjust, then they ought follow "the way of love," seek the welfare of their prince, and obey him without scruples—being certain that their souls are not in danger.[97]

---

[94] "Let all obedience to government, father and mother, and even the church that is disobedience of God be cursed to the depth of hell. . . . I do not recognize the authority of father, mother, friends, government, or the Christian Church, if they forbid me to hear God's word. In that case, the fourth commandment is set aside and I have no duty to obey. Christ himself declares: they are no longer father and mother, government, or Christian Church. For obedience to God . . . takes precedence over all other obedience." *WA* 28, 24; *WA* 43, 507; *LW* 5, 113–14.

[95] *WA* 31^I, 253; *LW* 14, 35.

[96] *WA* 6, 265; *LW* 44, 100; *WA* 11, 277; *LW* 45, 125; *WA* 19, 656; *LW* 46, 130; *WA* Br 10, 36.

[97] *WA* 11, 277; *LW* 45, 125; *WA* 19, 657; *LW* 46, 131.

Although Luther says that a government which persecutes the gospel is no longer exercising valid authority and its subjects need not obey it,[98] he does not mean to say that such a government no longer has any kind of authority at all. Rather, such a government is no longer a governing authority in its battle against God's word and we ought not obey it in *this* battle. We have very clear evidence for Luther's position on this point. A draft of the regulations (*Kirchenordnung*) for the church in Brandenburg and Nürnberg of 1532 asserts the following, on the basis of Romans 13:3, 4: "Any government that uses its power in such a way that someone must be afraid because he is doing what is right, is no longer a government in God's sight." When asked for their opinion of this draft, Luther and the other theologians at the University of Wittenberg replied that although the statement could be properly interpreted, they recommended omitting it in view of the possibility of misunderstanding. "Evil authority remains an authority, as every rational man knows; for if God no longer regarded evil authorities as valid authorities, all subjects would be absolved of their duty."[99] Even though a government acts unjustly and protects injustice, it does not totally abrogate its character and authority as a government instituted by God. And the fact that a Christian must sometimes refuse to obey a specific order does not totally absolve him of his obligation to obey.

These are Luther's basic ideas, and he maintained them throughout his life. He did not abandon them even when confronted by the difficult situation of the evangelical princes and territories after the Diets of Speyer in 1529 and Augsburg in 1530. At that time the evangelicals were considering whether they could offer armed resistance against the oppressive use of force by the emperor. Luther said they had no right to do so. According to Scripture, he concluded, there are no circumstances under which a Christian may rebel against his government even when it acts unjustly: "Rather, a Christian ought to endure oppression and injustice, especially at the hands of his government." The fact that the emperor acts unjustly does not abrogate his imperial authority or absolve his subjects of their duty to obey, as long as the empire and the imperial

[98] See above, p. 126.
[99] *WA* Br 6, 341.

electors treat him as their emperor and do not depose him. Emperors and princes frequently break God's commandments but they remain emperors and princes. Their "sin does not put an end to government and the obedience due it." And resisting the emperor with armed force would be rebellion.[100]

Nevertheless, Luther does more than advice the patient endurance of suffering.[101] The opinion of 1529 just referred to demonstrates this. There Luther asserts that the imperial electors not only elect the emperor but can also depose an emperor who misuses his power. During the following years Luther developed this position more fully. The lawyers pointed out that imperial law and the constitution of the empire itself permitted the use of force in resisting an obviously unjust use of power. Luther took this into account but did not reach any conclusion as to whether this juridical approach was valid, since as a theologian he was neither competent nor responsible in this area. Luther recognized that a prince when acting as a prince is a "political person," that is, he does not act in his own behalf but fulfills his official duty of protecting his subjects. A prince is therefore not limited simply by the commandment of the Sermon on the Mount, which forbids every Christian to resist evil. As a result, Luther no longer proposed to exercise a definitive theological veto in case the princes decided, on the basis of the legal reasoning referred to above, to resist the emperor with force. He made them responsible for their own decision and left it up to their judgment and consciences. "I will let them do it, I am not responsible." At the same time, however, Luther leaves no doubt that the true Christian attitude would be to depend on God's assistance and to avoid resistance as unnecessary. This was his position in 1531.[102]

In an opinion issued in 1539 (written by Melanchthon but also signed by Luther) the Reformers deal with the question of resistance to the emperor on the basis of common and natural law. According to natural law, the obvious use of violence by one in

---

[100] *WA* Br 5, 259–60; *S-J* 2, 519–22.

[101] Johannes Heckel, *Lex charitatis. Eine juristische Untersuchung über das Recht in der Theologie Martin Luthers* (Munich: Verlag der Bayerischen Akademie der Wissenschaften, 1953), pp. 184 ff. Additional references are given there.

[102] *WA* Br 6, 16–17. See also Luther's *Warning to His Dear German People* (1531), *WA* 30[III], 291 ff.; *LW* 47, 30 ff.

authority abrogates all the subject's obligations to him. It is the business of a father and of a government to protect against violence the people entrusted to them—whether the violent man is a private individual or the emperor. And if the emperor wants to start a war for reasons of faith, he does not act in his office as emperor but rather as a tool of the pope. He thus acts contrary to his imperial duties. Under those circumstances resistance is just.[103] And yet, as Karl Holl says, Luther "never reached the point of advocating resistance enthusiastically and with full inner conviction."[104] He encouraged the princes to participate in the wars against the Turks but issued no similar statements encouraging the evangelical princes and cities to resist the emperor.

Luther knew that the Christian who refuses to obey the government when it orders him to transgress God's commandment or to deny the truth of the gospel will get into trouble. Under some circumstances he may even be required to make very great sacrifices. For the government will not tolerate such disobedience and will punish it. The Christian must then be prepared to make any sacrifice. "In such cases we should indeed give up our property and honor, our life and limb, so that God's commandments remain."[105] The Christian is forbidden to resist his government actively. "Outrage is not to be resisted but endured." The only alternative is to emigrate.[106]

Except in those cases where our duty to obey God prevents us from obeying the government, Christians should even obey an evil and tyrannical government which corrupts the country and the people. We are to obey and endure it as a plague sent to us by God—and we sinners always deserve it.[107] The preachers and all who are called to do so must address the conscience of the governing officials and admonish them to stop administering justice arbitrarily for their own profit and to begin administering the laws in the service of their subjects. When such exhortations do

---

[103] Ernst Ludwig Enders et al., *Dr. Martin Luthers Briefwechsel* (Leipzig: Verein für Reformationsgeschichte, 1910), 12:78–80 (no. 2678 is not in *WA Br*).
[104] *GA* 1, 269.
[105] *WA* 6, 265; *LW* 44, 100; *WA* 11, 267; *LW* 45, 112.
[106] *WA* 11, 267; *LW* 45, 112; *WA* 18, 322; *LW* 46, 36; *WA* 19, 633 ff.; *LW* 46, 103 ff.
[107] *WA* 19, 637; *LW* 46, 109.

no good, however, the people must endure whatever the government does. "For the governing authority must not be resisted by
force, but only by confession of the truth. If it is influenced by
this, well and good; if not, you are excused; you suffer wrong for
God's sake."[108] The attempt of the subjects to act in their own
behalf, as happened in the Peasants' War, is explicitly rejected as
unchristian and a sin against God's commandment. It is equally
contrary to nature for a subject to revolt against his government
as for a servant to revolt against his master, a maid against her
mistress, children against their parents, or students against their
teacher.[109] Even if the officials are marvels of incompetence, and
in spite of all distortion of their office, they continue to exercise
divine authority. Their subjects acknowledge this divine authority
by not resisting, by enduring this distortion. However, they do this
not by abandoning the truth in the face of injustice but by freely
confessing the truth.[110]

The government has been directly established by God and is
directly responsible to God. Therefore, God is its only judge.[111]
Revolution and rebellion against the political authority thus constitute an encroachment on God's juridical function.[112] God will
punish those officials who use their authority to tyrannize their
people. But their subjects do not have the right to judge and to
punish such officials; instead, they ought to obey and endure them.
God uses one scoundrel to punish another. For example, he used
the rebellious peasants to punish the princes and the lords. The
peasants were instruments of God's wrath against the princes and
lords; at the same time, however, they remained rebels who committed a grave sin against God. For God uses human sin for his
own purposes in history, but it remains sin which both deserves
and results in punishment.[113] Luther threatens the princes by saying that the people are going to revolt, but at the same time he
forbids the people to do so. God brings about revolutions through
earthly forces.[114] We ought not try to bring them about. God will

108 *WA* 11, 277; *LW* 45, 124–25.
109 *WA* 19, 641; *LW* 46, 114.
110 *WA* 28, 283.
111 *WA* 31^I, 192–93; *LW* 13, 45; *WA* 39^{II}, 41.
112 *WA* 19, 640–41; *LW* 46, 112–13; *WA* 39^{II}, 41.
113 *WA* 19, 634, 636, 643–44, 652; *LW* 46, 104–5, 107, 115–16, 125–26.
114 *WA* 31^I, 214; *LW* 13, 68; *WA* 51, 228; *LW* 13, 182.

punish the officials of government who forget their duties, but we do not have the right to take the initiative. The theological perspective on history goes beyond the ethical perspective but does not abrogate it.

Luther does not grant the right to rebel even when the prince breaks laws he has sworn to uphold.[115] He does not even exclude the war which the Swiss waged to gain their freedom. Seen in the long perspective, all revolutions have cost heavily and brought their own vengeance. This makes it possible for us to see that God does not will them. Revolutionaries dream that they are going to improve the world, but men who overthrow the government succeed only in changing the government, not in improving it. Improvement comes about only through the will and action of God himself.[116]

Luther's position consistently reflects his deep theological pessimism about this world and its history. This world is the devil's cabaret. God has subjected it to the lordship of the devil. Under these circumstances we can expect nothing except disaster—for example, the tyranny of rulers. A Christian ought not to be amazed by this but rather should marvel that through the goodness and mercy of God the situation is still as good as it is.[117]

LAW AND THE ADMINISTRATION OF JUSTICE[118]

"Who can doubt that law is a good thing and a gift of God?"[119] Law is a good thing because no country and no community can survive without it.[120] It is God's gift because God has implanted it

---

115 *WA* 19, 640; *LW* 46, 113; *WA* Br 5, 258; *S-J* 2, 519–20.

116 *WA* 19, 635, 639; *LW* 46, 106–7, 112.

117 "God has thrown us into the world, under the power of the devil. As a result, we have no paradise here. Rather, at any time we can expect all kinds of misfortune to body, wife, child, property, and honor. And if there is one hour in which there are less than ten disasters or an hour in which we can even survive, we ought to say, 'How good God is to me! He has not sent every disaster to me in this one hour.' " *WA* 19, 644; *LW* 46, 117.

118 The most important passages in Luther's writings dealing with this theme have been collected by Hermann Wolfgang Beyer, *Luther und das Recht. Gottes Gebot, Naturrecht, Volksgesetz im Denken Luthers* (Munich: Chr. Kaiser, 1935) and Karl Holl, *GA* 1, pp. 269 ff. See also Hermann Wolfgang Beyer, "Glaube und Recht im Denken Luthers," *Luther-Jahrbuch* 17 (1935): 56–86.

119 *WA* 7, 581; *LW* 21, 335.

120 *WA* 31I, 200; *LW* 13, 53–54.

into human reason through his act of creation. Thus law is simultaneously human and divine, for it both is contained in human reason and at the same time expresses divine wisdom. Luther is speaking here of the natural law. Natural law was given and recognized long before there were lawyers. We must distinguish natural law from written or positive laws. The formulation of natural law and its codification in the form of positive laws is the business of lawyers and legislators.[121] Men do this work by using the reason which God has given them. "Secular or imperial law is nothing else than what human reason has built on, concluded from, and spun out of natural law."[122] The form of such positive laws has varied according to the particular country and time. Positive law is thus historically conditioned and therefore also subject to change in the course of history.[123]

Germany was at that time governed by the recently introduced Roman law of the empire. At first, Luther rejected the proposal to adopt the Roman law.[124] Later he changed his position on this point.[125] After this change Luther spoke very highly of the Roman law, as he did of the laws of classical antiquity in general. "Whoever wants to learn and become wise in secular government, let him read the heathen books and writings. They have truly painted it and portrayed it quite beautifully and generously, with both verses and pictures, with teachings and examples; and they became the source for the ancient imperial laws."[126] But Luther continued to criticize individual provisions of the ancient Roman laws, as well as of the ancient German laws and laws that were binding during his own lifetime.[127]

In order to administer justice it is absolutely necessary to study traditional legal precedents and to refer to the law books. For the

121 *WA* 40III, 221–22; *WA* TR 4, no. 3911; *LW* 54, 293.

122 *WA* TR 6, no. 7013.

123 *WA* 30III, 225; *LW* 46, 291; *WA* TR 1, no. 349; *WA* TR 4, no. 4733.

124 He does so, for example in *To the Christian Nobility of the German Nation concerning the Reform of the Christian State* (1520) *WA* 6, 459–60; *LW* 44, 203–4.

125 "Since the government in our German land is supposed to be guided by the imperial law of Rome, and this law is our government's wisdom and reason, given it by God. . . ." *WA* 30II, 557; *LW* 46, 239; *WA* 51, 242; *LW* 13, 198.

126 *WA* 51, 242; *LW* 13, 199.

127 *WA* 14, 591; cf. *LW* 9, 57; *WA* 14, 714; *LW* 9, 241; *WA* 12, 243; *LW* 45, 157; *WA* 16, 537, 542. See Karl Holl, *GA* 1, 272.

gift of arriving at a just decision by oneself and without help is
very rare. It is therefore not permissible for anyone who is responsible for the administration of justice simply to rely upon his
reason, as if reason had natural law at its disposal. Only a very
few are able to rely on their inherent knowledge of natural law.
So it is ordinarily advisable to administer justice "by the book."[128]
At the same time, Luther demands that judges not be mere
slaves of the written law and apply it rigidly. The judge is called
to make his own personal decision. "For judges are living laws or
the soul of the law." And God established judges before he gave
written laws.[129] That says it well enough. There are always special
cases that are not foreseen in the necessarily general rules and in
which a just decision cannot be made by a strict application of
these rules.[130] In such cases the judge must be free to decide the
case on the basis of reason, that is, on the basis of knowledge of
natural law, whose content is love. That is the ultimate authority
of all law books. One may not make this law "a captive of
letters."[131] "Therefore, a prince must have the law as firmly in
hand as the sword, and determine in his own mind when and
where the law is to be applied strictly or with moderation, so that
law may prevail at all times and in all cases, and reason may be

---

128 "Men must learn and know the law and wisdom of our worldly government. It is a fine thing, to be sure, if an emperor, prince, or lord is by nature so
wise and able that he can instinctively hit upon what is right." *WA* 30[II], 558;
LW 46, 239; *WA* 51, 212, 242; *LW* 13, 161, 199.
129 *WA* 14, 554; *LW* 9, 20. "But what does it mean to be a good magistrate
or a good prince? I answer: he is the living law. If he wishes to act as a dead
law and only be guided by that which is written in the book, he is often a bad
ruler." *WA* TR 6, no. 7031.
130 *WA* 11, 272; *LW* 45, 118–19; *WA* 19, 630–32; *LW* 46, 100–2.
131 *WA* 11, 272; *LW* 45, 119. One should administer justice in such a way
"that love and natural law may always prevail. For when you judge according
to love you will easily decide and adjust matters without any law books. . . .
A good and just decision must not and cannot be pronounced out of books,
but must come from a free mind, as though there were no books. Such a free
decision is given, however, by love and by natural law, with which all reason
is filled." In discussing a correct verdict, Luther says: "It sprang from untram-
meled reason above the law in all the books, and is so excellent that everyone
must approve it and find the justice of it written in his own heart. . . . Therefore, we should keep written laws subject to reason, from which they originally
welled forth as from the spring of justice. We should not make the spring
dependent on its rivulets, or make reason a captive of letters." *WA* 11, 279–80;
LW 45, 128–29. "Whatever is done with nature's power succeeds very smoothly
without any law; in fact, it overrides all the laws." Luther goes on to contrast
natural law and written law by characterizing them as "healthy" law and "sick"
law. *WA* 51, 214; *LW* 13, 164.

the highest law and the master of all administration of law."[132]
Finally, Luther makes the same demands upon the administration
of justice that he does upon the ethical life: in both, Luther always
leaves a person free to reach his own decision.

This freedom from law books and from the letter of the law
and this flexibility in the administration of justice are to be
demonstrated in terms of equity, mildness, and love.[133] Luther
here uses the traditional Aristotelian concept of *epieikia* (equity).[134] Luther repeatedly quotes the rule that "the strictest law is
the greatest injustice." He also cites Ecclesiastes 7:16: "Be not
righteous overmuch."[135] A judge acts wisely when, as often as
possible, he does not render a decision strictly according to the
law, but rather moderates his decision in terms of what is just and
equitable.[136] The law must "leave room for love."[137] For love is
the highest authority and stands above both natural and positive
law. And justice administered according to the law without love
becomes "a plague and disaster" for men: "the greatest calamity,
the greatest injustice, and the deepest misery imaginable on this
earth."[138] However, God gave his commandments in order to help
men, not to injure them.[139] Thus whoever administers justice must
consider whether the law and its strict application to a particular
person will help or injure him. For this reason Luther advises
punishing too little rather than too much.[140] All this, Luther feels,
is not primarily a Christian principle; it is universally valid on the

132 *WA* 11, 272; *LW* 45, 119; *WA* 14, 555; *LW* 9, 20. In this quotation
(as in *WA* 27, 362) Luther speaks not only of the prince but also of the
father of the household.
133 "Justice in this case must correct the law." *WA* 19, 631; *LW* 46, 102;
WA 37, 157.
134 *WA* 6, 166; *LW* 39, 44; *WA* 7, 514; *WA* 19, 632; *LW* 46, 101; *WA*
27, 363; *WA* TR 1, no. 315; *LW* 54, 43–44; *WA* TR 6, no. 7031.
135 For example, *WA* 17[II], 92; *WA* 19, 630; *LW* 46, 100.
136 *WA* 10[III], 255. "Judges and lords must be wise and pious in this matter
and mete out reasonable justice, and let the law take its course, or set it aside,
accordingly." *WA* 19, 632; *LW* 46, 102.
137 "Thus people must live and act according to the law whenever they can
and it is good for them to do so. On the other hand, where it would be harmful
for them to do so, the law must be flexible enough to give; and the ruler must
be wise enough to leave room for love and to set aside specific works and the
laws which demand them." *WA* 17[II], 96.
138 *WA* 17[II], 91–92. In this context Luther comments on Jesus' decisions in
Matthew 12:3–4 and Mark 2:25–26: "Love was empress over the law and
subdued it. . . . Love is the mistress of all laws." *WA* 17[II], 91–92.
139 *WA* 10[III], 256.
140 *WA* 11, 261; *LW* 45, 104.

basis of natural law and applies to all earthly administration of justice.

Equity must keep the law and justice under control. Beyond this, however, mercy is needed side by side with law and justice. Luther lays this on the hearts of the princes and lords. Justice and mercy must be combined in the proper proportions. "If there is only mercy . . . all discipline and honor will come to an end. On the other hand, if there is only anger and punishment or too much of it, then tyranny will result, and the pious will be breathless in their daily fear and anxiety." But Luther also says that "too much mercy is better than too much punishment." For if mercy is misused, it can be withdrawn or reduced. Punishment, however, is irrevocable, especially corporal or capital punishment.[141]

The government's authority to punish includes the right to inflict capital punishment. Luther has no doubt that this is part of the office of government. For this is the office of the "sword," as Paul says in Romans 13:4. Unlike Thomas Aquinas—and the majority of Catholic theologians who have adopted his position—Luther does not derive capital punishment from natural law or sociological considerations but from the Bible. Like government itself, capital punishment is based on God's explicit command. Luther cites Genesis 9:6: "Whoever sheds the blood of man, by man shall his blood be shed." This statement is confirmed by Exodus 21:14 and by Christ's statement to Peter in Matthew 26: 52: "All who take the sword will perish by the sword."[142] In Genesis 9:6, God places the sword in man's hand and thereby institutes law and government. Originally, in the time before the flood, God had reserved judgment on crimes to himself. Now, however, God has said that the blood of the murderer is to be shed through men. He thereby gives government a share in his authority over life and death.[143]

---

[141] *WA* 51, 205–6; *LW* 13, 152–53.
[142] *WA* 11, 248; *LW* 45, 86.
[143] "Here, however, God shares his power with man and grants him power over life and death among men, provided that the person is guilty of shedding blood. Whoever does not have the right to kill human beings and yet kills a human being, him God makes liable not only to his [God's] own judgment but also to the human sword. Therefore if such a person is killed, even though he is killed by the human sword, he is nevertheless correctly said to have been killed by God. . . . Here we have the source from which stem all civil law and the law of nations." *WA* 42, 360; *LW* 2, 140; *WA* 24, 203; *WA* 37, 383.

When the government executes a man in obedience to God's commandment, then it is really God himself who puts the murderer to death by the hand of man. The executioner administers God's wrath in God's name, and his sword is the sword of God himself. Execution "preaches," that is, it proclaims God's wrath over evil.[144] The fifth commandment, which forbids us to kill, and Jesus' statements in the Sermon on the Mount, which forbid retribution and revenge, do not cause any more difficulties for Luther at this point than they do for Paul. We must, in accordance with the doctrine of the two governments, distinguish between the things that we do privately to one another in our own behalf and our official acts, which we carry out as God's representatives.[145]

WAR [146]

Luther felt that the responsibilities which God has given to government may under certain circumstances require it to wage war. Luther's affirmation of this possibility is based on government's responsibility to protect and defend its subjects against injustice and violence. Sometimes the government cannot do that without using force, just as it cannot protect its citizens within its own borders without sometimes using force.[147] Luther thus sees war as the extension of government's authority to punish outside its borders for the purpose of preserving peace against aggression and breaking the peace.[148] Understood in this way, even waging war is a work of love, and a soldier can be "blessed," that is, he can be and remain a Christian.[149]

Implicit in what Luther says is that he recognizes only a defensive war which is forced upon us by an aggressor. War is right

---

[144] *WA* 37, 383, 385.

[145] *WA* 30¹, 157; *BC*, 389.

[146] *Temporal Authority: To What Extent It Should Be Obeyed, WA* 11, 276–80; LW 45, 123–29. *Whether Soldiers, Too, Can be Saved* (1526), *WA* 19, 623–62; *LW* 46, 93–137. *On War against the Turk* (1529), *WA* 30ᴵᴵ, 107–48; *LW* 46, 161–205. *Sermon on War against the Turks* (1529), *WA* 30ᴵᴵ, 160–97.

[147] "Thus it is also a work of Christian love to protect and defend a whole community with the sword and not let the people be abused." *WA* 12, 330; *LW* 30, 76; *WA* 19, 648; *LW* 46, 121.

[148] "What else is war but the punishment of wrong and evil? Why does anyone go to war except because he desires peace and obedience?" *WA* 19, 625; *LW* 46, 95; *WA* 19, 628; *LW* 46, 98–99.

[149] *WA* 19, 625–26; *LW* 46, 95–96.

only when it is "our only miserable way of defending ourselves" and has been forced upon us.[150] Luther knows that most wars are waged for quite different reasons: selfish motives of princes and lords, lust for the property and possessions of others, desire for glory, the feeling that our honor has been insulted, wrath, and the desire for revenge.[151] However, a Christian prince is forbidden to wage war for such reasons. The one and only purpose of a war must be to protect his subjects against attack. In this sense the decision to go to war and the decisions about how war is to be waged must be quite "simple."[152]

Luther admonishes the princes not to follow the advice of the "fire-eaters" among his counselors, when these try to provoke him to start a war for some minor and insignificant reason. He also ought to respond with a cool head to provocations from outside his own country.[153] Remembering that Jesus blesses the peacemakers, he should seek peace above everything else, even when his cause is just and he must make sacrifices for peace. No matter how right one's cause may be, the man who seeks justice for himself by violence makes his own just cause into an unjust one; for he thereby assumes unto himself the majestic power that belongs to God and, contrary to Romans 12:19, makes himself judge and executioner.[154] "Whoever starts a war is in the wrong."[155] Thus one always ought to offer to negotiate the conflict and to reach agreement with his opponent according to Deuteronomy 20: 10 ff.[156] Luther did more than assert this as a general principle. In 1542 he clearly and dramatically summoned the elector John

---

150 *WA* Br 10, 33; *WA* 19, 645–48; *LW* 46, 118–21.

151 *WA* 30[II], 130; *LW* 46, 185.

152 "This fighting under the emperor's banner and obedience to him ought to be true and simple. The emperor should seek nothing else than simply to perform the work and duty of his office, which is to protect his subjects; and those under his banner should seek simply to do the work and duty of obedience." *WA* 30[II], 130; *LW* 46, 185.

153 "Therefore, he must not follow the advice of those counselors and fire-eaters who would stir and incite him to start a war, saying: 'What, must we suffer such insult and injustice?' He is a mighty poor Christian who for the sake of a single castle would put the whole land in jeopardy." *WA* 11, 276; *LW* 45, 124; *WA* 19, 649; *LW* 46, 123.

154 "You need more to start a war than having a just cause." *WA* 32, 330; *LW* 21, 39; *WA* Br 10, 33–35.

155 *WA* 19, 645; *LW* 46, 118. "God desires peace and is the enemy of those who start wars and break the peace." *WA* 19, 646; *LW* 46, 119; *WA* 31[I], 203; *LW* 13, 57; *WA* 30[II], 111; *LW* 46, 165.

156 *WA* 11, 277; *LW* 45, 125; *WA* 19, 651; *LW* 46, 125; *WA* Br 10, 33.

Frederick and Duke Moritz, who were ready to go to war with each other about a very insignificant matter, to maintain the peace. Luther felt that his pastoral responsibility to these Christian princes required this admonition. And as a servant of Christ, as a preacher of the gospel, he claims to speak his warning with the authority of God's word.[157]

If negotiations do not succeed in their purpose of preventing war, then whoever is unjustly threatened and attacked has the clear duty of defending his land and people and thus of waging defensive war.[158] He is then involved in a "war of necessity" that has been forced upon him. Luther contrasts this kind of war with one which has been begun deliberately and intentionally—this latter kind of war is from the devil and "God will not let the devil succeed." In contrast to this, a war of necessity is a "human accident, in which we can expect God's help." If the whole land is in danger, then the prince must wage war; and he must do it "joyfully and with a good conscience," with the decisiveness and energy that comes from the knowledge that he is fighting a war of necessity.[159] Luther felt that the clergy also had the duty to admonish the princes seriously and urge them to wage war whenever they were lazy and did not decisively fulfill their duty to defend their subjects with the sword when they were attacked.[160] Luther himself did exactly this both in the Peasants' War and when the Turks were threatening to attack.[161]

---

157 *WA* Br 10, 32–36 (letter of April 7, 1542).

158 *WA* 32, 330; *LW* 21, 40.

159 *WA* Br 10, 35; *WA* 19, 648; *LW* 46, 121–22. "Since your entire land is in peril you must make the venture, so that with God's help all may not be lost. If you cannot prevent some from becoming widows and orphans as a consequence, you must at least see that not everything goes to ruin until there is nothing left except widows and orphans." *WA* 11, 277; *LW* 45, 125.

160 "But since it is and remains uncertain whether the princes are Christians, and it is certain that they are emperors and princes, that is, that they have God's command to protect their subjects and are duty bound to do so, we must let the uncertainty go and hold to the certain, urge them with continual preaching and exhortation, and lay it heavily upon their consciences that it is their duty to God not to let their subjects perish so terribly." *WA* 30^{II}, 131; *LW* 46, 186–87.

161 *Against the Robbing and Murdering Hordes of Peasants* (1525), *WA* 18, 357–61; *LW* 46, 49–55. "For I think . . . that neither emperor nor princes themselves believe that they are emperor and princes. They act as though it were up to them whether to rescue and protect their subjects from the power of the Turk or not; and the princes neither care nor think that they are bound and obligated before God to counsel and help the emperor in this matter with body and goods. Each of them passes it by as though it were no concern of his and

But decisiveness ought not to be confused with foolhardiness. Anyone who trusts in his own cause and his own power is foolhardy.[162] As seriously as Luther admonishes a prince to do his duty in a specific instance and to use his weapons to protect his subjects, and as strongly as he emphasizes the prince's responsibility for his country, he in no way creates the expectation that the prince whose "cause is just" will win. Luther says to the prince: Because your whole country is threatened, you must take the risk and see whether God wants to help you.[163] Luther speaks of risk because no one knows how the conflict will end. Even the fact that one has been attacked and has good reason to defend himself does not guarantee his success. It is of no use to emphasize the justice of one's cause, for this, like all pride, stubbornness, and security, is an abomination to God. We ought not to rely on the justice of our cause, only on God's grace and mercy. In this case, too, God wants us to fear him. Thus a Christian prince who finds himself waging war for a just cause will be courageous and fainthearted at the same time. He will be courageous against his opponents who are in the wrong, but he will be humble and fainthearted before God, who alone gives the victory.[164]

In 1525 Luther summoned the lords and princes to intervene against the plundering and burning mobs of peasants. He says: It is now clearly your duty, as the government instituted by God, to draw the sword; you are God's instrument, and he wants to use you to save the country. Then Luther immediately goes on to say that the outcome is uncertain and that the whole matter must be committed to God's will. Thus the princes will learn whether or not God wants them to be princes and lords. Perhaps God will give victory to the revolutionaries. He may even use this as a preliminary to the Last Judgment and destroy all order and create chaos in the world.[165] The mere fact that the princes are now fulfilling their clear and present duty and therefore have a just cause

---

as though he were forced neither by command nor necessity, but as though it were left up to him to do it or not." *WA* 30^{II}, 131; *LW* 46, 187. See also *WA* 30^{II}, 129, 132–33, 145–47; *LW* 46, 184, 188–89, 202–4.

162 *WA* 30^{II}, 135; *LW* 46, 198–99.

163 *WA* 11, 277; *LW* 45, 125.

164 "It is indeed true that you have a really good reason to go to war and to defend yourself, but that does not give you God's guarantee that you will win." *WA* 19, 649; *LW* 46, 123; *WA* 19, 650–51; *LW* 46, 123–25.

165 *WA* 18, 359–60; *LW* 46, 52–54.

does not in any way guarantee their victory. The outcome lies in
God's hands and must be committed to him. The princes must
wait to see what kind of an outcome God will give.

Just as one ought not to trust in his own cause, one ought not
to trust in his own power. One ought indeed to use all possible
power, but in the end not depend upon that; one ought to consider
that everything depends on God's help and remember that he
wants us to pray for this.[166] This is what Luther means when he
says that a war should be fought and won "with fear and humility."[167] Thus Luther combines the strongest appeal to human responsibility with the strongest assertion that God remains free to
direct the course of history as he wills. The most earnest human
determination is to be accompanied by the fear of God.[168]

Luther's demand that war be waged "simply" took on special
significance in the context of the war against the Turks. He felt
that it was a terrible falsification to present this war as a concern
of Christianity instead of as a purely political matter. Luther ob-
jected to the fact that the emperor had been urged to go to war
"as head of Christendom and as protector of the church and defender of the faith," rather than in his office as the emperor whom
God had established as the protector of Germany.[169] Luther says:
"Not so! The emperor is not the head of Christendom or defender
of the gospel or the faith. The church and the faith must have a
defender other than emperors and kings."[170] At this point Luther
specifically applies his doctrine of the two governments. It is not
the task of Christendom as such to wage war against the Turks.
Christendom fights only with the sword of the Spirit, that is, "it
fights against the devil with the word of God and with prayer."[171]

---

[166] *WA* 30[II], 136; *LW* 46, 191; *WA* 30[I], 441; *LW* 14, 119.

[167] "It is not enough for you to know that God has committed this or that to
you; you should do it with fear and humility, for God commands no one to do
anything on the basis of his own wisdom or strength. He too wants to have a
part in it and be feared. He wants to do it through us and wants us to pray to
him so that we will not become presumptuous or forget his help." *WA* 30[II],
135; *LW* 46, 190–91.

[168] *Theology*, 107–8.

[169] *WA* 30[II], 111–14, 129, 133–34; *LW* 46, 164–69, 185, 188–90.

[170] *WA* 30[II], 130, 133; *LW* 46, 185, 188–89.

[171] *WA* 30[II], 111; *LW* 46, 165. "The church ought not to strive or fight with
the sword. It has other enemies than flesh and blood; their name is the wicked
devils in the air [Ephesians 6:12]; therefore, the church has other weapons and
swords and other wars; it has enough to do and cannot get involved in the wars
of the emperor or princes." *WA* 30[II], 114; *LW* 46, 158.

"The emperor's sword has nothing to do with the faith; it belongs to physical, worldly things." Otherwise, God's order will be confused and destroyed, and this will provoke his wrath.[172]

Luther said all this even though he recognized that the growing power of the Turks threatened not only the empire but also Christianity and the church. He knew that the Turks were enemies of Christ; but at the same time he recognized that God was using them to discipline Christendom and that Christendom ought to respond to such discipline in a Christian way, that is, with repentance and prayer. Although the spiritual task of Christendom in relationship to the Turks and the secular political task of the emperors were to be differentiated and separated from each other, they also belonged together. Christendom and political power carry on the conflict in different ways: Christendom with the weapons of repentance, conversion, and prayer; the emperor with his military power. But Luther concludes that military power alone will hardly be very effective against the Turks. For the Turk who is an enemy of Christ is at the same time God's instrument of discipline, and behind his power stands the devil. This theological dimension of the secular and political opposition between the empire and the Turks must be recognized. It means that only repentance, conversion, and prayer—not military force—have the power "to take the rod out of God's hand, so that the Turk may be found only, in his own strength, all by himself, without the devil's help and without God's hand."[173]

Thus the spiritual battle of Christendom has decisive significance for the secular conflict against the Turks—at least insofar as one could hardly resist the Turks without it. For one could not come to terms with God's wrath, which was using the Turks as a rod of discipline, except by fearing God and humbly hoping in him. Luther reminds his readers of Psalms 147:10–11: "His delight is not in the strength of the horse, nor his pleasure in the legs of a man; but the Lord takes pleasure in those who fear him, in those who hope in his steadfast love." On this basis Luther asserts that this battle must be won with "Christian weapons and power." This does not mean that these Christian weapons guar-

---

172 *WA* 30[II], 129–31; *LW* 46, 186–88.
173 *WA* 30[II], 116–17; *LW* 46, 170–75.

antee the earthly victory but that, since God will not grant the
victory without them, they are the indispensable condition of
victory. Luther bases these assertions on the history of Israel and
on the words the prophets spoke to the people of Israel.[174]

Thus the spiritual and the secular are, in spite of all their
differences, closely related to each other. And the kingdom of
Christ has significance for secular government; the fear of God
and faith are significant for the political world. For Luther, the
God who directs the course of political history remains by and
large a hidden God, but ultimately he is the same God who encounters us in his word.

The political world has changed considerably since Luther's
time. As a result, his ideas no longer provide an adequate basis
on which to respond to contemporary questions of political ethics.
Luther's ideas must now, as in the past, be applied in new ways
in terms of the situations currently confronting us. His basic concepts, however, remain valid even for the modern world: (1)
The Christian as a politician must be primarily concerned with
peace, and war can be defended only when it is a war of necessity.[175] (2) Waging war is entirely the responsibility of secular
government and is a *completely secular matter*, whose secularity
ought not to be distorted by a religious or pseudoreligious ideology.
Luther thereby rejects every concept of a "Christian war" or a
"holy war" and all the ideology of a crusade. (3) We are warned
not to rely on our own just cause as meaning that we deserve the
victory and as a guarantee of victory for us—God's direction of
history goes far beyond such moralizing.

THE SOCIAL ORDER

Luther proclaims the freedom of the Christian. This freedom
is the freedom of faith. For Luther, as for Paul, it is entirely an
inner, spiritual matter. The Christian is lord of all things, all
relationships, and all destiny because nothing can prevent him
from maintaining faith, love, and hope and thereby being saved.
On the contrary, everything must help him to maintain such faith,

---

[174] Ibid.
[175] "One must not begin a war or work for it; it comes unbidden, all too
soon. One must keep peace as long as one can." *WA* 31^1, 203; *LW* 13, 57.

hope, and love and thus help him to achieve salvation. However, Luther passionately objects to every confusion of this Christian freedom with social demands. Luther does not do this because he is indifferent toward the form of social life. He affirms natural law and in all decisive points equates it with the "law of love" proclaimed in the gospel. On this basis he distinguishes between righteousness and unrighteousness in men's relationships to one another and in the relationships of the various stations. Nor was Luther reluctant to criticize existing conditions. In spite of his pessimistic attitude toward everything earthly, he did not feel that social unrighteousness and oppression could not be changed and improved.

However, Luther could—in accordance with his patriarchal understanding of the state—expect such obvious abuses to be reformed or completely abolished only by the authorities who were responsible for the country. As a result, he discussed them only with the lords and princes—but those discussions were very sharp and to the point. This is already clear in his treatise *Temporal Authority: To What Extent It Should Be Obeyed* of 1523. He threatens the princes with the rebellion of the oppressed people: "The common man is learning to think, and the scourge of princes (that which God calls *contemptum*) is gathering force among the mob and with the common man. I fear that there will be no way to avert it, unless the princes conduct themselves in a princely manner and begin again to rule decently and reasonably. Men will not, men cannot, men refuse to endure your tyranny and wantonness much longer. Dear princes and lords, be wise and guide yourselves accordingly. God will no longer tolerate it. The world is no longer what it once was, when you hunted and drove the people like game."[176]

In 1525 Luther wrote his *Admonition to Peace, a Reply to the Twelve Articles of the Peasants in Swabia*. He points out that many demands of the peasants are basically selfish; but he also says that some of their demands are very valid. He recognizes that the tax burden laid upon the peasants is unbearable, that it consumes all their profits, and that it only serves to support the inappropriate

---

[176] *WA* 11, 270; *LW* 45, 116.

luxury of the courts of the princes. The peasant earns his profit with bitter labor, only to have it taken from him and "squandered . . . on clothes, food, drink, and buildings as though it were chaff." Luther demands that the princes reduce their expenditures so that the poor people can keep something for themselves.[177]

That is how Luther speaks to the lords and princes about the situation of the peasants. However, although he lays this upon the princes as their *duty*, he does not grant the peasants the *right* of demanding it for themselves. This means that Luther recognizes that the lords have Christian, brotherly responsibilities. But he does not recognize that there are any human rights to which the peasants could appeal and which the oppressed could even assert by trying to help themselves with a revolution. It is the Christian's vocation to suffer injustice and to hope in God, just as the patient psalmists did—and God will then certainly give victory to their cause. The peasants, however, make their just cause an unjust one as soon as they use violence. And they will finally fail disastrously, or in any case be subject to God's eternal judgment, because they have been disobedient to God's order. It is bad enough that the lords and the peasants oppose each other like two parties, that right is opposed to right and interest is opposed to interest, so that some compromise must be found to resolve the dispute. That situation alone contradicts the true Christian attitude. At this point Luther's opinion corresponds to that of Paul in 1 Corinthians 6. It would be Christian if the princes were really fathers of their countries, recognized their responsibility for the condition of their subjects, and sought their best interests; and it would be Christian if the peasants endured patiently, called upon God, and waited.[178]

Luther's statements are ultimately based on the Sermon on the Mount, which he took with complete seriousness. Does anyone fail to recognize the basic justice of this viewpoint in comparison with the wild and shameful struggles of interest groups in our modern society? At the same time, however, we have moved beyond the patriarchal state of Luther's time. As far as Luther was concerned, the lords and princes bore sole responsibility for

---

[177] *WA* 18, 298–99; *LW* 46, 22–23.
[178] This is the basic theme of Luther's *Admonition to Peace. WA* 18, 291 ff.; *LW* 46, 17 ff.

social conditions. History has since developed in such a way that all citizens, in varying degrees, share responsibility for the conditions of our society. As a result, when the current "prince" or party in power fails to meet its responsibilities, it can be the task of other elements of the people to form a movement and to engage in a political struggle to change the future of oppressed and underprivileged groups in the nation. In Luther's terms, advocates who take the initiative in seeking the welfare of their fellowmen are no less officials than the princes were. Their service is no longer the service of private persons, and their political and social struggles cannot be forbidden and condemned on the basis of the Sermon on the Mount.[179]

Something else has happened to change the situation since Luther's time. As we have said, Luther follows Paul in defining Christian freedom under the gospel as a purely spiritual freedom. Paul has said that the slave who was not free in this world had become a "freedman of the Lord" (1 Corinthians 7:22). Luther accordingly responded to the peasants' demands that serfdom be abolished by saying that they had made "Christian freedom a completely physical matter." "A slave can be a Christian, and have Christian freedom, in the same way that a prisoner or a sick man is a Christian, and yet not free."[180] Neither Paul nor Luther had the slightest intention of demanding social emancipation in the name of Christianity. There is deep truth in this understanding of freedom and of the corresponding attitude of the Christian. That truth will always remain. However, since then Christianity has moved beyond the old understanding of the relationship between spiritual and secular freedom.[181] It has recognized that the freedom which the gospel gives to the Christian must also express itself as political and social freedom. As a result, Christianity today holds that slavery and similar conditions are unjust violations of human dignity. For a long time Christianity has felt called to

---

179 See Paul Althaus, *Religiöser Sozialismus. Grundfragen der christlichen Sozialethik* (Gütersloh: Bertelsmann, 1921), pp. 91 ff.; idem, *Luthers Haltung im Bauernkreig*, 2d ed. (Darmstadt: Wissenschaftliche Buchgesellschaft, 1958), especially pp. 22 ff.

180 *WA* 18, 326–27; *LW* 46, 38–39.

181 See H.-D. Wendland, "Sklaverei und Christentum," in *Die Religion in Geschichte und Gegenwart*, 3d ed. (Tübingen: J. C. B. Mohr, 1962), 6:101–4.

participate in abrogating slavery. Although one may surely possess Christian freedom in the deepest sense of the term even though he lives in a condition of social bondage, it is also true that the logical consequence of Christian freedom is social freedom.

CHRISTIAN MINISTRY TO POLITICAL OFFICIALS

Luther constantly emphasizes the distinction between the two kingdoms and disapproves any intervention by the one in the realm of the other. However, this does not by any means indicate that the areas and powers of these kingdoms are completely separated and unrelated. On the contrary, Luther feels that there are vital connections between the political office and the office of the ministry.[182] He recognizes that the spiritual office has a ministry to those who rule and that those who rule have a ministry to the word of God and to the church. This has nothing to do with a false confusion between the two and does not represent any intervention in an alien office. Luther is not proposing that someone might rule in alien territory, but rather that he will serve God who is the highest authority and the lord of both offices and powers. Both offices have the duty of serving God. One way in which they serve is by "helping the other to be obedient."[183]

The decisive question then is whether people in both governments have subjected themselves to the word of God and seek to serve God, or whether they glorify themselves by placing themselves above and seeking to rule God and his word. Such autonomy of the offices and powers results in infringements on the area of the other and in mutual conflict. The willingness to serve and obey prevents these difficulties from arising. "Therefore, in service or submission to God there can be no rebellion among the spiritual or the secular authorities. Even in the world, rebellion never stems from obedient service but from an ambitious desire to rule."[184] On this basis we can decide what is an improper confusion of the powers and what is not.

---

[182] See above, pp. 59–61.
[183] *WA* 51, 240; *LW* 13, 196.
[184] Ibid.

The question of competency or incompetency is decided on the basis of how the person speaking and acting relates to the word of God. Domination is incompetent; service is competent. In warning against improper confusion and intervention of the two governments, Luther was thinking less of the relationship of the political office to the spiritual office, or of the state to the church, than he was of the relationship of both offices to the word of God. His decisive concern was not that a prince might say and do something that only the spiritual office or the church ought to say and do but that he might not submit himself to the autonomous authority of God's word. The political office is limited not by the inherent independence of the ecclesiastical office but by the authority of the word of God. Spiritual government and the ecclesiastical institution are not simply one and the same. Luther is ultimately interested in limiting the state not with respect to the ecclesiastical institutions but with respect to God's word and the lordship of Christ in the church. Now, this certainly implies also a limitation on the state with respect to the office of the word. However, just as the office of the ministry of the word does not have its freedom from interference by the state simply as a result of an ecclesiastical regulation but only through the word of God—because it serves and insofar as it serves that word—so the prince is also not forbidden to concern himself about that word, to remind people of it, and to call people to hear it. Rather, he is forbidden to do only one thing, and that is to dominate it. Luther's definition of the relationship of two offices is something different from the modern idea of the "separation of church and state."

The political office and the preaching office of the ministry encounter each other at the point of God's law. Political authority is basically the office of the law. However, both the gospel and the preaching of the law have been committed to the church. And the preaching of the law has been committed to the church not merely insofar as, understood in its depth, it reveals the sin of men and leads them toward the gospel but also insofar as it is intended to preserve order in the world.

For this reason the office of preaching has an important task in the political order. It instructs people in all the stations of life that the orders in which they act are the work of God. Admittedly, this is not the unique and primary theme of preaching, but there is no doubt that it is one of the tasks of preaching. "For a preacher confirms, strengthens, and helps to sustain authority of every kind, and temporal peace generally. He checks the rebellious; teaches obedience, morals, discipline, and honor; instructs fathers, mothers, children, and servants in their duties; in a word, he gives direction to all the temporal estates and offices."[185] This means that the office of preaching does not merely issue a general proclamation that all the orders are God's great gifts and gracious ordering of our world—even though we so often fail to recognize them as such; it also specifically instructs each station about God's will for it and calls each of the stations to order when it ignores God's will. It also does this in relationship to the political office.[186]

This does not in any way mean that the spiritual office should give detailed instructions about politics and government and thereby absolve the prince of the necessity of making his own decisions. God's word and the office of the word are not in a position to do that. What Luther says at this point corresponds exactly to his teaching about the relative significance of faith and reason for government. The word of God does not intend to instruct political *understanding* but to summon the conscience before God and to remind it that the meaning of the political office lies in its character as *service*.

It is the task of reason and rational evaluation to decide what is to be done here and now in a specific situation. Reason has been given in greater or lesser measure to all people and all nations. Luther emphasizes that it is also to be found among the Turks and the heathen. For this reason they too have been able to establish good governments which are sometimes and in some ways superior to the governments established by Christian nations. They do not need Christ to do that. But political understanding must be guided by conscience and by the knowledge of God's will for the office of the prince. "For this reason I know of no law to prescribe for a prince; instead, I will simply instruct his heart and mind on

185 The text continues: "Of all the good things a pastor does these are, to be sure, the least. Yet they are so high and noble that the wisest of all the heathen have never known or understood them, much less been able to do them." *WA* 30ᴵᴵ, 537; *LW* 46, 226.
186 *WA* 31ᴵ, 196; *LW* 13, 49; *WA* 32, 519–20; *LW* 21, 265–67.

what his attitude should be toward all laws, counsels, judgments, and actions."[187]

This is necessary in view of the constantly threatened misuse of the orders created by God and the demonic temptations of power. Luther himself energetically exercised this office of instruction and rebuke from the word of God. He did it in his public writings and also very specifically in his letters to lords and princes. He denies that political authorities have the right to reject such instruction, criticism, and reminders of God's will as an improper intervention in their affairs or even as rejection of and rebellion against their authority or as an insult to their honor. "It would be far more seditious if a preacher did not rebuke the sins of the rulers."[188] "Now, if a preacher in his official capacity says to kings and princes and to all the world: 'Thank and fear God, and keep His commandments,' he is not meddling in the affairs of secular government."[189] For although the political office certainly does not stand under the church, it does stand under God and his word. For this reason the office of the word must speak to the government, and the government must listen. The same word which instituted and established the authority of government continues to stand above it and judge it. Government, therefore, must permit itself to be judged, condemned, created, and instructed by this word of God.[190]

In saying this, we must emphasize that Luther also says the office of preaching does not call politicians to obey the gospel, the Sermon on the Mount, or a Christian law but rather the secular

---

187 *WA* 11, 273; *LW* 45, 119. In speaking of the war against the Turks, Luther says: "It is not proper for me to say anything more about it other than to point out everyone's duty and to instruct his conscience." *WA* 30[II], 129; *LW* 46, 184.

188 *WA* 31[I], 190, 197; *LW* 13, 43, 50. (The quotation is to be found in the second reference.)

189 *WA* 51, 240; *LW* 13, 195.

190 *WA* 31[I], 191; *LW* 13, 44. "For God keeps the upper hand over them and the right to judge them and does not make them gods in such a way as to abolish his own Godhead and let them do as they please, as if they alone were gods over God. On the contrary, it is his will that they be subject to his word and either listen to it or suffer all misfortune. It is enough that they have rule over everything else; over God's word they are not to have it. For God's word appoints them, makes them gods, and subjects everything to them. Therefore they are not to despise it, for it is their institutor and appointer; but they are to be subject to it and allow themselves to be rejudged, rebuked, made, and corrected by it." *WA* 31[I], 195; *LW* 13, 48.

law. God has established this law in secular government, and it
is basically known and to be kept by everyone whether he is a
Christian or not. The office of preaching thus does not serve the
lordship of Christ in the orders—as the modern christocratic doctrine asserts—but rather the lordship of natural law over the
political office.

In Luther, none of this has the slightest clerical overtone. For
the word confronts the institutional church with the same seriousness as it confronts the state. The ecclesiastical organization does
not stand over against the state as though it has the task of super-
vising and evaluating the state; rather, the office of the word
instituted by Christ has the task of proclaiming God's will to both
the state and the church. Demonic forgetfulness of God and his
will can be found in one as well as in the other. But Luther does
feel that the misuse of spiritual power is a more serious matter
than the misuse of secular power, because it is more dangerous.
For the spiritual office is concerned with the eternal salvation of
men and the secular office is not.[191] Luther feels that a prince may
even need to remind the church of the obedience which it owes
to God.

The office of preaching has a task to fulfill even for the great
men of history, who otherwise do not need human counsel.[192]
For they "need instruction from the word of God to ascribe their
success and great achievement to God, to give honor to him from
whom they receive it, and not to praise and glorify themselves.
They do not do this without the word of God, nor do they know
how to do it."[193] God's word proclaimed to them through the
office of preaching preserves them in humility.

POLITICAL POWER AND THE CHURCH

There are decisive differences between Luther's concept of the
relationship of the government to the church and our contemporary
ideas of church and state. First, Luther does not think of "the
state," but of the person of the prince. He then distinguishes two
types of situations: in one the prince is God-fearing and in the

---

[191] *WA* 6, 259; *LW* 44, 93.
[192] See chapter 9.
[193] *WA* 51, 207, 215; *LW* 13, 155, 166.

(2) | other he is godless. (Luther includes among the godless the adherents of another faith, such as the Turks or the idolatrous kings of the Old Testament.) The relationship between the political authority and the church varies according to the kind of prince involved. Luther does not yet consider the possibility of a religiously neutral state.

(1')   Luther uses King David as an example of a God-fearing prince, with particular reference to Psalm 101. David rules his kingdom not only according to his secular station but also according to his spiritual station, that is, he preserved it through God's word. Luther does not consider the fact that David understood and exercised his government in this twofold way as an Old Testament limitation. A God-fearing prince has a task in relationship to God's word and in relationship to the worship of his people: to support God's word and pure doctrine, to provide opportunity and freedom for those who teach the truth, and to prevent false teachers from doing their work. The princes "should seek the kingdom of God and his righteousness first [Matthew 6:33], and keep their subjects loyal to the word of God and to the ministers and preachers."[194] This is the gospel ministry of a godly prince.

(2')   The other case is that of a godless prince. Here the pattern is not Psalm 101 but Psalms 2:2: "The kings of the earth set themselves, and the rulers take counsel together, against the Lord and his anointed."[195] Luther leaves no doubt about the fact that this latter situation is the more common and that a God-fearing prince is an exception, even a divine miracle.[196] Luther feels that it is the very nature of the political authorities to be indifferent or antagonistic toward the word of God.[197] This opinion is unquestionably

---

194 *WA* 51, 216, 234–35, 238; cf. *LW* 13, 166, 189, 193; *WA* 31[I], 199, 204; *LW* 13, 52, 57.

195 *WA* 51, 217, 234; *LW* 13, 167, 188.

196 "Emperors and kings are usually the worst enemies of Christendom and of the faith." *WA* 30[II], 130; *LW* 46, 185; *WA* 19, 643; *LW* 46, 115. "But if there are some among the kings, princes, and nobles who seriously—yes, I say seriously—concern themselves about God and his word, you may well regard such as extraordinary leaders from God and call them a rare dish in the kingdom of heaven. They do not do this by virtue of their reason or noble wisdom. God touches their hearts and directs them in a special way so that they do not resist him the way other kings and lords do. Instead, they follow David's example and promote the cause of his word, to the extent that God gives them the ability and help." *WA* 51, 217; *LW* 13, 168.

197 "Such tyrants are acting as worldly princes are supposed to act, and worldly princes they surely are. But the world is God's enemy; hence, they too

conditioned by Luther's bitter experiences with the resistance of many lords and princes to the Reformation. Above and beyond this, however, it is meant as a basic judgment: Luther concludes that the blindness and enmity against the word of God which is common to all natural men is particularly apparent and effective in people who hold power.

This enmity means that Christianity will repeatedly find itself involved in a passionate struggle with the political authorities and that it cannot avoid being persecuted. That is the law of Christ for his congregation. It is his will, for he finds his martyrs and saints in the suffering church and it is with them that he fills his kingdom.[198] Here, too, we find Luther's theology of the cross. But we dare not forget that Luther felt that the Christian community would repeatedly suffer persecution not only by the political authorities but also by the official institution of the church. For the basic characteristics of natural humanity—which is antagonistic to God's word—can make themselves felt in the church as well as in the political authorities.[199] Both are constantly threatened by demonic distortion.

When Christendom suffers in its struggle with the political powers, the opposition of the two kingdoms in their absolute

---

have to do what is antagonistic to God and agreeable to the world, that they may not be bereft of honor, but remain worldly princes. Do not wonder, therefore, that they rage and mock at the gospel; they have to live up to their name and title." *WA* 11, 267; *LW* 45, 112–13. "Therefore it is no wonder that worldly kings, princes, and lords are enemies of God and persecute his word. This is the natural thing for them; they are born that way. It is a natural and innate characteristic of reason that it has neither grace nor intelligence to think or to act otherwise." *WA* 51, 217; *LW* 13, 168.

198 "Christ must have martyrs. It is for this reason that he has at all times permitted his people to be physically weak and has made his enemies mighty and victorious. This is the way in which he cleanses and purifies his people." *WA* 30^{II}, 170. "Christ intends to be weak upon earth and to suffer with his people so that he may make shameful fools out of those who are mighty and use their rage in such a way that they (without knowing it) fill heaven with martyrs and saints. Thus his kingdom will be filled all the sooner and he may come to judgment." *WA* 30^{II}, 173. "Christ intends to suffer and be weak here on earth and must even permit himself to be killed so that his kingdom may speedily increase and be filled. For his kingdom is not physically present here upon earth. It is for this reason that he is most energetically at work when there is much suffering and many martyrs, as 2 Corinthians 12:9 says: 'My power is made perfect in weakness.' " *WA* 30^{II}, 178.

199 *Theology*, 341 ff. Luther places the secular and spiritual "great ones" alongside each other as those who are to be expected to be opponents of the gospel. Speaking of both he says: "The world cannot tolerate what comes from God." The "world" is also active in the ecclesiastical institution. *WA* 6, 274; *LW* 44, 112.

sense of the kingdom of God and the kingdom of Satan become
manifest. And yet even when this is taken into consideration, we
cannot combine and identify the basic relationship of the two
governments, as Luther understands them, with the struggle
between God and Satan. According to Luther, even an unjust
government that is antagonistic toward Christianity remains a
government commissioned by God. We ought to obey it insofar
as this specific conflict is not involved and to endure its injustice
without resisting. No matter how much Satan and the world may
work through its activity, such a government is not as such a
totally satanic power. For this reason, Christianity, in spite of
everything, stands in a different relationship to such a government
than it does to Satan, the opponent of God. For even such a corrupt government has still been instituted and established by God.
Secular government is never simply to be equated with the world
that is at enmity with God. Luther felt that Christianity is far
more seriously threatened through the antichrist who "sits inside
the church" than through persecution by the political powers.[200]
Only in the former do we confront the total and complete
incarnation of Satan.

---

[200] *Theology*, 421–22.

9

GREAT MEN IN
POLITICAL HISTORY

L UTHER WAS very much interested in the history of nations. He was acquainted with the history of classical antiquity and the biblical history of the Old Testament. As a result, he knew that each historical moment and every prince or statesman is unique. At very special and rare times God gives us a "healthy hero or a wondrous man," that is, a creative statesman.[1] The world needs such exceptional people from time to time. The times that come before and after such men are not very important. People must be governed even when there is no great man, of course, but then there is no central thrust and no creative power to government; the situation is dominated by books and traditions. At such times we become aware of what a poor thing this world really would be if God did not repeatedly intervene and again send us a great man.[2]

Luther thus does not intend to ignore the political history of the nations in his theology or to avoid interpreting it. His God

---

[1] *WA* 51, 207, 214–15; *LW* 13, 154–55, 163 ff.

[2] "The world is indeed a sick thing; it is the kind of fur on which neither hide nor hair is any good. The healthy heroes are rare, and God provides them at a dear price. Still, the world must be ruled, if men are not to become wild beasts. So things in the world in general remain mere patchwork and beggary; it is a veritable hospital, in which princes, lords, and all rulers lack wisdom and courage—that is, success and direction from God—even as the sick person lacks strength and power. So here one must patch and darn and help oneself with the laws, sayings, and examples of the heroes as they are recorded in books. Thus we must continue to be disciples of those speechless masters which we call books. Yet we never do it as well as it is written there; we crawl after it and cling to it as to a bench or to a cane. In addition, we also follow the advice of the best people who live in our midst, until the time comes in which God again provides a healthy hero or a wondrous man, in whose hand all things improve, or at least fare better than is written in any book. Either he changes the law, or he overrules it in such a way that all things flourish and prosper in the land with peace and discipline, protection and punishment. Thus you have what may be called a wholesome regime. Moreover, during his lifetime he is feared and honored and loved in the highest degree; and after his death he is eternally praised." *WA* 51, 214; *LW* 13, 164–65.

does not merely direct the history of the church, he also guides political history. As clearly as Luther distinguishes God's dealing with his church from his dealing with the world of politics, it is still one and the same God who acts in both places. In both we find instruments of God, vocations, and God's direction and blessing. Speaking of creative geniuses in the history of the world, Luther says: "Some have a special star before God; these he teaches himself and raises them up as he would have them. They are also the ones who have smooth sailing on earth and so-called good luck and success. Whatever they undertake prospers; and even if all the world were to work against it, it would still be accomplished without hindrance."[3] Thus Luther asserts that God inspires, teaches, and drives these people to carry out their political plans and activity, and he permits them to succeed in spite of all opposition.

Luther refers the inspiration of great men back to God's Spirit, the Holy Spirit. His thinking at this point is determined by the Old Testament, and he shares its broad concept of the activity of the Spirit of God.[4] The Spirit thus works not only in salvation history but also in the political history of the world, not merely in the area of the church but also in this profane, godless world. The heathen recognized that this was the case with their great men. Luther agrees.[5] The Holy Spirit works in a different way, of course, when he leads a man to faith in Jesus Christ, puts love in his heart, and thus creates and establishes the congregation. However, God's Spirit also works by raising up great men in history and driving and inspiring them to carry out their work. They too require a kind of faith, an extraordinary confidence in what they are doing, if their work is to succeed.[6] And the very same God who gives saving faith also places this special confidence in their hearts. Such confidence is not saving faith but rather that special

---

[3] *WA* 51, 207; *LW* 13, 154. The context makes it clear that Luther is not thinking exclusively of lords and princes, but of people "in all walks of life"; however, the people to whom he primarily refers are lords and princes.

[4] *Theology*, pp. 439 ff.

[5] The heathen know "from experience that there never has been a man of great deeds or an extraordinary man without a special inspiration from God, even though there have always been men who were powerful, very wise, and highly intelligent." *WA* 51, 222; cf. *LW* 13, 174; *WA* 39[II], 198, 237; *WA* 40[III], 209.

[6] *WA* 39[II], 237. Luther speaks of a "heroic faith." *WA* 39[II], 247.

kind of confidence without which no one can do any great historical work.

Since the very same God works both in politics and for our eternal salvation, his activity in political history—in spite of all the differences—corresponds at decisive points to his saving work. Thus Luther's theology of history also proclaims the same great theme which dominates his doctrine of justification: "Let God be God."[7]

God's activity in history is characterized by the same sovereign freedom with which he shows grace to the sinner. God raises up wondrous men where and when he wills. From our human viewpoint, it would seem to be rational and appropriate that anyone given an office in this world would have the understanding and the competence to carry it out. But God does not act as we expect. Here too he goes his own way. He could indeed direct history in such a way that it would seem reasonable to us, but he does not intend to do so. Here too he demonstrates that he is God. He uses the painful lack of reason in history, the distorted relationship between office and person, position and ability, to announce that he retains his freedom as the creator and is not accountable to men. Even though God has created the historical institution of government, he does not feel himself so bound to it that he needs to provide only administrators who are competent to fill their positions.[8] This totally corresponds to what Luther says about

---

[7] *Theology,* 118–19.

[8] "It is true, and it should be, that prominent personages—like kings, princes, lords, and noblemen, high and low—ought to be shrewd and devout, everyone according to his station. This is why they have a high and noble title, a shield and helmet ahead of others. They have the power, wealth, and honor of the world, so that they ought to rule well alone. But what is missing is the fact that our Lord God makes up his own mind. He regards us all as one dough, one like another, and does with us as he pleases. Therefore, to a noble he often gives wisdom and virtue as he does not give to three princes, and to a commoner such as he does not give to six nobles. As a real God, he wants to be free and unbound and not subordinate to the human creature, as Saint Peter calls it [1 Peter 2:13], even though it be pretty and fair. Who would not wish that the higher the standing by birth, the higher the wisdom and virtue might be? But it cannot be and never will be thus. This is our Lord God's fault, not ours. He could do it that way if he wanted to; we cannot do it that way, no matter how anxious we might be to do so. For it is written [Psalms 100:3]: 'He makes us, and we do not make ourselves.'" *WA* 51, 255; *LW* 13, 214. Luther frequently uses this verse from Psalm 100 in condemning work-righteousness. *WA* 39^I, 48; *LW* 34, 114; *WA* 40^{II}, 457; *LW* 12, 402.

God's freedom in *The Bondage of the Will*. He there teaches that
God remains free to grant and to refuse salvation.[9]

Through this free creating activity, God sets limits for all
human attempts to devise curricula and methods of education that
will train people for political competence. We ought indeed to do
all these things as well as we are able. However, we will not be
able to create any great man, but at best will only train people to
learn from the history and the example of people to whom God
has been gracious. Genuine political talent cannot be developed
by any kind of training or education. God gives great men to the
nations directly and unpredictably. Luther reminds us that when
David stood before Goliath, "he was not an apprentice, trained in
this craft [of warfare]; he was a master, created for it by God."
The same is true of Naaman.[10] This then is the contrast: either
one is equipped for a particular task by training or he is created
with the necessary ability. Luther describes Fabian von Feilitzsch,
counselor of elector Frederick the Wise, as a man who "was no
doctor of laws, but when he heard a case, he gave his advice
directly and to the point." Yet, as Luther says: "He was not a
jurist by education or training; rather, he was a born jurist."[11]
Speaking of great statesmen in general, Luther says: "I do not call
such people trained or made but rather created; they are princes
and lords, directed by God."[12] God gives them to us through his
own act of creation. Luther's God is thus a living God who acts
in history and does wonderful things.

However, we cannot institutionalize such wonders. Even the
wonderful talent of the great man cannot be inherited. What the
fathers have earned can be dissipated and destroyed by their children, even though they may work harder than their parents did.[13]
This depends not only on human work but also on God's blessing

---

[9] *Theology*, 280 ff.
[10] *WA* 51, 208; *LW* 13, 156. "If the king of Syria had put in Naaman's
place a man who was much wiser and much more clever than seven Naamans,
he would not have been able to manage so nicely and so well in Syria through
such a person. Neither Syria nor the king had trained Naaman; according to the
Scriptures, God brought success and prosperity to Syria through Naaman. He
would not have done it through another, even as it is not written of any other."
Ibid.
[11] *WA* 51, 209; *LW* 13, 157.
[12] *WA* 51, 207; *LW* 13, 155.
[13] *WA* 51, 209; *LW* 13, 107.

—the latter, however, is free and beyond our control. "God's miracles are not inherited; they do not belong to us, nor are they subject to us the way possessions, house, and home are. God wants to be free to give such extraordinary leaders, such jewels, when, where, and to whom he pleases."[14] Thus even in terms of political history, Luther confronts us with the free and living God. This is an awe-inspiring freedom, because God does not give us such heroes very often and their hour comes to an end. If and when God gives us such heroes, we should thank and praise this freedom.

Thus the historical life of nations is also governed by the rule which dominates Luther's concept of salvation: nothing depends on past achievements but rather on the person whom God creates;[15] nothing depends on human activity but rather on a previously given nature which is the necessary source of all activity. God makes good persons and then their deeds are good. The reverse is not true; works do not make men good. This is also true in history.[16] Just as the individual person must wait for God to give him a new nature, so a nation must wait for God to give it a great man who has the kind of greatness that is beyond all the possibilities of human education and training. Luther explicitly emphasizes this correspondence between God's activity in salvation and his activity in political history. Luther sometimes speaks of "apes" who imitate great men. Such "apes" act as though they too were inspired and had no need of human advice. In reality, they are controlled by the devil and are his great people. They are like the people who want to become saints by doing good works.[17]

Truly great men have the wonderful certainty of sleepwalkers. However, they can lose both this confidence and their power. God has given his gifts and he can take them away. He withdraws these gifts when the "heroes" lose their humility before him, when they

---

14 *WA* 51, 209; *LW* 13, 157.

15 "If two people happen to be doing exactly the same kind of work, still it is said that the one is doing right while the other is doing wrong; for it depends on the person. If God wants a person to succeed, then he will succeed, even though he be as stupid as Claus Narr [a court fool]. But if he is not the person or the man, then he will not succeed." *WA* 51, 212; *LW* 13, 161.

16 *WA* 39I, 46; *LW* 34, 111; *WA* 51, 210–12; *LW* 13, 159–61.

17 "The apes really ought to let them do the advising and speaking, and they could very well do so. But they refuse. Instead, they want to be like the really extraordinary leaders and do everything they do, since the devil rides and leads them." *WA* 51, 212; *LW* 13, 161–62; *WA* 51, 210; *LW* 13, 159.

become proud and ascribe their success to themselves instead of
receiving it as a gift from God. They thereby insult God's deity
and honor. That is the danger of being a great man. It is very easy
for great men to praise themselves instead of God. As a result,
they seldom come to a good end. "When their time is up and God
withdraws his hand because of their presumptuousness and ingrati-
tude, they fall in such a way that no advice or reasoning can help
any longer."[18] Then they fall and are destroyed. Thus does Luther
understand God's activity in history in terms of the concept of
God's being God—the concept that plays such an important role
in his doctrine of justification.

---

[18] *WA* 51, 207, 212; *LW* 13, 155, 162.

INDEXES

INDEX OF AUTHORS

INDEX OF SCRIPTURE REFERENCES

Indexes   163

INDEX OF SUBJECTS